GMAT®
Verbal Workbook
Fifth Edition

The Staff of Kaplan Test Prep and Admissions

KAPLAN

PUBLISHING

New York

© 2008 Kaplan, Inc.

Published by Kaplan Publishing, a division of Kaplan, Inc.
1 Liberty Plaza, 24th Floor
New York, NY 10006

Printed in the United States of America

August 2008
10 9 8 7 6 5 4 3

ISBN-13: 978-1-4195-5305-9

Kaplan Publishing books are available at special quantity discounts to use for sales promotions, employee premiums, or educational purposes. Please email our Special Sales Department to order or for more information at kaplanpublishing@kaplan.com, or write to Kaplan Publishing, 1 Liberty Plaza, 24th Floor, New York, NY 10006.

Table of Contents

KAPLAN

KAPLAN

kaptest.com/publishing

The material in this book is up-to-date at the time of publication. However, the Graduate Management Admission Council may have instituted changes in the test after this book was published. Be sure to carefully read the materials you receive when you register for the test.

If there are any important late-breaking developments—or any changes or corrections to the Kaplan test preparation materials in this book—we will post that information online at **kaptest.com/publishing**. Check to see if there is any information posted there regarding this book.

kaplansurveys.com/books

We'd love to hear your comments and suggestions about this book. We invite you to fill out our online survey form at **kaplansurveys.com/books**. Your feedback is extremely helpful as we continue to develop high-quality resources to meet your needs.

How to Use This Book

Welcome to Kaplan's *GMAT Exam Verbal Workbook*. You have just wisely purchased the most comprehensive book on the market focusing specifically on the verbal portion of the Graduate Management Admissions Test (GMAT). Kaplan has prepared students to take standardized tests for over 60 years, longer than the GMAT has been around. Our team of researchers and editors knows more about preparing for the GMAT than anyone else, and you'll find their accumulated knowledge and wisdom here in this book.

This book is designed to benefit anyone who needs to increase his or her scores on the GMAT, whether on the Verbal Section, the Analytical Writing Assessment (AWA) Section, or both. You may have already taken the GMAT, or at least a simulated GMAT, and you're comfortable with your quantitative score on the test, but need to boost your verbal score in order to get into the M.B.A. program of your choice.

If so, this book is for you. If you want a book that covers the entire GMAT, we recommend Kaplan's *GMAT* (with or without CD-ROM); for a book that focuses on math content and strategies for the GMAT, pick up a copy of Kaplan's *GMAT Math Workbook*.

This book is designed to raise your verbal score on the GMAT regardless of your present skill level. Some of our readers may have relatively strong verbal skills, but know they could still be scoring higher, while others may not be native English speakers and can use serious help with English grammar and idioms. This book is designed to help in either situation. And almost all test takers, no matter their proficiency in English, can use solid strategies for dealing with the dense reading passages and arguments found on the GMAT—as well as techniques for cranking out superior AWA essays.

With this understanding of our readers' differing needs and skill sets, we have divided the book into several parts.

PART ONE: GETTING STARTED

The first step to a higher score is to know exactly what you can expect to find on the GMAT. In part one of this book, we'll provide you with background information on the different sections of the test, what they cover, and how they're organized. We'll explain how the Computer Adaptive Test (CAT) format differs from traditional pencil-and-paper tests in the way it determines your score, and how you can use the CAT format and scoring method to your advantage.

KAPLAN

PART TWO: VERBAL STRATEGIES

Once you have the big picture, it's time to focus on the specifics of the verbal portions of the GMAT. Part two examines the three question types that constitute the 75-minute Verbal Section: Sentence Correction, Reading Comprehension, and Critical Reasoning. We dedicate a chapter to each, examining first the question format and then exactly what is tested by the question type. Finally, we give you our best Kaplan methods and strategies for handling each, along with plenty of testlike examples on which to practice. We also devote a separate chapter to "Reading the GMAT Way," which is designed to help you develop the very specific reading skills that you need to read Reading Comprehension and Critical Reasoning passages with better efficiency and understanding.

PART THREE: PRACTICE SETS

After you're comfortable with our Kaplan methods and strategies for handling Verbal question types, you'll want to try them out with more questions. The practice sets contained in part three contain hundreds of Sentence Correction, Critical Reasoning, and Reading Comprehension questions complete with detailed explanations. As you go through these, look for patterns of questions that you tend to get right and wrong. Take notice of your areas of strength, but focus the bulk of your studies on your areas of weakness. With sufficient practice, you'll be ready for anything that could appear on the GMAT Verbal Section.

PART FOUR: PUTTING IT ALL TOGETHER

Part four contains our best effort (on paper) to replicate the experience of taking an actual GMAT Verbal Section, mixing the Verbal types in the same manner that an actual GMAT would. Here's your chance to bring together all your newly acquired verbal strategies and get a sense of what the GMAT Verbal Section feels like.

PART FIVE: ANALYTICAL WRITING ASSESSMENT

Part five focuses on the essay portion of the GMAT, known as the Analytical Writing Assessment (AWA). It contains descriptions and examples of the two essay question types, along with an explanation of how the essays are graded and strategies for successfully completing each. Finally, you'll see sample essay topics and sample essays, along with a scoring guide that will enable you to see how your practice essays measure up to the ETS scoring formula.

PART SIX: APPENDIXES

The appendixes contain additional materials to help you fine-tune your skills and address any verbal weak spots. We especially recommend that all readers take a look at the list of common GMAT idioms in appendix 3. There is also an extensive grammar reference guide, as well as a guide to usage and style that presents 16 principles of good writing and exercises to help you sharpen your writing skills. Spending time with these guides will help you develop skills that will serve you long after you've taken the GMAT. Good luck with your studies.

A Special Note for International Students

The M.B.A. (Master of Business Administration) has become a degree of choice for businesspersons around the globe. Variations of U.S.-style M.B.A. programs exist in Asia, Europe, and the Americas. In recent years, hundreds of thousands of international students have studied business and management in the United States.

As the United States increases its participation in the global economy, U.S. business schools are reaching out to attract exceptional international candidates to their graduate programs. However, competition for admission to prestigious programs is heavy and international students need to plan carefully if they wish to enter a top U.S. graduate management program.

If you are not from the United States, but are considering attending a graduate management program at a university in the United States, here is what you'll need to get started:

- If English is not your first language, start there. You will probably need to take the Test of English as a Foreign Language (TOEFL®) or show some other evidence that you are proficient in English prior to gaining admission to a graduate program in business. The ability to communicate in English, both verbally and in writing, is extremely important to your success in an American M.B.A. program.

- You may also need to take the GMAT® (Graduate Management Admissions Test). Some graduate business programs may require you to take the GRE® (Graduate Record Examination) as well.

- Since admission to many graduate business programs is quite competitive, you may wish to select three or four programs you would like to attend and complete applications for each program.

- You should select a program that meets your current or future employment needs, rather than simply a program with a big name. For example, if you hope to work in the hotel and tourism industry, make sure the program you choose specializes in that distinct area.

- You need to begin the application process at least a year in advance. Be aware that many programs only offer August or September start dates. Find out application deadlines and plan accordingly.

- Finally, you will need to obtain an 1-20 Certificate of Eligibility from the school you plan to attend if you intend to apply for an F-1 Student Visa to study in the United States.

KAPLAN ENGLISH PROGRAMS*

If you need more help with the complex process of business school admissions, assistance preparing for the TOEFL or GMAT, or help improving your English skills in general, you may be interested in Kaplan's programs for international students.

Kaplan English Programs were designed to help students and professionals from outside the United States meet their educational and career goals. At locations throughout the United States, international students take advantage of Kaplan's programs to help them improve their academic and conversational English skills, raise their scores on the TOEFL, GMAT, and other standardized exams, and gain admission to the schools of their choice. Our staff and instructors give international students the individualized instruction they need to succeed. Here is a brief description of some of Kaplan's programs for international students:

General Intensive English

Kaplan's General Intensive English classes are designed to help you improve your skills in all areas of English and to increase your fluency in spoken and written English. Classes are available for beginning to advanced students, and the average class size is 12 students.

General English Structured-Study

For students needing a flexible schedule, this course helps improve general fluency skills. Kaplan's General English Structured-Study course employs the communicative approach and focuses on vocabulary building, reading, and writing. You will receive books, and audio and video materials as well as three hours of instructor contact per week.

TOEFL and Academic English

This course provides you with the skills you need to improve your TOEFL score and succeed in an American university or graduate program. It includes all the skills tested on the new test.

TOEFL Test Preparation Course

Kaplan's TOEFL course can help you learn test-taking skills and strategies to raise your TOEFL score. This course is for intermediate to advanced English learners.

GMAT for International Students

The Graduate Management Admissions Test (GMAT) is required for admission to many graduate programs in business in the United States. Hundreds of thousands of American students have taken this course to prepare for the GMAT. This course, designed especially for non-native English speakers, includes the skills you need to succeed on each section of the GMAT, as well as access to Kaplan's exclusive computer-based practice materials and extra verbal practice.

*Kaplan is authorized under federal law to enroll nonimmigrant alien students. Kaplan is accredited by ACCET (Accrediting Council for Continuing Education and Training).

OTHER KAPLAN PROGRAMS

Since 1938, more than 3 million students have come to Kaplan to advance their studies, prepare for entry to American universities, and further their careers. In addition to the above programs, Kaplan offers courses to prepare for the SAT®, GRE®, LSAT®, MCAT®, DAT®, USMLE®, NCLEX®, and other standardized exams at locations throughout the United States.

Applying to Kaplan English Programs

To get more information, or to apply for admission to any of Kaplan's programs for international students and professionals, contact us at:

Kaplan English Programs
700 S. Flower, Suite 2900
Los Angeles, CA 90017, USA
Telephone: (213) 385-2358
Fax: (213) 383-1364
Website: www.kaplanenglish.com
Email: world@kaplan.com

| PART ONE |

Getting Started

Chapter 1: **About the GMAT**

Before we start preparing for the verbal portions of the GMAT, let's get a sense of the big picture. In this chapter we'll discuss the content and structure of the GMAT. We'll also explain strategies for making the computer-adaptive format of the exam work to your advantage.

WHAT'S ON THE GMAT?

Pearson Vue administers the Graduate Management Admissions Test (GMAT) for the Graduate Management Admission Council (GMAC), the association for graduate business schools around the world. The GMAT consists of two 75-minute multiple-choice sections (one Quantitative and one Verbal) and two 30-minute essays known as the Analytical Writing Assessment. The two multiple-choice sections are made up of five question types: Problem Solving, Data Sufficiency, Sentence Correction, Reading Comprehension, and Critical Reasoning. The two essays are administered first, followed by a 5-minute break. A second 5-minute break is given between the Quantitative and Verbal Sections.

QUANTITATIVE SECTION

There are 37 questions on the 75-minute Quantitative Section, of which 9 are "experimental," meaning that they don't count towards your score but are put into the test in order to calibrate their difficulty level for inclusion in future tests. Since there's no way to know for sure which questions are experimental, you should try to give each question your best effort.

Problem Solving: You'll see approximately 23 Problem Solving questions in the classic five-answer-choice format. The concepts and skills tested are taken from the broad areas of arithmetic, algebra, and geometry—essentially the math we all studied in high school. This doesn't mean, however, that the GMAT rewards you solely for your knowledge of that material. The most successful test takers organize available data and efficiently use an arsenal of math tools and test-taking strategies. Why does the GMAT test you on word problems and triangles? The GMAC figures that the best managers find the speediest, most efficient solutions to business problems. Business schools also want to test your ability to convert real-life situations (such as those found in word problems) into mathematical models that can be analyzed and solved.

 RUSSIAN ROULETTE

Don't try to figure out which questions on your test are experimental. What if you guess wrong? Just try to give every question your best shot, and hope that the questions that give you trouble won't count towards your score.

Data Sufficiency: Data Sufficiency is a "fixed-format" question type, meaning that every question has the same five answer choices. You'll see about 14 of these questions. Each consists of a question and two pieces of data. You must determine whether the given data are sufficient to answer the question at hand. The premise behind this question type is that Data Sufficiency tests not only your math abilities but also your ability to know when you can answer a question—or, by analogy, make a management decision. You exercise this skill every time you delegate responsibilities. A manager must know what information is necessary to make a business decision before asking an employee to gather that data.

VERBAL SECTION

There are 41 questions on the 75-minute Verbal Section, of which 11 are experimental. The three question types described below are mixed throughout the section.

Sentence Correction: The Verbal Section will present you with about 15 Sentence Correction questions. In each of these, part or all of a sentence is underlined. Your job is to select the best of five versions of that underlined portion, according to the conventions of "standard written English." Although grammar is at the heart of this section, good style and efficiency also contribute to success here. The good news: Not all grammar rules are tested, and the GMAT will not test you on any grammar terminology. However, you do need to recognize "GMAT style"—the kind of sentence that the test writers consider to be correct and effective—as well as the classic errors that appear over and over on this question type. Why does the GMAC consider grammar and style important for your business career and your business school efforts? A business leader is only as effective as his or her ability to communicate goals and agendas clearly and effectively to colleagues and employees.

Reading Comprehension: On your Verbal Section you can expect to see four Reading Comprehension passages (each approximately 200–300 words long) with three or four questions based on each. The passages are written in difficult, often technical prose, adapted from books and journals in the broad areas of business, the social sciences, and the natural sciences. You shouldn't take the Reading Comprehension challenge lightly. The reading skills you developed in college and use for your personal pleasure are ill suited to success on the GMAT. Reading Comp on the GMAT requires a different, more aggressive kind of reading that this book teaches. Reading Comp questions are designed to see whether you can get the gist of the prose—its underlying purpose and principal ideas—quickly and accurately. In much the same way, managers need to pare down volumes of reports and data to the key facts that contribute to a decision.

Critical Reasoning: Critical Reasoning tests your ability to judge the merits of an opinion or idea. A short argument forms the basis of each of the approximately 13 questions. The most commonly tested skill is the ability to break down an argument in order to strengthen or weaken it or to identify the author's assumptions. Success in Critical Reasoning hinges on developing a systematic approach to analyzing arguments with a trained, or at least intuitive, grasp of proper logic. Those experienced in debate tend to do well here. We will show you how to develop a core set of skills and a winning strategy for Critical Reasoning questions. The GMAC includes this question type because business managers need to apply these same critical thinking skills every time they evaluate the merits of a business proposal or plan.

ANALYTICAL WRITING ASSESSMENT (AWA)

In addition to multiple-choice questions, the GMAT includes two scored typewritten essays. As this section's name suggests, the essays test your analytical as well as writing skills. On Test Day, you'll need to complete writing samples on the following two topic types, either of which can come first:

Analysis of an Issue: The "Analysis of an Issue" topic will present you with a few sentences discussing a broad, general issue. You will be asked to present and explain convincingly your viewpoint on the issue. To succeed, you'll have to analyze different sides of the issue, present a convincing case for your point of view, and support your argument with good examples or reasons taken from your own experience or education.

Analysis of an Argument: The "Analysis of an Argument" topic will be a brief argument that expresses one point of view. Your essay will have to explain how logically persuasive you find the argument. A good essay will critique the argument's line of reasoning and use of evidence. You should also identify what would make the argument more convincing or help you better evaluate its conclusion.

Obviously, the Analytical Writing Assessment is designed to test your ability to communicate effectively—something you'll have to do as a manager. Business schools also treat your essay as an example of your capacity for incisive thought under pressure. In both business school and your career, you'll need to be able to analyze an issue and reason through a response quickly and clearly.

 PREDICTABLE

The GMAT tests the same principles over and over. Every GMAT is virtually the same as every other one because the format must be consistent from year to year to yield dependable results.

SCORING

The score report you receive, and that ETS will send to the business schools you choose, will contain four separate scores. The most important is the overall scaled score. This is reported on a 200–800 scale.

You will also be given verbal and quantitative subscores for the multiple-choice sections. The range of the subscores is 0–60, but scores below 10 and above 46 are infrequent. The subscores are less important factors in your business school application than your overall score, but some schools look at them to make sure your skills in a particular section are up to par.

The separate AWA score is in a 0–6 range, although scores from 0–1.5 are reserved for essays that don't address the stimulus in any meaningful way. Your AWA score is an average of the scores you were awarded for the two essays you completed, each of which is reviewed by one human grader, as well as a computer program called the E-rater. If the human grader and E-rater disagree by more than one point, a second human grader is brought in to resolve the difference. The human grader uses holistic grading, which considers an essay in its entirety. Some of the more important holistic grading criteria are organization, clarity, concision, grammar, and sentence structure. The e-rater is designed to mimic human graders, but, of course, a computer program isn't a great judge of humor or creativity. Don't worry, we'll show you how to get a high score from both the human grader and the computer grader.

While you'll get your 200–800 score before you leave the test center, your essay results will be sent to you at a later date. A percentile ranking accompanies all four scores, showing the percentage of test takers who scored below you. When the GMAT was first administered, the scaled scores were pegged to certain percentile ranks (a 500 referring to the 50th percentile, for example). However, after many years, the scaled scores and percentile ranks have tended to separate a bit. Thus business schools also use percentile ranks to evaluate your GMAT performance.

HOW DO I REGISTER?

The GMAT is administered at special computerized testing centers six days a week during regular business hours. To register for the GMAT, call 800-GMAT-NOW.

You can also register by mail, using the forms in the most recent GMAT *Information Bulletin*, which is published by ETS every summer for the forthcoming academic year. It's free and available at Kaplan centers and most colleges, but you can receive one by mail by writing to:

> Graduate Management Admissions Test
> Educational Testing Service
> P.O. Box 6103
> Princeton, NJ 08541-6103 USA

Alternatively, you can access the *Bulletin* online by visiting the GMAC website at www.gmac.com.

You can also order a copy by phone, 24 hours a day. Call ETS at (609) 771-7330.

To contact ETS by courier or by fax, address your correspondence to:

> Educational Testing Service
> Distribution and Receiving Center
> 225 Phillips Boulevard
> Ewing, NJ 08628-7435 USA
> FAX (609) 883-4349

You should plan to take the GMAT no later than two weeks after you've finished going through your test-prep materials. Some time slots fill up quickly, so register soon!

HOW DOES THE CAT FORMAT WORK?

The CAT format takes some getting used to—in fact, it's pretty weird at first. Here's how it works. You will see only one question at a time. Instead of having a predetermined mixture of basic, medium, and hard questions, the computer will select questions for you based on how well you are doing.

The first question will be of medium difficulty. If you get it right, the second question will be selected from a large pool of questions that are a little harder; if you get the first question wrong, the second will be a little more basic.

If you keep getting questions right, the test will get harder and harder; if you slip and make some mistakes, the test will adjust and start giving you easier problems, but if you answer them correctly, it will go back to the hard ones. Ideally, the test gives you enough questions to ensure that scores are not based on luck. If you get one hard question right, you might just have been lucky, but if you get ten hard questions right, then luck has little to do with it. So the test is self-adjusting and self-correcting.

Because of this format, the GMAT CAT is very different structurally from the paper-based test. After the first problem, every question that you see is based on how you answered the prior one. Consequently, you are not allowed to return to a question once you've answered it, because that would throw off the sequence. Once you answer a question, it's part of your score, for better or worse. This means you can't skip around within a section and do questions in the order that you like.

Another major consequence of the CAT format is that hard problems count more than easy ones. It has to be this way, because the very purpose of this adaptive format is to find out at what level you reliably get about half the questions right; that's your scoring level.

Imagine two students: One who does ten basic questions, half of which she gets right and half of which she gets wrong; and one who does ten very difficult questions, half of which she gets right and half of which she gets wrong. The same number of questions has been answered correctly in each case, but this does not reflect an equal ability on the part of the two students.

In fact, the student who answered five out of ten very difficult questions incorrectly could still get a very high score on the GMAT. But in order to get to these hard questions, she first had to get medium-difficulty questions right.

What this means for you is that no matter how much more comfortable you might be sticking to the basic questions, you definitely want to get to the hard questions if you can, because your score will be higher.

HOW SHOULD I ATTACK THE VERBAL SECTION?

In the chapters that follow, we'll cover techniques for answering various question types that you'll see on the Verbal Section of the GMAT. But you'll also need strategies for managing a section as a whole. Here are some strategies for attacking either multiple-choice section of the GMAT.

Be Systematic

Because it's so important to get to the hard questions as early as possible, work systematically at the beginning of a GMAT section. Use scratch paper to organize your thinking. If you're not 100 percent sure of the correct answer to a question, eliminate choices by crossing them off on your scratch paper, and guess intelligently. The first 10–15 questions of a section are crucial in determining your ability estimate, so invest the time necessary to try to answer these questions correctly. You also don't want to get several questions wrong in a row, so if you know that your answer to the previous question was a rough guess, invest a little extra time to get the next question right. You must, however, leave enough time to mark an answer for every question in the section. You will be penalized for questions you don't reach.

Draw a Grid

Using the process of elimination is especially essential when you're working your way through the Verbal Section of the GMAT. Your job always is to find the best choice of the five choices offered, and often it's easier to spot what makes an answer choice wrong than what makes one choice best. If crossing off wrong answer choices on paper tests helps you to keep track of your thinking, you may want to consider making a grid on your scratch paper before you begin the CAT (taking advantage of the fact that one side of the scratch paper you are given will be graph paper). Use the grid to mark off answer choices that you have eliminated, as shown below. This way you'll be able to tell at a glance which choices are still in the running. If you end up using it often, it'll be worth the ten seconds it takes to draw a simple grid, like this one:

A	X	X		X		X			X		X		
B		X	X	X			X	X	X	X		X		
C					X				X					X
D	X			X		X			X		X		X	
E	X	X			X			X			X			

Pace Yourself

Of course, the last thing you want to happen is to have time called before you've done half the questions. On the other hand, it's also tragic to rush through a section and have lots of time left over that you could have spent making sure you got the tough questions right. It's essential, therefore, that you learn to pace yourself, keeping in mind the general guidelines for how long to spend on any individual question or passage.

No one is saying that you should spend, for instance, exactly 90 seconds on every Critical Reasoning question. But you should have a sense of how long you have to do each question, so you know when you're exceeding the limit and should start to move faster. You'll develop this sense if you time yourself while working on practice GMAT questions.

Stop the Clock

The timer in the corner of the computer screen can work to your advantage, but if you find yourself looking at it so frequently that it becomes a distraction, you should turn it off for 10 or 15 minutes and try to refocus your attention on the test, even if you lose track of time somewhat. The CAT rewards focus and accuracy much more than it does speed.

Don't Waste Time on Questions You Can't Do

We know that forgoing a possibly tough question is easier said than done; we all have the natural instinct to plow through test sections, answering every question as it appears. But this approach often doesn't pay off on the GMAT. If you dig in your heels on a tough question, refusing to move on until you've cracked it, you're letting your test-taking mojo get in the way of your score. Like life itself, a test section is too short to waste on lost causes.

Remain Calm

It's imperative that you remain calm and composed while working through a section. You can't let yourself be rattled by one hard question or Reading Comp passage to such a degree that it throws off your performance on the rest of the section. Expect to find some hard questions, but remember that you won't be the only one encountering difficult problems. The test is designed to challenge everyone who takes it. Having trouble with a difficult question isn't going to ruin your score, but getting upset about it and letting it throw you off track will. You should recognize that part of the test maker's goal is to reward those who maintain their composure, so it's essential that you take it in stride when you run into challenging material.

HOW DO I MOVE AROUND ON THE CAT?

Let's preview the primary computer functions that you will use to move around on the CAT. ETS calls them "testing tools," but they're basically just boxes that you can click with your mouse. The screen below is typical for an adaptive test.

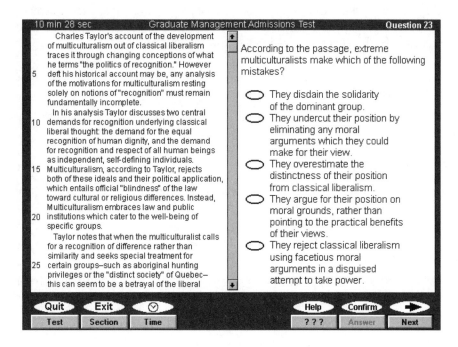

Here's what the various buttons do.

The *Time* Button

Clicking on this button turns the time display at the top of the screen on and off. When you have five minutes left in a section, the clock flashes and the display changes from Hours/Minutes to Hours/Minutes/Seconds.

The *Exit* Button

This allows you to exit the section before the time is up. If you budget your time wisely, you should never have to use this button—time will run out just as you are finishing the section.

 NO SKIPPING AROUND

You can't skip questions on the GMAT CAT; you have to answer every question you get. But you do get more time per question on the CAT than on the formerly offered pencil-and-paper test.

The *Help* Button

This one leads to directions and other stuff from the tutorial. Again, you should never have to use this button because you should know all this already. And besides, the test clock won't pause just because you click on Help.

The *Quit* Button

Hitting this button ends the test. You should never, ever use this button. You always have the option of canceling the score at the end of the GMAT, and even if you're convinced that you're bombing the exam, you should relax and view the rest of the test as a learning experience. If you do decide to cancel your score, you'll be better prepared for the next time you take the GMAT.

The *Next* Button

Hit this when you want to move on to the next question. After you press Next, you must hit Confirm.

The *Confirm* Button

This button tells the computer you are happy with your answer and are really ready to move to the next question. You cannot proceed until you have hit this button.

The *Scroll* Bar

Similar to the scroll bar on a Windows-style computer display, the scroll bar is a thin, vertical column with up and down arrows at the top and bottom. Clicking on the arrows moves you up or down the page you're reading.

PROS AND CONS OF THE GMAT CAT

There are both good and annoying things about the GMAT CAT. The following are a few things you should be thankful for or watch out for as you prepare to try your luck on the test.

Eight Good Things about the CAT

1. There is a little timer at the top of the computer screen to help you pace yourself (you can hide it if it distracts you).

2. There will be only a few other test takers in the room with you—it won't be like taking it in one of those massive lecture halls with distractions everywhere.

3. You get a pause of five minutes between each section. The pause is optional, but you should always use it to relax and stretch.

4. You can sign up for the CAT either a few days or a few weeks before the test (depending on the time of year and the availability of test centers in your area), and registration is very easy.

5. The CAT is much more convenient for your schedule than the pencil-and-paper exam was. It's offered at more than 175 centers three to six days a week (depending on the center) all year long.

6. The CAT gives you more time to spend on each question than you got on the paper-based test (almost an additional 30 seconds per question) and there are fewer questions to answer.

7. You can see your scores before you decide where you want to send them.

8. Perhaps the CAT's best feature is that it gives you your scores immediately and will send them to schools just 10 to 15 days later.

 NO DISTRACTIONS

One advantage of the GMAT CAT is that it gives you the chance to work methodically on one question at a time with no other questions there to distract you.

Seven Annoying Things about the CAT

1. You cannot skip around on this test; you must answer the questions one at a time in the order the computer gives them to you.

2. If you realize later that you answered a question incorrectly, you can't go back and change your answer.

3. If the person next to you is noisy or distracting, the proctor cannot move you or the person, since your test is on the computer.

4. You can't cross off an answer choice and never look at it again, so you have to use your scratch paper to keep track of the answers you've eliminated.

5. You have to scroll through Reading Comprehension passages, which means you won't be able to see the whole thing on the screen at once.

6. You can't write on your computer screen the way you can on a paper test (though some have tried), so you have to use scratch paper they give you, which will be inconveniently located away from the computer screen.

7. Lastly, many people find that computer screens tire them and cause eye strain—especially after almost four hours.

KAPLAN CAT STRATEGIES IN A NUTSHELL

Using certain CAT-specific strategies will have a direct, positive impact on your score:

- At the beginning of the section, each question you get right or wrong will rapidly move the computer's estimate of your score up or down. A key strategy for doing well on the CAT is to get the computer's estimate of your score up to where you are handling the hard questions. This is because getting a hard question right will help your score a lot, but getting a hard question wrong will hurt your score only slightly. Thus, it pays to spend more time on those early questions, double-checking each answer before you confirm it. Getting to the hard questions as soon as possible can only help your final score.

- As you progress through the middle part of the section, try to avoid getting several questions in a row wrong, as this will sink your score on the CAT. If you know that the previous question you answered was a blind guess, spend a little extra time trying to get the next one right.

- The CAT will switch from one question type to another within a section (going from Reading Comprehension to Sentence Correction, for example) without automatically showing the directions for each new question type. Knowing the format and directions of each GMAT question type beforehand will save you a lot of time and avoid possible confusion during the exam.

- Because the level of difficulty of questions on the CAT will not be predictable, always be on the lookout for answer-choice traps.

- Because each right or wrong answer directly affects the next question you get, the CAT does not allow you to go back to questions you've already answered to double-check your work. So be as certain as possible that you have answered a question correctly before moving on.

- The CAT does not allow you to skip questions. So if you are given a question you cannot answer, you'll have to guess. Guess intelligently and strategically by eliminating any answer choices that you know are wrong and guessing among those remaining.

- Don't get rattled if you keep seeing really, really difficult questions. It just means you're doing very well on that section. Keep it up!

- At the end of the section, you are penalized more heavily for not getting to a question at all than for answering it wrong. So if you have only a minute or two left and several questions remaining, you should guess at random rather than leave anything unanswered. And if you're down to the very last question and have almost no time left, pick a response (but do not confirm it!) and then attempt to answer the question.

PART TWO

Verbal Strategies

Chapter 2: **GMAT Sentence Correction**

Many people are surprised to discover that Sentence Correction questions are the most common question type on the Verbal Section of the GMAT. You'll probably see about 15 or 16 Sentence Correction questions out of the 41 questions on the Verbal Section of your GMAT, so they account for almost 40 percent of the entire section.

So why is grammar such a big deal on the GMAT? The GMAC and the schools it represents believe that the best managers are those who can communicate effectively, and knowing the rules of standard written English is part of being an effective communicator. The bad news about Sentence Correction questions is that they cover a range of grammar and style errors, some of which are so obscure that even good writers commit them.

The good news about Sentence Correction is that you don't need to be a grammar maven to do well on this question type. While there are lots of rules of standard written English, the GMAT most commonly concentrates on the following five:

1. Verb usage (proper agreement and correct tense)
2. Reference (proper use of pronouns and modifiers)
3. Parallel structure (consistency among items in a list or comparison)
4. Idioms (proper use of idiomatic expressions)
5. Style (avoiding excess verbiage, using active verbs, etc.)

Developing a method for attacking Sentence Correction questions and reviewing the five rules of GMAT English will help you to maximize your performance on this question type.

ANATOMY OF A SENTENCE CORRECTION QUESTION

The first step towards doing your best on GMAT Sentence Corrections is to get familiar with the format. Let's take a look at the various parts of a typical Sentence Correction question.

The Directions

The directions for these questions look something like this:

Directions: Each question presents a sentence, part or all of which is underlined, beneath which you will find five ways of phrasing the underlined part. The first repeats the original; the other four are different. If you think the original is best, choose the first answer. Otherwise, choose one of the others.

This is a test of correctness and effectiveness of expression. In choosing your response, follow the rules of standard written English; that is, pay attention to grammar, word choice, and sentence construction. Choose the answer that yields the most effective expression; this answer should be clear and exact, without awkwardness, redundancy, or ambiguity.

The directions go on and on, and they're definitely not something you want to spend your precious test-taking time reading. Here's the important news. First, note that the first answer choice repeats what's underlined in the original sentence. Since the first thing you should do on a Sentence Correction question is to read the entire original sentence, this means you should *never bother reading the first answer choice*.

Second, always remember that you are looking for the best answer, not the right answer. The test makers are skilled at finding sentences that obey the rules of standard written English without sounding particularly appealing. If the original sentence doesn't sound great, but you can't find anything specifically wrong with it and none of the other choices sound better, stick with the first choice.

Finally, note the wording the test makers use in distinguishing what makes one answer best. It should be "clear and exact, without awkwardness, redundancy, or ambiguity." Basically, this boils down to following the five basic rules of GMAT grammar (which we'll discuss later in the chapter), but if you're still struggling between two answer choices, go for the shortest answer that doesn't sound awkward and doesn't leave anything in doubt.

The Question and Answer Choices

1. A recent spate of news reports questioning the long-term health benefits of high-fat diets <u>have done little to convince its practitioners that they should follow more traditional weight-loss plans</u>.

Here's what a typical Sentence Correction sentence looks like. The first thing you should do on a Sentence Correction question is to *read the sentence in its entirety* and try to spot an error. If you spot an error, eliminate choice (A). Can you spot you spot any errors in this sentence? If you can't, there's another way to get to the correct answer . . .

(A) have done little to convince its practitioners that they should follow more traditional weight-loss plans.

(B) have done little to convince their practitioners to follow more traditional weight-loss plans.

(C) has done little to convince its practitioners to follow more traditional weight-loss plans.

(D) has done little to convince practitioners of these diets to follow more traditional weight-loss plans.

(E) has done little to convince practitioners of these diets they should follow more traditional weight-loss plans.

Go to the answer choices! Here's where you can isolate any error being tested, even if you couldn't spot it in the original sentence. The key is to scan the answer choices, looking for differences. Try reading vertically. What's the first difference you can spot among the answer choices? If you spotted *have* versus *has*, then you simply have to figure out which is correct, and eliminate answers with the wrong verb. You'll be left with either two or three choices.

Time to read vertically again and spot any other differences in the remaining choices. Eliminate choices as soon as you find a mistake, until only one choice remains. Then read your selected choice back into your sentence just to confirm that it makes sense. This is the gist of the Kaplan Three-Step Method for Sentence Corrections.

THE KAPLAN THREE-STEP METHOD FOR SENTENCE CORRECTIONS

1. Read the original sentence carefully.

If you find an error in the sentence, cross out choice (A) immediately because you know it repeats the original sentence and won't be the correct answer choice. You should also eliminate any other answer choice that repeats the original error.

2. Scan the answer choices for differences that can help you zero in on what types of errors are being tested.

If the answer choices present a variety of verb tenses or pronouns, for instance, you'll know where to focus your attention.

3. Eliminate a choice as soon as you find *one* error in it.

If you spot any error in an answer choice, eliminate that choice and any other choices that repeat the same error. Then scan the remaining answer choices for other differences by which you can zero in on other errors. You should be able to eliminate enough to come up with the correct answer, or at least to take a good guess. Make sure to confirm your answer by reading your selected choice back into the sentence; if it makes sense, move on.

USING THE KAPLAN THREE-STEP METHOD

Now let's apply the Kaplan method to our question:

1. A recent spate of news reports questioning the long-term health benefits of high-fat diets <u>have done little to convince its practitioners that they should follow more traditional weight-loss plans.</u>

    (A) have done little to convince its practitioners that they should follow more traditional weight-loss plans.

    (B) have done little to convince their practitioners to follow more traditional weight-loss plans.

    (C) has done little to convince its practitioners to follow more traditional weight-loss plans.

    (D) has done little to convince practitioners of these diets to follow more traditional weight-loss plans.

    (E) has done little to convince practitioners of these diets they should follow more traditional weight-loss plans.

1. Read the original sentence carefully.

There's a good chance you'll notice that one error lies in the first underlined word, *have*. The subject of the sentence is *spate*, which is singular, so the verb should also be singular, *has*. You can get rid of choice (A), and choice (B) as well, which repeats the error.

2. Scan the answer choices for differences.

If you hadn't spotted the above error in step one, you would have caught it here. Now that you've eliminated the first error, scan the remaining answer choices for other differences. For instance, choice (C) refers to *its practitioners*, whereas the remaining choices refer to *practitioners of these diets*. Which is correct here?

3. Eliminate a choice as soon as you find *one* error in it.

You can eliminate (C) because the pronoun *its* cannot refer to *high-fat diets*, which is plural. And in (D) and (E) you have, respectively, *convince practitioners . . . to follow* versus *convince practitioners . . . they should follow*. If choice (D) sounds better to you, you should learn to trust your ear, as (D) is idiomatically correct, and therefore the right answer.

THE FIVE FUNDAMENTAL RULES OF GMAT ENGLISH

It's time for a quick grammar review. Fortunately, as noted earlier, GMAT Sentence Corrections do not test every variety of grammatical error. In fact, the test makers tend to recycle the same classic errors over and over again. Get to know the five fundamental rules of GMAT English and you'll do well on this question type. Let's take a look.

Rule 1: Verb Usage (agreement, correct tense)

Just about everyone knows that a verb should agree with the subject (singular or plural) of the sentence. So how do the GMAT writers manage to catch so many test takers with this rule? By finding ways to confuse the issue by separating the verb from the subject or by putting it before the subject, that's how. Take a look. Choose the best response in each of the following sentences:

 RULE

Make sure that each verb matches its subject, and that its tense fits the rest of the sentence.

1. Each of the entertainers involved in the festivities (was, were) paid in advance.
2. A series of sightings of UFOs (has, have) turned the sleepy town into a tourist mecca.
3. Neither the prosecutor's eloquent closing argument nor the mountains of incriminating evidence (was, were) able to convince the jury to find the defendant guilty.
4. There (is, are) a number of delicious ways to prepare artichokes.

You also have to make sure that the verb tense agrees with the sequence of events in the rest of the sentence. Depending on the sentence, the appropriate verb tense may be past, present, future, or something a bit more complicated. As a rule, you should keep the verb tense as simple as possible while still allowing for the sequence of events to make sense. Choose the right verb tenses in the following sentences:

5. The criminal escaped from custody and is believed (to flee, to have fled) the country.
6. I (did not see, had not seen, have not seen) him since last Saturday.
7. She already (closed, has closed, had closed) the door behind her when she realized that she (wasn't, won't be, wouldn't be) able to get back in later.

Answers and Explanations

1. *Each . . . was* paid in advance. "Each" is always singular. Ignore the prepositional phrases containing plurals that follow the subject. They're there to confuse you.
2. A *series . . . has* turned the sleepy town . . . . The subject is *series*, which is always singular. Watch out for subjects like *series, string, spate,* and *succession,* which are often followed by prepositional phrases containing lots of plurals, but are still singular subjects.
3. Neither the prosecutor's eloquent closing argument nor the *mountains* of incriminating evidence *were* able to convince the jury to find the defendant guilty. In *neither . . . nor* sentences, the verb has to agree with the subject following *nor*—in this case *mountains,* which is plural. Likewise in *either . . . or* sentences, the verb must agree with the subject following *or.*
4. There *are a number* of delicious ways . . . . In "There is . . . " and "There are . . . " sentences, the subject follows the verb; here the subject "a number of delicious ways" is plural ("a number of"—meaning "several"—will always signal a plural subject on the GMAT).
5. The criminal escaped from custody and is believed *to have fled* the country. The criminal has already *escaped,* and so the logical belief is that he has already *fled* the country.
6. I *have not seen* him since last Saturday. The "since last Saturday" in the sentence tells you that the (non)activity under discussion began in the past and continues into the present; thus you should use the present perfect tense, *have not seen.*

7. She already *had closed* the door behind her when she realized that she *wouldn't be* able to get back in later. When the rest of the sentence is in the past tense (as in "she realized") and the verb in question refers to an action that occurred *before* that, you should use the past perfect tense (here, it's *had closed*). And when the verb in question refers to the future as contemplated in the past, you should use the past tense of *will*, *would*, as in *wouldn't be*.

For a more exhaustive review of verb tenses and agreement, check out the Grammar Reference Guide in appendix 1 of this book.

Rule 2: Reference (proper use of pronouns and modifiers)

 RULE

Make sure that each pronoun clearly and correctly refers to one and only one thing (or group), and that each modifying phrase is placed as close as possible to what it modifies and clearly and correctly refers to what it modifies.

To break down this rule a bit, there are two things to look for when you see a pronoun underlined (especially *it*, *its*, *they*, *them*, *their*, *that*, *those*, and *which*). First, does the pronoun agree with the noun it is replacing (singular with singular and plural with plural)? Second, is it absolutely clear what noun the pronoun is replacing? If there's any doubt or ambiguity, the pronoun use is wrong. Choose the best response in each of the following sentences:

1. Although the company had promised to maintain operational factories within the city limits, (it, they) later reneged on the agreement.
2. If the partners cannot resolve their differences, the courts may have to do (it, so).
3. After Orson Welles created an unflattering portrait of newspaper mogul William Randolph Hearst in the movie *Citizen Kane*, (he, Hearst) set about to destroy (his, Welles's) career and reputation.

Modifying phrases must also clearly and correctly refer to what they modify, which means they should be placed as close as possible to what they modify. On the GMAT, these phrases most often begin the sentence and are followed by a comma; what follows the comma should be the subject of the phrase. For instance, if a sentence begins "Born in a log cabin," you should expect that "Abraham Lincoln" will follow that comma.

Misplaced modifiers can occur anywhere in a sentence, however, so the best rule once again is to avoid any possibility of ambiguity. And if a phrase seems to occur in different parts of the sentence as you examine the answer choices, ask yourself: What does that phrase modify? Where does it belong? Finally, you may have to choose between an adverb (which usually ends in *-ly*) and an adjective; if so, ask yourself whether the word modifies a noun (in which case it should be an adjective) or a verb or another adjective (in which case it should be an adverb). Try your hand at the following:

4. While eating spaghetti, (a meatball rolled, I let a meatball roll) off my plate.
5. He laid the trousers (flat, flatly) upon the table.

Answers and Explanations

1. Although the *company* had promised . . . , *it* later reneged . . . . Watch out for collective nouns like *company*, *committee*, *group*, *gang*, etc., which require singular pronouns.
2. . . . the courts may have to do *so*. Using *it* would make no sense here. What does *it* refer to? Since we're not referring to an antecedent noun here, the proper choice is *so*.

3. After Orson Welles created an unflattering portrait of newspaper mogul William Randolph Hearst in the movie *Citizen Kane, Hearst* set about to destroy *Welles's* career and reputation. Using pronouns would have led to ambiguity in this sentence as either man could have set out to destroy the other's (or even his own) reputation.

4. While eating spaghetti, *I let a meatball roll* off my plate. Unless the meatball was in fact eating spaghetti as it rolled off the plate, it should be assumed that the subject of the modifying phrase "While eating spaghetti" is "I."

5. He laid the trousers *flat* upon the table. The modifier here refers to the *trousers*, and not the verb *laid*, and so adjective form *flat* is correct. How do you lay something flatly, anyway?

Rule 3: Parallel Structure (consistency among items in a list or comparison)

 RULE

Make sure that similar elements in a list or series have similar constructions, and that comparisons are made only between the same sorts of elements.

The basic idea behind parallel structure is pretty simple: Ideas with the same importance and function in a sentence should be expressed in the same grammatical form: all nouns, all verbs, or all whatever. Any time you recognize items being listed, be on the lookout for parallel structure. Try to pick the correct responses to the following:

1. The city's decay stems from governmental mismanagement, increasing unemployment, and (downtown businesses are relocating, the relocation of businesses) outside the city.

2. I remember my aunt making her own dandelion wine and (playing, that she played) the fiddle.

3. To visualize success is not the same as (to achieve, achieving) it.

Likewise, comparisons must also exhibit parallel structure—and more than that. Most faulty comparisons relate to the notion that you can't compare apples and oranges. You don't merely want comparisons to be grammatically similar; they must be logically similar as well. You have to compare one individual to another, one quality to another, one verb to another, etc. Be on the lookout for faulty comparisons, and try the following out for size:

4. Even though our stands stood side by side, I sold more lemonade than (the girl next door, the girl next door did).

5. The article questioned the popularity of jazz compared to (classical music, that of classical music).

6. The challenger weighed 20 pounds less than (the defender, that of the defender).

Answers and Explanations

1. The city's decay stems from governmental *mismanagement*, increasing *unemployment*, and *the relocation of downtown businesses* outside the city. The list here is of nouns: mismanagement . . . unemployment . . . relocation.

2. I remember my aunt *making* her own dandelion wine and *playing* the fiddle.

3. *To visualize* success is not the same as *to achieve* it.

4. Even though our stands were side by side, *I sold more* lemonade *than the girl next door did.* When you are comparing actions as here (how much *I sold* to how much *the girl next door sold*), you need to include that second verb "did" to make the comparison clear.

5. The article questioned *the popularity of jazz* compared to *that of classical music*. Otherwise, the article would be comparing *popularity* to *music*.

6. The *challenger* weighed 20 pounds less than *the defender*. Here, you're comparing people.

Rule 4: Idioms (proper use of idiomatic expressions)

 RULE

Use correct idioms. There really is no rule for idiom usage, just a "right" way of saying things. Certain expressions, often involving prepositions, have established themselves as correct in standard English.

As anyone who's ever studied a foreign language can attest, learning proper idioms can be extremely annoying because there is no general rule, only lists to memorize. When it comes to GMAT English, either your ear will recognize the correct idiom, or you should take the time to learn the idioms that appear over and over again on the GMAT. Try out your ear for idioms on the following:

1. Matthew Brady is regarded (as, to be) one of the greatest nineteenth-century American photographers.

2. The destruction of the tropical rainforest is generally (considered, considered as, considered to be) a major threat to the environment.

3. It took me four times as long to write the report collaboratively (as, than) it would have taken by myself.

4. Her client didn't tell her (if, whether) he had sent his payment yet.

5. The movie's ending was different (than, from) that of the book.

Also note that many idioms also set up comparisons, and thus must be followed by parallel constructions (e.g., "<u>both</u> A <u>and</u> B"). Try the following.

6. Jewel is not only a great singer, (and also, but also, but is also) a talented poetess.

7. I (either must read, must either read, must read either) the newspaper or listen to the radio before I go to work.

Answers and Explanations

1. Matthew Brady is *regarded as* one of the greatest nineteenth-century American photographers.

2. The destruction of the tropical rainforest is generally *considered* a major threat to the environment. (While "considered to be" is also technically correct, it will never be correct on the GMAT.)

3. It took me four times *as long* to write the report collaboratively *as* it would have taken by myself. (Use *than* when preceded by an *-er* word and *as* when preceded by *as* or *so*, e.g., *longer than*, *as long as*.)

4. Her client didn't tell her *whether* he had sent his payment yet. (On the GMAT, *whether* will always beat *if*.)

5. The movie's ending was different *from* that of the book.

6. Jewel is *not only* a great singer, *but also* a talented poetess. (not only *A* but also *B*)

7. I *must either read* the newspaper or listen to the radio before I go to work. (either *A* or *B*)

For a more exhaustive list of idioms that commonly appear on the GMAT, be sure to check out the GMAT Idioms List in appendix 3 of this book.

Rule 5: Style (effective expression)

Some errors are best classified as problems of "style"—that is, as problems of ineffective expression. The most common of these on the GMAT is using too many words to get an idea across. Sometimes the problem is outright redundancy, but more often the wording is just needlessly verbose. Another common style error is using a passive verb when the sentence could easily be written using an active verb.

 RULE

Eliminate unnecessary wording and redundancy. Avoid passive verbs wherever possible.

Try rewriting the following sentences to correct for errors of style, and then compare your final versions to ours:

1. There are many children who believe in Santa Claus but there are few adults who do.

   _____

2. The country's procedures for the processing of visas are extremely inefficient.

   _____

3. The shrine is at least 2,000 years old or older.

   _____

4. Because I have studied the five rules of GMAT grammar, therefore I will do well on Sentence Correction.

   _____

5. *A Confederacy of Dunces* has been bought and enjoyed by millions of readers since it was first published in 1974.

   _____

Answers and Explanations

1. Many children believe in Santa Claus but few adults do. "There is/are" sentences are often needlessly wordy and therefore wrong on GMAT Sentence Correction.
2. The country's procedures for processing visas are extremely inefficient.
3. The shrine is at least 2,000 years old. The redundant phrase *or older* is already implied by *at least*.
4. Because I have studied the five rules of GMAT grammar, I will do well on Sentence Correction. *Because* implies that the second part of the sentence is the conclusion, so *therefore* here is redundant and wrong.
5. Millions of readers have bought and enjoyed *A Confederacy of Dunces* since it was first published in 1974.

PRACTICE QUESTIONS

Now that you know the five big rules of GMAT English, it's time to try out your knowledge on some practice Sentence Correction questions. Although the five big rules explain the great majority of Sentence Correction errors, the Grammar Reference Guide in appendix 1 of this book offers a more thorough treatment of these rules, as well as all the possible grammatical rules and errors that could appear in these questions. Make sure to apply the Kaplan Three-Step Method as you answer the following questions. Answers and explanations follow.

1. Nineteenth-century authors often included encyclopedic information in their novels; Melville's famous chapter of the physiology on whales, <u>contained as it is in</u> his masterwork *Moby-Dick*, serves as a perfect example of this phenomenon.

    (A) contained as it is in
    (B) contained as it is within
    (C) contained in
    (D) found contained in
    (E) being found contained in

2. Due to the limitations imposed by the speed of light, the visible universe <u>is estimated as</u> a mere fraction of the total universe.

    (A) is estimated as
    (B) is estimated to be
    (C) is estimated at
    (D) estimated to be
    (E) estimated at

3. For over thirty years, Dr. Jane Goodall has conducted field studies of large primate species and <u>shares her findings with the general public in an effort</u> to promote conservation of these species and their habitats.

    (A) shares her findings with the general public in an effort
    (B) has shared her findings with the general public so as
    (C) shared her findings with the general public in an effort
    (D) will share her findings with the general public so as
    (E) would share her findings with the general public in an effort

4. Cattle were domesticated both for the uses made of the animal—food and leather—<u>but also for</u> the labor the animal could provide.

    (A) but also for
    (B) and for
    (C) or for
    (D) but also
    (E) and also

5. Recent surveys indicate that, contrary to popular belief, total abstinence from alcohol does not correlate <u>as strongly with good health as does moderate drinking</u>.

    (A) as strongly with good health as does moderate drinking

    (B) strongly with good health, like moderate drinking does

    (C) as strongly with good health as does moderately drinking

    (D) as strongly with good health as with moderate drinking

    (E) as strongly with good health as moderate drinking

6. Despite <u>the platform of the Republican Party supporting the measure, they keep voting</u> against campaign finance reform in Congress.

    (A) the platform of the Republican Party supporting the measure, they keep voting

    (B) the Republican Party's platform supporting the measure, they keep voting

    (C) the Republicans' platform supporting the measure, it keeps voting

    (D) the Republican Party's platform supporting the measure, party members keep voting

    (E) the supporting measure of the platform of the Republican Party, they keep voting

7. <u>The creation of an independent treasury, establishing lower tariffs, and purchasing</u> the Oregon Territory, all credited to the presidency of James Knox Polk, are among the significant accomplishments that persuade historians to rank this former governor of Tennessee well as a U.S. president.

    (A) The creation of an independent treasury, establishing lower tariffs, and purchasing

    (B) The creation of an independent treasury, securing lower tariffs as well as purchasing

    (C) The creation of an independent treasury, the establishment of lower tariffs, and the purchase of

    (D) Creating an independent treasury, securing lower tariffs, and purchasing

    (E) Creating an independent treasury, the securing of lower tariffs, and the purchasing of

8. In many coastal New England towns, <u>the fisherman still operates as they have</u> for generations, displaying and selling their catch dockside at the end of each day.

    (A) the fisherman still operates as they have

    (B) the fisherman still operates as was done

    (C) fishermen still operate as they have done

    (D) the fisherman still operates as he has

    (E) fishermen still operate as they had

KAPLAN)

9. The average salary of new jobs <u>is expected to rise in the near future as jobs become available in high-paying industries</u>.

   Ⓐ is expected to rise in the near future as jobs become available in high-paying industries

   Ⓑ are expected to rise in the near future as jobs become available in high-paying industries

   Ⓒ are expected to rise in the near future through jobs becoming available in high-paying industries

   Ⓓ would be expected to rise in the near future through jobs becoming available in high-paying industries

   Ⓔ will rise in the near future because jobs in high-paying industries are expected to become available

10. Pablo Picasso's genius is fully revealed only when one considers the various facets of his work as they developed through many artistic phases, <u>beginning with his Red period, continuing through his Blue period, and finishing with his period of Cubism.</u>

   Ⓐ beginning with his Red period, continuing through his Blue period, and finishing with his period of Cubism

   Ⓑ beginning with his Red period, continuing through his Blue period, and finishing with his Cubist period

   Ⓒ beginning with his Red period, and continuing through his Blue period and his Cubist period

   Ⓓ beginning with his Red period phase, his Blue period phase, and his phase of Cubism

   Ⓔ beginning with his Red period, his Blue period, and his period of Cubism

11. Many climatologists now suspect that the effects of global warming will include unusual temperature fluctuations throughout the northern and southern hemispheres that <u>far exceeds what scientists at the Kyoto Summit were predicting only a few years ago.</u>

   Ⓐ far exceeds what scientists at the Kyoto Summit were predicting only a few years ago

   Ⓑ far exceeds those predicted by scientists at the Kyoto Summit only a few years ago

   Ⓒ exceeds by far that which scientists at the Kyoto Summit had predicted only a few years ago

   Ⓓ exceed by far those that scientists at the Kyoto Summit had predicted only a few years ago

   Ⓔ far exceed what scientists at the Kyoto Summit were predicting only a few years ago

12. The ancient Sumerians are credited <u>as having</u> created the first phonetic writing system as long ago as 3100 B.C.

   Ⓐ as having

   Ⓑ to have

   Ⓒ for having

   Ⓓ with having

   Ⓔ as being the ones who

13. Several stock market analysts now report that the plummeting <u>values of many high-tech stocks have fallen so as to make</u> them once again attractive to investors.

(A) values of many high-tech stocks have fallen so as to make

(B) high-tech stock values have fallen, making

(C) descent of many high-tech stock values have made

(D) values of many high-tech stocks are making

(E) values of many high-tech stocks have fallen, which has made

14. Unlike <u>its fellow Baltic nations, Latvia and Lithuania, the economy of Estonia grew at an astonishing rate in the late 1990s, and at the end of the decade it was placed on the fast track to join</u> the European Union.

(A) its fellow Baltic nations, Latvia and Lithuania, the economy of Estonia grew at an astonishing rate in the late 1990s, and at the end of the decade it was placed on the fast track to join

(B) its fellow Baltic nations, Latvia and Lithuania, Estonia's economy grew at an astonishing rate in the late 1990s, and at the end of the decade was placed on the fast track to join

(C) its fellow Baltic nations, Latvia and Lithuania, Estonia's economy grew at an astonishing rate in the late 1990s, and at the end of the decade they were placed on the fast track to join

(D) Latvia and Lithuania, its fellow Baltic nations, the economy of Estonia grew at an astonishing rate in the late 1990s, and at the end of the decade was placed on the fast track to join

(E) Latvia and Lithuania, its fellow Baltic nations, Estonia possessed an economy that grew at an astonishing rate in the late 1990s, and at the end of the decade the country was placed on the fast track to join

15. <u>By the number of carbons in the compound's longest chain, a hydrocarbon's standard name is partly determined.</u>

(A) By the number of carbons in the compound's longest chain, a hydrocarbon's standard name is partly determined

(B) The number of carbons in the compound's longest continuous chain enables partial determination of the standard name of a hydrocarbon

(C) The standard name of a hydrocarbon is partly determined by the number of carbons in the compound's longest continuous chain

(D) Counting the number of carbons in the compound's longest continuous chain enables partially determining a hydrocarbon's standard name

(E) As the carbons on a hydrocarbon's longest continuous chain are counted, so that partially determines the compound's standard name

ANSWERS AND EXPLANATIONS

1. C	6. D	11. E
2. B	7. C	12. D
3. C	8. C	13. D
4. B	9. A	14. E
5. A	10. B	15. C

1. Choice (C) is correct.

When you suspect that excess verbiage may be at issue, check to see whether the shortest choice makes sense. In this case, it does.

2. Choice (B) is correct.

The correct idiom is "estimate(d) to be" (and of course you need "is estimated to be" because it's not the universe that's doing the estimating).

3. Choice (C) is correct.

Sometimes determining the proper verb tense is simply a matter of maintaining the same tense as the other verbs in the sentence (parallel structure), as in "Dr. Jane Goodall has *conducted* . . . and *shared* . . . ." Choice (B), with "has shared," would also work, but it contains that awkward construction "so as"—which is never correct on the GMAT (although "so . . . as to be . . . " often is correct).

4. Choice (B) is correct.

The key here is to recognize that the "both" in the sentence sets up the parallel-structure idiom "both A and B," so we can anticipate the correct answer here to be "*both* for the uses . . . *and* for the labor," which is exactly what (B) gives us. By the way, "and also" is considered redundant on the GMAT. Moreover, phrases between dashes, as in "—food and leather—" here, are usually thrown into Sentence Correction sentences just to confuse the issue. They should always be ignored on your first reading of the sentence.

5. Choice (A) is correct.

The first thing to recognize is that there's a comparison going on here, so we need to make sure that it's an appropriate comparison. The comparison here is between how strongly total abstinence from alcohol correlates with good health and how strongly moderate drinking correlates with good health. Choices (B) and (D) mangle the sense of that comparison. Choice (C) is out because "drinking" here is being used as a noun, so it should be modified by the adjective "moderate," not the adverb "moderately." Finally, (E) is out because that second verb, "does," is necessary to convey the sense that the comparison is between how one "correlates" and how the other "correlates."

6. Choice (D) is correct.

Be suspicious anytime you see *they* or *it* in the underlined portion of the sentence or among the answer choices. For starters, (A) is out because there is no antecedent plural noun that "they" could be referring to. (B) and (E) are out for the same reason. And (C) is out because the "it" here makes it sound as if the platform is doing the voting in Congress. Only (D) avoids these pronoun pitfalls.

7. Choice (C) is correct.

Look for consistency among items in a list. (A) and (B) are out, "The creation . . . securing . . . purchasing," as is (E), "Creating . . . the securing of . . . the purchasing of . . . ." Both (C) and (D) are internally consistent, but since the list is supposed to refer to accomplishments, (C), a list of nouns, "The creation . . . the establishment . . . the purchase," makes more sense than (D), a list of gerunds, "Creating . . . establishing . . . purchasing." (Standard noun forms are generally considered preferable to gerunds on the GMAT.)

8. Choice (C) is correct.

You have to read the entire sentence to know whether to go singular or plural here. Because the sentence refers to "their catch," you need plural "fishermen" and plural "they." That eliminates everything but (C) and (E). And (E) is out because under discussion is a practice that has continued from the past into the present, so the proper verb tense is present perfect, as in "fishermen still operate as they *have done* . . . ."

9. Choice (A) is correct.

The subject is "salary," so the verb should be singular, which eliminates (B) and (C). As written, "is expected to rise in the near future" makes good sense; there's no need to complicate the verb tense, as (D) does. (E) scrambles the meaning of the sentence, turning an expectation into a fact.

10. Choice (B) is correct.

Again, we're looking for consistency throughout this sequence. (A) is out because after "Red period" and "Blue period," why change it to "Period of Cubism"? Choices (D) and (E) have similar inconsistencies. Choice (B) makes the fix we want: "Red period . . . Blue period . . . Cubist period." Choice (C) also has this fix, but loses the sequential sense contained in the original sentence of "beginning with . . . continuing with . . . and finishing with . . . ."

11. Choice (E) is correct.

A vertical scan reveals a choice between *exceeds* and *exceed*, so ask yourself, what is the subject of the verb? The answer is *fluctuations*, which is plural, so the proper verb form is *exceed*—(A), (B), and (C) are out. And (D) is not only wordier than (E), but it also makes inappropriate use of the past perfect verb tense *had predicted* (which should be used only when you're discussing something that occurred before something else you're also discussing that occurred in the past).

12. Choice (D) is correct.

The idiom is "credit(ed) with"—don't ask us why, just learn it.

13. Choice (D) is correct.

In this sentence, there's an out-and-out redundancy; "plummeting" means falling, so get rid of any answer choices that discuss falling, including (A), (B), and (E). Choice (C) is also a bit off, with its "plummeting descent." Choice (D) is the only choice that avoids redundancy and makes sense.

KAPLAN

14. Choice (E) is correct.

Be on the lookout for modifying phrases followed by commas at the beginning of a sentence. In this case, all the sentences begin with variations of "Unlike its fellow Baltic nations, Latvia and Lithuania," so what follows this introduction should in fact be a Baltic nation—that is, Estonia, not Estonia's economy. Only (E) corrects this misplaced modifier error.

15. Choice (C) is correct.

When the entire sentence is underlined, style problems are often found in many of the answer choices, so read and eliminate aggressively. Here choice (A) needlessly complicates the sentence by sticking the long and confusing prepositional phrase "By the number . . . ") at the beginning of the sentence (it's also a misplaced modifier, as the phrase should be next to "determined"). In choice (B), does the wording "enables partial determination of the standard name" strike you as a bit off? Surely there must be a better way of phrasing this sentence. Choice (C) is the first version that makes sense. Choice (D) is off: "Counting . . . enables . . . partially determining . . . ." And (E) not only mangles the sense of the sentence, but is not even a complete sentence. Moral of the story: You don't have to know what stylistic error a sentence is committing, so long as your ear can distinguish effective expression from ineffective expression. (Also, note that the passive voice is not *always* wrong. In this case, the clearest way to express the idea was to use the passive *"is . . . determined."*)

Chapter 3: **Reading the GMAT Way**

If you find it difficult to slog through all the dense reading passages that appear on the GMAT Verbal Section, you are not alone. This chapter is designed to help you develop the very specific reading skills that you need to read with better efficiency and comprehension on the GMAT. First and foremost, "reading the GMAT way" means reading with different goals, and employing different techniques, from your reading in everyday life. As a rule, we read for one or both of two simple reasons: to learn something, or to pass the time pleasantly. Needless to say, neither of those has anything to do with the GMAT!

Furthermore, we typically tend to read for content. "What's this author saying?" we ask ourselves, or, "What's this book about?" But anyone who tries to read for content on the GMAT is missing the point. There's just no time under strict test conditions to understand everything that's being said—and there's no payoff in it, either.

So what does GMAT reading, as distinct from everyday reading, involve? Broadly stated, it involves two things:

1. Reading for the author's purpose—the "why" of the text
2. Reading for the passage's structure—the "how" of the text

Almost every single GMAT Reading Comprehension question—and Critical Reasoning question, for that matter—fundamentally hinges on your ability to step back from the text and analyze why the author is writing in the first place, and how she puts her text together. Why these particular skills being tested? Apparently, the GMAT writers figure that requiring us to determine the author's purpose and passage structure is the best way to test how we think about the prose we read. And thinking is always being tested, one way or another, on every GMAT question.

Look at it this way. The entire purpose of the GMAT is to sort test takers along a gradient from lesser to greater ability. Since most test takers are perfectly adequate readers in everyday life, the GMAT writers have to come up with a way to complicate the task. Therefore, in order to set up the questions—to test how we think about the prose we read—the GMAT passage authors hide or disguise their statement of purpose, and challenge us to find it. Take a look at this, the first sentence of a typical GMAT passage:

> The great migration of European intellectuals to the United States
> in the second quarter of the twentieth century prompted a transmuta-
> tion in the character of Western social thought.

We can already begin to figure out why the author is writing. The purpose, we might say, is "to explore how the arrival of European eggheads during the period 1926–1950 changed Western social thought"

(your phrasing might be a bit different, but the gist is probably the same). And notice the implied structure of what will follow. We can expect that the author will first describe the migration westward, and then explain what the "transmutation" was. And it probably will be in that order—GMAT authors are nothing if not logical. So there is a definite purpose and structure implied here; we just have to work at figuring them out.

The first task of GMAT reading is to use the clues provided by the author to figure out what she has in mind as she strings sentences together to create a unified whole—a full passage. Reading in this way is the first step towards raising your GMAT verbal score.

TOPIC AND SCOPE

While you're trying to figure out the author's purpose, you should also take note of the topic and scope of the passage. The topic of the passage is the raw subject matter. The scope of the passage is the fraction of the topic that interests the author.

Normally, we read without paying attention to the scope of what we're reading. But on the GMAT, you'll want to establish precisely what the author does and does not choose to cover. In order to answer many GMAT Verbal questions, you need to stick to the scope of the passage. Sound easy? Sometimes it is, but it's often easy to miss the forest for all the trees. For instance:

> Genetic engineering may offer the best hope of improving yields of *Oryza sativa* (cultivated rice) and perhaps, in time, other important U.S. crops. The insertion of foreign genetic material into the DNA of cultivars appears to confer an herbicidal protection on the resultant plants, enabling them to compete successfully for nutrients with uncultivated grasses . . . .

Even a confirmed "sciencephobe" should be able to cut past the jargon to see that the topic here is genetic engineering or, to paraphrase it in simple terms (a habit you should start getting into), "mucking about with genes." And what aspect of that topic is the author interested in? The scope of the discussion is cultivated rice, specifically, improving cultivated rice through mucking about with its genes. That's what the bulk of the discussion is going to deal with. Note also that the reference at the end of the first sentence signals that the scope is likely to extend, before the passage ends, to other crops. But the qualifier "perhaps, in time" suggests that those other crops, if they're mentioned at all, will be of only passing interest; cultivated rice is likely to stay the main center of attention. Most readers of the passage above would be content to know the general topic, but in your GMAT reading, you'll want to identify the scope of the passage, as this will allow you to answer the questions quickly and accurately. On Reading Comprehension, and especially on Critical Reasoning, wrong answers typically stray beyond the scope of the passage.

GETTING THE GIST

Most test takers make the mistake of trying to understand every bit of the text in Reading Comprehension and Critical Reasoning. Terrified of "missing something," they muscle their way through, hanging on to every word and every thought, as if every sentence were of equal importance. But critical reading demands the opposite strategy. When you read critically, you must recognize some sentences as really important (because they announce major themes or ideas), some as secondary (in that they present evidence for larger points), and some as tertiary, trivia, or filler. Worse yet, the GMAT's timed conditions make it virtually impossible for most people to absorb every single sentence in the time allotted, let alone have time to answer the questions.

Here are a few ways to get into the habit of reading for the gist:

- Recognize that not all sentences are created equal. Some are more important than others, and you are the one who has to judge which information is vital.
- Give only a cursory reading to secondary or trivial details.
- Zero in on the topic sentence in each paragraph.
- Read the important stuff carefully, and paraphrase it to be sure you understand it.

To see why getting the gist is so important, suppose you're reading the following paragraph:

> The Davis-Bacon Act was originally intended to favor white laborers, who at the time of its passage constituted the overwhelming majority of trade union memberships. While the requirement that laborers on federally funded or assisted construction projects in the inner city be paid the local "prevailing wage" might seem likely to benefit minority workers as well as the minority-owned contracting firms that are often awarded preference points in the bidding process for such contracts, in practice such requirements thwart the economic advancement of minority laborers. For its part, the AFL-CIO is committed to enlarging the scope of the regulations.

Many test takers stop dead to read that middle sentence in detail, and the clock runs out on them as they fail to see the forest for the trees. In your first pass through this paragraph, you should read for the gist. You read that the intent of the Act was "to favor white laborers," and you figure that it either did, or did not, achieve that intent. Skim, skim, skim through that subordinate "while" clause, looking for something that relates to the ultimate effect of the Act, and you make your way to this: " . . . in practice such requirements thwart the economic advancement of minority laborers." "So," you say to yourself, "not only was it intended to favor white workers, but it out-and-out 'thwarted' minority workers too." And then the final sentence makes sense: The AFL-CIO's attempt to broaden the scope of the Davis-Bacon Act must really be an attempt to make the Act work for all workers, regardless of race.

What this little example illustrates is that those who get the gist of difficult text, and put it into their own, simpler language, are empowered to keep moving forward. They're secure in the knowledge that they've read and understood the most important points, and that if a question demands a closer reading, then and only then will they go back and read in (slightly) more depth. The best test takers know how to read for the gist and how to paraphrase, and they exercise those skills at every opportunity. We encourage you to make paraphrasing a habit.

Here's an exercise designed to give you some additional practice at "getting the gist" of GMAT text. When tackling GMAT prose in this way becomes second nature, your timing improves—you get through the passages much faster—and your ability to answer questions improves as well, because getting the gist is all about thinking about difficult prose and interpreting it.

> The "Robber Baron" industrialists of the late 19th and early 20th centuries are often portrayed as having no interest in the well-being of society as a whole in their ruthless pursuit of power and personal fortunes. Quite apart from the incidental benefits they provided to society through industrial development, this view ignores the philanthropic endeavors with which most of the Robber Barons were associated. Admittedly a good deal of their philanthropy took the form of bequests; still, these industrialists are responsible for many of our best museums and symphony halls, and the foundations they established continue to rank among the most important sources of charity to this day.

Keeping in mind the issues of topic, scope, and purpose, sum up the gist of this paragraph in one sentence, using your own words as much as possible. Then read on to compare your version with ours.

What this author is basically saying is:

_____

_____

Here's one way to sum up that paragraph:

> Contrary to popular belief, turn-of-the-century "fat cats" did a lot of things (like donating money) to make society better.

This version has hit on the right topic ("Robber Baron" industrialists) and scope (their concern, or lack of same, for society during the late 19th and early 20th centuries). Just as importantly, it's got the author's purpose right. It would be a distortion, for instance, to say that this author is out to whitewash the Robber Barons, to argue that they were totally selfless. There's no attempt here to deny that these guys were out to make money for themselves. What the author wants to do is acknowledge that they also score some points on the "Helping Society" side of the ledger, in contrast to the prevailing view. "They weren't all bad" is the bottom line.

What's important to note is that this paragraph, like so many other GMAT passages (in both Reading Comprehension and Critical Reasoning), is contrasting a common view with the author's own view; and as long as you get the gist of each of those viewpoints, you'll be okay. You don't have to underline or memorize all the details—all the specific examples of Robber Baron largesse—unless and until questions demand it. As long as you've gotten the gist of the text, you're armed well enough to move on.

Try the same process with the following paragraphs, reading and distilling them one at a time. Remember:

- Think of the topic, scope, and purpose.
- Put the prose into your own, casual words.
- Cut through the details—think about why they're there, and not so much what they're saying.

1. It is a commonplace observation that people have become much more sophisticated about evaluating media-delivered messages than used to be the case. But take a closer look. Media celebrities still act as spokespeople to persuade the public to buy every kind of product from automotive parts to phone cards. Political campaigns are waged entirely on the basis of 30-second television spots. People can be stirred to favor foreign intervention in response to television images. How sophisticated is that?

    What this author is basically saying is:

    _____

    _____

    _____

2. Observers moved by the plight of a country in the throes of famine will sometimes call for the international community to act. Unfortunately, the solution is often more complicated than first appears; if it weren't, the country would be able to solve the problem itself. Famines are usually caused by civil strife. In order to alleviate the famine, the international community must send in a "peace-keeping force" to resolve the dispute. That means they must either come down in favor of one side, often without understanding the issues at stake, or try to keep either side from winning, and as a result, artificially prolong the war.

    What this author is basically saying is:

    _____

    _____

    _____

3. When people get older, their memories of "the good old days" are not always accurate. They may remember that a movie cost a quarter and a trolley ride cost a nickel, but they forget that those amounts represented an appreciable part of the average person's hourly wage. They remember living in close-knit communities, but they forget the depressions and wars that sometimes struck those communities.

    What this author is basically saying is:

    _____

    _____

    _____

4. Last week I got a letter from Leon saying that he has finally found the perfect house, and he'll never move again. I've gotten similar letters from him on at least two other occasions. He began praising the house, the neighborhood, and the town to the skies. But there always turned out to be something wrong. Once he moved because the winters were too harsh where he was living; another time, the house was too small after he got married. So I'll wait and see.

    What this author is basically saying is:

    _____

    _____

    _____

Explanations

Here are some possible statements of the gist of each of the paragraphs on the previous page. Your versions will surely differ from these, probably in major ways. But see how many of the key issues you picked up on.

1. People probably are no better at resisting TV sales pitches than they used to be.

Once again, the "commonplace" view is contrasted to the author's view. She uses several examples of how the media (mostly TV) sells us products or ideas in quick, unsophisticated snippets, and ends with a rhetorical question, "How sophisticated is that?" to evoke the response: Not very. It's easy to overlook the implied comparison in the first sentence ("much more sophisticated . . . *than used to be the case*" [emphasis ours]), but that comparison is important to the scope.

2. Would-be international rescuers of countries suffering famine and civil wars inevitably get caught up in those wars.

The "inevitably" is justified by the painful choice offered in the last sentence: Countries trying to relieve famine, the author says, "must" send in peacekeepers and "must" either favor one side or prolong the war through their efforts at neutrality. Other issues raised in the paragraph—the motives for international relief efforts; the deceptive complexity of the situations; the causes of famine—are secondary to, or supportive of, the key point made above.

3. Older people sometimes remember only the "good parts" of their youth.

That the gist of this paragraph is merely a paraphrase of the first sentence is no surprise: The second and third sentences are simply acting as evidence for the opening assertion. This happens a lot on the test, especially in Critical Reasoning. These last two examples were written in much more casual language, but that doesn't mean that you shouldn't continue to use your own casual language to paraphrase them.

4. Despite his claim, Leon may very well move again.

This paragraph shouldn't be read as "Leon will move again" or even "he will probably move again." It would be a mistake to infer that the author would take any kind of a bet on Leon's relocation. The gist of the paragraph is simply that there has been a historical disjunction between Leon's previous expressions of homeowner satisfaction and his subsequent behavior. With Leon's claim to love his current home, the pattern may be on its way to repeating itself.

KEYWORDS

The best GMAT test takers are anticipatory readers. They know that every passage is more than the sum of its parts—that the parts must fit together to create a unified whole. To better understand the function of each part within the passage, they keep asking themselves, "Where is this going?" In other words, they try to sense how each piece of information helps the author set up the next. These readers know that because GMAT prose is extremely logical, the passage will almost always go where logic dictates. Occasionally, the author may surprise you—but if you know what to expect, his taking a different tack will be all the more striking. And all this means you can stay on top of the author instead of several steps behind.

The best GMAT readers also think structurally. They do so by picking up the clues left by the author, structural clues that we at Kaplan call Keywords. Keywords are the structural signals that every author uses: The words and phrases whose only purpose is to organize and shape the text. For example . . . hey wait a second, that's a Keyword phrase right there! The moment you see the phrase "For example," you know that it signals an upcoming illustration of whatever was just said. And that's what we mean by thinking structurally.

We generally respond to Keywords unconsciously. But that's not good enough. Those who are best at GMAT Verbal locate, interpret, and use Keywords knowingly. Keyword signals exist only because they have a function: to help the author structure the prose. By concentrating more on the function of words than on their information content, the GMAT Verbal champs save themselves an awesome amount of time, and are rewarded with faster and better answers. Check out how meaningful these important categories of Keywords are to you. Jot down as many examples as you can think of for each category, and then compare your responses to what we've provided.

Illustration Keywords

For example

_____   _____

Sequence Keywords

First of all

_____   _____

Continuation Keywords

And

_____   _____   _____   _____

_____   _____

Contrast Keywords

On the other hand

_____   _____   _____   _____

_____   _____   _____   _____

Conclusion Keywords

Therefore

_____   _____   _____   _____

Evidence Keywords

Because

_____   _____

Emphasis Keywords

Most of all

_____   _____

(Now read on.)

KAPLAN)

Illustration Keywords signal that an example is about to arrive. *For example* and *for instance* are the most obvious. But think about these:

> *In the words of Jean-Paul Sartre*
> *As Maya Angelou says*

In each case, what's about to follow is an example of that person's thinking.

Sequence Keywords are the author's way of telling you, "Hey, there's some sort of order at work here." They announce that a logical arrangement of the author's reasoning is taking place. These are the most common:

> *Second (third, fourth, etc.)*   *Next*   *Finally*

Continuation Keywords announce that more of the same is about to come up. *And* is the most common one in English; others include:

> *Also*   *Likewise*   *In addition*   *At the same time*
> *As well as*   *Furthermore*   *Moreover*

Also (there's a signal for you!), the colon usually does the same job: It tells you that what follows expands upon, or continues, what came before. Note that some Continuation Keywords can also function as Sequence Keywords.

Contrast Keywords signal an opposition or shift. There are lots of these besides the one we provided:

> *Although*   *By contrast*   *However*   *Conversely*   *Still*   *Yet*   *Whereas*
> *But*   *Despite*   *Nevertheless*   *Otherwise*   *Though*   *Notwithstanding*

Contrast Keywords are among the most significant in both Reading Comprehension and Critical Reasoning, because so many passages are based on contrast or opposition. Almost certainly, something important is happening when a Contrast Keyword shows up.

Conclusion Keywords signal that the author is about to sum up or announce her thesis. The most common one is *therefore*, to which we can add:

> *Consequently*   *Thus*   *It can be seen that*   *We can conclude that*
> *As a result*   *Hence*   *So*   *In conclusion*

Since these Keywords have to do with the author's logic, it's small wonder that they're especially crucial for Critical Reasoning. No less important are:

Evidence Keywords, which tell you that the author is about to provide support for a point. Here are the most important Evidence Keywords:

> *Because*   *Since*   *For*   *Given that*

When all is said and done, **Emphasis Keywords** may be the most welcome. If we're supposed to read for author point of view, and we are, what better than to stumble across words and phrases whose sole purpose is to announce "I, the author, find this important"? Note these well:

Above all	*Most of all*	*Essentially*
Primarily	*Indeed*	

KEYWORDS EXERCISE

Each of the following pieces of text—any of which might be found in a Reading Comprehension passage or Critical Reasoning argument—ends with a familiar Keyword or phrase. After you read it, try to formulate an idea of what ought to follow the Keyword; then look at the three possibilities listed. Choose the one that would be the most logical completion of the sentence: Which one (if any) comes the closest to your expectation?

1. The latest research seems to suggest that people who consume alcohol in moderation may be healthier, on average, than either teetotalers or heavy drinkers. Hence,

    (A) people who enjoy a single glass of wine with dinner need not fear that they are endangering their health.

    (B) at least one clinical study rates both nondrinkers and heavy drinkers as less psychologically stable compared with moderate drinkers.

    (C) without more data, it would be premature to change one's lifestyle on the basis of these findings.

2. The photograph being copied must be in good condition; otherwise,

    (A) it should be examined with a magnifying glass under strong white light.

    (B) its dimensions must be identical to those of the desired duplicate.

    (C) the duplicate will exhibit the same scratches or smears as the original.

3. After Giotto's death, the fresco was completed by an apprentice whose skills were not quite up to the task, and

    (A) he clearly attempted to imitate the master's strokes.

    (B) neither the perspective nor the colors are convincing.

    (C) he had studied with the master for only a short time.

4. The evidence suggesting that the two species of felines may have existed simultaneously on the African veldt is purely circumstantial. For example,

   (A) with no direct proof to the contrary, many experts still believe that the giant cats died out long before their smaller relatives appeared.

   (B) fossil traces of both species have been found in separate areas in sediments that are thought to have been laid down by the same floodwaters.

   (C) since all of the giant fossils found so far have been male, some scientists suspect that the smaller ones represent the females and young of the same sexually dimorphic species.

5. Only one day-care facility in this city bases its fees on a sliding scale according to family income, and there are over three hundred children on its waiting list. Consequently,

   (A) it is nearly impossible for most poor mothers to work outside the home while providing care for their children.

   (B) the blame for the lack of affordable childcare alternatives must be placed on state legislators, who have stymied every attempt to redress the situation.

   (C) the number of high- and middle-income families who place their preschool children in day care primarily to give them an educational advantage continues to rise.

6. The purpose of the proposed advertising campaign is, first, to increase public awareness of the company's new logo. For instance,

   (A) it is hoped that the new commercials will reinforce brand loyalty among consumers.

   (B) a major portion of the budget has been allocated to create a striking and memorable design.

   (C) television viewers should be able to identify the design correctly after seeing the commercial only once.

7. Tobacco companies often advertise cigarettes with filter tips or with lower levels of tar and nicotine as "lighter," implying that they are less damaging to health than regular cigarettes. But

   (A) several studies have shown that people who smoke such cigarettes tend to inhale more deeply, thereby delivering at least as much tar and nicotine to their lungs as if they were smoking regular cigarettes.

   (B) in manufacturing and marketing these products, the tobacco companies are responding to the widespread awareness and fear, even among habitual smokers, of the harmful effects of smoking.

   (C) the impression created by these advertisements is that people—particularly young women—who care about their health may smoke these cigarettes without having to worry about developing cancer or emphysema.

8. Many methods of contraception work by preventing sperm from fertilizing the ovum. Alternatively,

    Ⓐ latex condoms and diaphragms present physical barriers to sperm; the contraceptive efficacy of these methods can be increased chemically via spermicides.

    Ⓑ these methods, however varied their mechanisms, are all prophylactic in nature, in that no embryo is ever created.

    Ⓒ pregnancy can be averted after fertilization by causing the fertilized egg to be expelled from the body, rather than implanting in the uterine wall.

9. That Nabokov's novels found a mass audience in the United States, a country in which relatively few people study foreign languages, is mystifying, especially given

    Ⓐ his appeal to academics and literary critics.

    Ⓑ his penchant for multilingual puns.

    Ⓒ the ribald adult content of his books.

ANSWERS AND EXPLANATIONS

1. A	4. B	7. A
2. C	5. A	8. C
3. B	6. C	9. B

1. Choice (A) is correct

Hence is a Conclusion Keyword, and (A) is the only one of the choices that can reasonably be deduced from the previous sentence. (B) provides additional evidence along the same lines, and would more logically follow a Continuation Keyword like *moreover*. (C), which takes a different view, would probably start off with a Contrast Keyword like *however*.

2. Choice (C) is correct

The Contrast Keyword *otherwise* warns of some undesired consequence to follow if the photo is in bad shape; (C) fits the bill. (A) is a precondition to ensure that the original photo is okay; it should take a Conclusion Keyword like *therefore*. (B) describes a second requirement that's distinct from the photo's condition; it needs a Continuation Keyword like *also* to set it up.

3. Choice (B) is correct

And expresses continuation, another piece of evidence that points in the same direction. Replacing *and* with a wordier Evidence Keyword, such as *as evidenced by the fact that*, would make (B) even more clearly correct. Contrast Keyword *although* would more appropriately introduce (A), which expresses a subtle contrast (the apprentice didn't succeed, though he tried). (C) attempts to explain why the apprentice wasn't up to snuff; an Evidence Keyword like *since* should set up this choice.

KAPLAN

4. Choice (B) is correct

For example, one of the most common Illustration Keywords, sets the stage for (B), a specific piece of the circumstantial evidence mentioned in the first part of the sentence. (A) suggests an opposing conclusion—that the two species did not coexist—and would probably be introduced by a Conclusion Keyword like *thus*. (C) reinforces the main clause's statement that only circumstantial evidence supports the conclusion that the two species coexisted; this choice raises additional evidence pointing to an alternative conclusion, and would be more effectively set up by the Continuation Keyword *in addition*.

5. Choice (A) is correct

The Conclusion Keyword *consequently* leads nicely to (A), a natural result of the first sentence. Placing blame, (B), is not a result but a conclusion, and can't be introduced by this Conclusion Keyword because it's buttressed by new evidence (the legislators have stymied every attempt to redress the situation). Emphasis Keywords like *in large measure* would serve better. (C) discusses a simultaneous but different trend. *At the same time*, a Continuation Keyword with subtle overtones of contrast, would set it up better.

6. Choice (C) is correct

Illustration Keywords *for instance* should lead to an example of how the campaign would increase public awareness; (C) would be a reasonable result to hope for. A Sequence Keyword like *secondly* would more effectively indicate that (A) raises a new issue, brand loyalty, that is an additional purpose of the campaign, unrelated to public awareness. (B) requires a Conclusion Keyword like *hence* to show that the previously stated objective mandates a hefty design budget for the new logo.

7. Choice (A) is correct

But, one of the bluntest Contrast Keywords in the English language, leads to (A), an outcome diametrically opposed to the claims in the cigarette ads. (B) is an attempt to infer why the tobacco companies would make such claims; Conclusion Keywords like *it can be concluded that* would clarify the logical connection. (C) continues the train of thought begun in the previous sentence, summarizing the subtext of the advertisements; Emphasis Keywords like *above all* would work well here.

8. Choice (C) is correct

The Contrast Keyword *alternatively* has to introduce contraceptive methods that don't rely on preventing fertilization; (C), preventing implantation after the fact, is a good alternative. (A), which describes specific contraceptive methods that prevent fertilization, would be better introduced by an Illustration Keyword like *for example*. An Emphasis Keyword like *essentially* would help (B) point out what all these methods have in common.

9. Choice (B) is correct

Especially is another Emphasis Keyword. (B) is the only choice that would make Nabokov's mass appeal in a linguistically provincial country even more mystifying. His appeal to academic and literary critics might explain his mass readership, or at least render it less mystifying; (A) should thus be introduced by a Contrast Keyword like *despite*. (C) would tend to work in favor of Nabokov's mass appeal, rather than against it; a combination of Contrast and Evidence Keywords—something like *though perhaps understandable, given*—would make for a better transition.

IN CONCLUSION

We've shown you the basic tools that will allow you to read GMAT passages more quickly and with a better grasp of the essentials. What we've basically been advocating is a different approach to reading, one specifically tailored to the demands of GMAT Verbal. This approach involves reading for the "why" and the "how" of the passage and giving less attention to the "what"—in particular, the details that weigh down the passage and aren't worth the time it takes to digest them.

The bad news about GMAT reading passages is that they tend to be dense with information and, for most test takers, deadly dull. The good news about these passages is that they are logically constructed, and the reader who reads for the gist and structure of the passage, who takes note of the Keywords that the author provides to facilitate this process, who mentally paraphrases the big ideas found within each paragraph, and who skips quickly over the details and filler until and unless they're needed to answer a question, is bound to do well on the GMAT Verbal Section.

Learning to read this way takes practice. You'll have plenty of opportunities to hone this approach to reading the GMAT way throughout this book, but you needn't stop there. In fact, if you're serious about really doing well on GMAT Verbal, you should also apply these principles to your general reading for a while and challenge yourself with some of the denser journals and magazines found on the newsstand.

If you don't do so already, get into the habit of reading *The Economist* or another serious business journal for practice reading business passages (this has the added benefit of giving you ideas and stories to use in your AWA essays). Reading literary journals such as *The New York Review of Books* can help you to sharpen your reading skills for just about any type of passage. And if science passages are your worst nightmare, try reading a serious science journal such as *Scientific American* or *Astronomy* (those GMAT writers just love astronomy passages). With practice, you'll find that you don't have to "get" the science to understand the author's main idea when you read an article in one of these journals—and the same is true of GMAT Science passages.

And after you've aced the GMAT, we promise you can go back to reading for fun.

Chapter 4: **GMAT Reading Comprehension**

Love it or hate it, there's no escaping it: Reading Comprehension is the only question type that appears in every single major standardized test. In theory at least, this makes sense, because whether you're interested in becoming a business manager, a doctor, a lawyer, an academic, or even a CIA agent, the ability to wade through volumes of information and understand the substance of what's been written is an essential skill.

The trouble is that Reading Comprehension is a rather artificial means of testing this skill. It's also the most time-consuming, and for many test takers the most intimidating, portion of the GMAT Verbal Section. This does not have to be the case, as we will show you.

On the Verbal Section you can expect to see four Reading Comprehension passages, each approximately 200–300 words long and paired with three or four questions. Reading Comprehension questions comprise roughly one third of the entire section, about 14 of the 41 questions you'll see.

Despite what many test takers seem to believe, Reading Comprehension questions do not test your ability to read and comprehend a passage so thoroughly that you practically memorize what you read. Nor do they test your ability to relate what you read to outside knowledge. And they most definitely do not test your ability to offer a creative or original analysis of what you read. What Reading Comprehension questions do test is your ability to understand the gist of the passage and, where necessary, to research the passage for specific information to answer the question before you.

Developing a method for handling Reading Comprehension questions quickly so that you don't get bogged down reading and rereading the passages will help you do well on this question type.

ANATOMY OF A READING COMPREHENSION QUESTION

Doing well on Reading Comprehension begins with understanding the format. Let's examine the various parts of a typical Reading Comp question.

KAPLAN

The Directions

The directions for this question type look something like this:

Directions: The questions in this group are based on the content of the passage. After reading the passage, choose the best answer to each question. Answer all the questions accompanying the passage on the basis of what's *stated* or *implied* in the passage.

There are two important facts to be gleaned from these directions. First, recall that here and throughout the Verbal Section, you are looking for the *best* answer to each question, not the *right* answer. In fact, the correct answer to a Reading Comprehension question tends to be fairly inconspicuous, while each of the four wrong answer choices contains something that makes it *wrong*. Therefore, using the process of elimination is essential on this question type. Second, you must answer each question based solely on what's stated or implied in the passage; applying outside knowledge can often get you into trouble.

The Passage

Here's the passage (don't bother trying to read it all now):

Congress has had numerous opportunities in recent years to reconsider the arrangements under which federal forest lands are owned and managed. New institutional structures merit development because federal forest lands cannot be efficiently managed under the hierarchical structure that now exists. The system is too complex to be under-
(5) stood by any single authority. The establishment of each forest as an independent public corporation would simplify the management structure and promote greater efficiency, control, and accountability.

To illustrate how a system for independent public corporations might work, consider the National Forest System. Each National Forest would become an independent public
(10) corporation, operating under a federal charter giving it legal authority to manage land. The charter would give the corporation the right to establish its own production goals, land uses, management practices, and financial arrangements, within the policy constraints set by the Public Corporations Board. To assure economic efficiency in making decisions, the Public Corporations Board would establish a minimum average rate of
(15) return to be earned on assets held by each corporation. Each corporation would be required to organize a system for reporting revenues, costs, capital investments and recovery, profits, and the other standard measures of financial health. While the financial objective would not necessarily be to maximize profit, there would be a requirement to earn at least a public utility rate-of-return on the resources under the corporation's control.

(20)   Such an approach to federal land management would encourage greater efficiency in the utilization of land, capital, and labor. This approach could also promote a more stable work force. A positive program of advancement, more flexible job classifications, professional training, and above all, the ability to counter outside bids with higher salaries, would enable a corporation to retain its best workers. A third advantage to this

(25)   approach is that federal land management would become less vulnerable to the politics of special interest groups.

Scintillating, isn't it? On the CAT, the passage will appear on the left side of the screen, and to read it all you will usually have to use a scroll bar found on the right-hand side of the passage. Reading Comprehension passages are written in dense, often technical prose, and are adapted from books and journals in the broad areas of (1) business, (2) the social sciences, and (3) the natural sciences. You can expect to get at least one of each type of passage on the GMAT you take. Time permitting, you are encouraged to read the entire passage when you first encounter it, but the focus of this reading should be on the main idea or gist of the passage, and not on the mass of supporting details that the passage will invariably contain.

The Question and Answer Choices

1. The primary purpose of this passage is to

Here's a sample question, and in this case it's asking about the author's primary purpose in writing the passage, which your initial quick reading of the passage should reveal. Most Reading Comprehension questions are either *global* questions like this one, which ask about the passage as a whole, or *detail* questions, which require you to locate information in the passage to answer very specific questions.

    (A) suggest that the National Forest System is plagued by many problems

    (B) argue that it is necessary to restructure the management of federal forest lands

    (C) insist that private corporations be allowed to manage the country's natural resources

    (D) discuss the role of private corporations in the management of the National Forest System

    (E) highlight the competing needs of public agencies managing communications, transportation, and national forests

Here are the answer choices. One reason you don't want to spend too much time reading the passage is that you need sufficient time to attack and eliminate wrong answers. Fortunately, there are ways to recognize and eliminate wrong answer choices that we can show you. It's time to develop a strategic approach to Reading Comprehension.

THE KAPLAN FOUR-STEP METHOD FOR READING COMPREHENSION

As noted in the previous chapter, reading for the GMAT means reading with different goals and employing different techniques than you do in the course of everyday life. This is in part because Reading Comprehension passages are designed not to be easily digestible reading matter for the average test taker. And furthermore, there's just no time under strict test conditions to understand everything that's being said in the passage. Time management is a critical issue in Reading Comprehension. How you approach reading the passage may vary depending upon time issues, where you are in the test, and the type of passage you have before you. Because most test takers spend far too much time reading the passage—and not enough time researching the answer to the question in the passage, scrutinizing the answer choices, and choosing the best response—Kaplan has developed the following Four-Step Method for handling Reading Comprehension questions.

1. Attack the opening paragraph of the passage.

As a general rule, when you first encounter a passage you'll want to get a sense of what it's about before you turn to the questions. The opening paragraph is particularly important for understanding the gist of the passage. The key is to be an active reader. This means thinking about what you're reading; paraphrasing the complicated parts; determining the topic, scope, and author's purpose in writing the passage; taking note of the tone; and asking yourself questions about the passage.

2. Create a mental road map.

As you read through the rest of the passage, try to get a general idea about what's covered in each paragraph and how the paragraph fits into the overall structure of the passage. This can help you to get a fix on the passage as a whole, as well as to locate specific details later on. You may want to jot some notes about each paragraph on your scratch paper as you read through the passage.

3. Stop to sum up.

After you've looked at the passage and before you attack the questions, take a few seconds to summarize your mental road map and paraphrase the main idea of the passage.

4. Attack the questions.

Make sure you read each question carefully. Sometimes the wording is tricky, and if you misread the question, you're guaranteed to pick the wrong answer. Some questions you'll be able to answer based upon your initial reading of the passage; others will require you to go back into the passage to research the answer. Once you've located the answer to the question in the passage, you should generally be able to find one answer choice that paraphrases what you found. Other times, you may have to apply the process of elimination to get to the correct answer.

TIME/SECTION MANAGEMENT

How you approach reading the passage may vary according to:

- Where you are in the Verbal Section
- Whether you're running into time trouble
- How long the passage is

Let's take a look at how your reading of the passage may change depending on time/section management issues and the difficulty of the passage.

Plan A: The Optimal Approach

If it's early in the Verbal Section (or if you know you have enough time to finish the entire section and you don't find reading the passage to be a major hardship), you'll want to read the entire passage. The key principle behind reading the GMAT way, as discussed in the previous chapter, is to read actively for the gist of the passage. Here is a review of the reading principles that will reward you in this effort:

Focus on the Author. GMAT Reading Comprehension tests your understanding of what the author is thinking and doing. Therefore, your focus as you read must always be on the author. The test writers may want you to draw conclusions about why the passage has been written and how it has been put together. Focusing on authorial intent will help you to better understand the passage in general—why it's organized the way it is and what the author's purpose is in writing it.

Don't Sweat the Details. Details are in the passage only to illustrate what the author's thinking or doing. Therefore, read over details quickly. Trying to comprehend and assimilate all of the content is a waste of time. Always boil down the passage to its basics.

Read the First Third Closely. The first third of the passage is far and away the most important. Therefore, you should read it more closely than the rest of the passage. Why? Because the topic and scope are revealed here, and—quite often—so are the purpose, the main idea, and the author's attitude towards the subject. Moreover, the first third provides very strong hints about the direction in which the text will go.

Note Paragraph Topics and Make a Road Map. Paragraphs are the fundamental building blocks of the passage. Therefore, as you read, take note of paragraph topics and make a mental road map. Ask yourself: "What's the purpose of this paragraph? What's its basic point? How does it fit into the overall structure of the passage?"

Note: It should not take you much more than two minutes to read through the passage in this manner. At the end of this reading, you should be able to state in your own words the main idea of the passage.

Here's the passage we saw earlier. Take a few minutes now to read it the GMAT way, and then paraphrase the main idea of the passage.

Congress has had numerous opportunities in recent years to reconsider the arrangements under which federal forest lands are owned and managed. New institutional structures merit development because federal forest lands cannot be efficiently managed under the hierarchical structure that now exists. The system is too complex to be under-
(5) stood by any single authority. The establishment of each forest as an independent public corporation would simplify the management structure and promote greater efficiency, control, and accountability.

To illustrate how a system for independent public corporations might work, consider the National Forest System. Each National Forest would become an independent public
(10) corporation, operating under a federal charter giving it legal authority to manage land. The charter would give the corporation the right to establish its own production goals,

KAPLAN)

land uses, management practices, and financial arrangements, within the policy constraints set by the Public Corporations Board. To assure economic efficiency in making
decisions, the Public Corporations Board would establish a minimum average rate of
(15) return to be earned on assets held by each corporation. Each corporation would be
required to organize a system for reporting revenues, costs, capital investments and recovery, profits, and the other standard measures of financial health. While the financial objective would not necessarily be to maximize profit, there would be a requirement to earn
at least a public utility rate-of-return on the resources under the corporation's control.

(20)   Such an approach to federal land management would encourage greater efficiency
in the utilization of land, capital, and labor. This approach could also promote a more
stable work force. A positive program of advancement, more flexible job classifications,
professional training, and above all, the ability to counter outside bids with higher salary, would enable a corporation to retain its best workers. A third advantage to this
(25) approach is that federal land management would become less vulnerable to the politics
of special interest groups.

Road map:

Paragraph 1 (in 2–5 words): _____

Paragraph 2 (in 2–5 words): _____

Paragraph 3 (in 2–5 words): _____

Main idea of the passage (in 10 words or less):

_____

Were you able to summarize the main idea of the passage in ten words or less? And did you find that
focusing on the gist of the passage and reading over the details helped you to get through the passage
more quickly? It may take some time before you're comfortable reading this way, but with practice
you'll find that by reading actively you'll be able to get through the passage more quickly. You'll have a
chance to compare your paraphrase with ours later when we attack the questions.

Sometimes reading the entire passage in this manner proves difficult, either because the passage
seems harder than normal (a very subjective matter), or because the passage is longer than normal
and you're running low on time. For this situation we have an alternative approach.

Plan B: The Alternative Approach

If you're running out of time or finding it difficult to make it through the entire passage, it's time to
move to Plan B. This involves skipping over the parts of the passage that are least likely to contain vital
information. Here's how it works.

Read the first third of the passage carefully, then read the first sentence of each subsequent paragraph and the last sentence of the passage. Once again, focus on the gist of the passage. Apply the same reading principles as before, namely:

- Read with authorial intent in mind: Ask yourself, "What is the author trying to convey? Why is the passage structured as it is?"
- Even in the first third that you will be reading, focus on the big idea(s), not the supporting details.
- If you're still unsure about the main idea of the passage from the first third of the passage, pay especially close attention to the last sentence of the passage; this is where many authors tie together the loose ends and clarify the main idea of the passage.

Note: This strategy is especially useful on longer passages, particularly difficult science passages or passages that are dense with details.

Here's what you would read in the same passage using Plan B (the portions that you wouldn't read are grayed out):

Congress has had numerous opportunities in recent years to reconsider the arrangements under which federal forest lands are owned and managed. New institutional structures merit development because federal forest lands cannot be efficiently managed under the hierarchical structure that now exists. The system is too complex to be

(5) understood by any single authority. The establishment of each forest as an independent public corporation would simplify the management structure and promote greater efficiency, control, and accountability.

To illustrate how a system for independent public corporations might work, consider the National Forest System. Each National Forest would become an independent public

(10) corporation, operating under a federal charter giving it legal authority to manage land. The charter would give the corporation the right to establish its own production goals, land uses, management practices, and financial arrangements, within the policy constraints set by the Public Corporations Board. To assure economic efficiency in making decisions, the Public Corporations Board would establish a minimum average rate of

(15) return to be earned on assets held by each corporation. Each corporation would be required to organize a system for reporting revenues, costs, capital investments and recovery, profits, and the other standard measures of financial health. While the financial objective would not necessarily be to maximize profit, there would be a requirement to earn at least a public utility rate-of-return on the resources under the corporation's control.

(20) Such an approach to federal land management would encourage greater efficiency in the utilization of land, capital, and labor. This approach could also promote a more stable work force. A positive program of advancement, more flexible job classifications, professional training, and above all, the ability to counter outside bids with higher salary, would enable a corporation to retain its best workers. A third advantage to this

(25) approach is that federal land management would become less vulnerable to the politics of special interest groups.

KAPLAN

Although not optimal, this approach to reading the passage is usually sufficient for the GMAT. You should still try to paraphrase the main idea of the passage before you tackle the questions.

If you're absolutely desperate and running into serious time trouble, there's one last approach to your initial reading of the passage.

Plan C: The Emergency Approach

If you're really, really pressed for time, you'll want to get to the questions as quickly as possible. You may still be able to glean the main idea of the passage just by reading the first and last sentences of the passage.

Note: This strategy doesn't always work, and is recommended only in emergency situations. Nonetheless, if you're ever stuck trying to locate the "main idea" or "primary purpose" of a passage, these two sentences, statistically speaking, are where this information is most likely to be distilled.

Here's how you would read the same passage using Plan C (the portions that you wouldn't read are grayed out):

Congress has had numerous opportunities in recent years to reconsider the arrangements under which federal forest lands are owned and managed. New institutional structures merit development because federal forest lands cannot be efficiently managed under the hierarchical structure that now exists. The system is too complex to be under-

(5) stood by any single authority. The establishment of each forest as an independent public corporation would simplify the management structure and promote greater efficiency, control, and accountability.

To illustrate how a system for independent public corporations might work, consider the National Forest System. Each National Forest would become an independent public

(10) corporation, operating under a federal charter giving it legal authority to manage land. The charter would give the corporation the right to establish its own production goals, land uses, management practices, and financial arrangements, within the policy constraints set by the Public Corporations Board. To assure economic efficiency in making decisions, the Public Corporations Board would establish a minimum average rate of

(15) return to be earned on assets held by each corporation. Each corporation would be required to organize a system for reporting revenues, costs, capital investments and recovery, profits, and the other standard measures of financial health. While the financial objective would not necessarily be to maximize profit, there would be a requirement to earn at least a public utility rate-of-return on the resources under the corporation's control.

(20) Such an approach to federal land management would encourage greater efficiency in the utilization of land, capital, and labor. This approach could also promote a more stable work force. A positive program of advancement, more flexible job classifications, professional training, and above all, the ability to counter outside bids with higher salary, would enable a corporation to retain its best workers. A third advantage to this

(25) approach is that federal land management would become less vulnerable to the politics of special interest groups.

Do you think you could paraphrase the main idea of the passage from these two sentences?

Admittedly, reading just these two sentences misses a lot, but you could probably still tell that the author is advocating a new approach to managing federal forests. Obviously, you would want to read the passage this way only if you're running very short on time. Now let's turn to the questions.

ATTACKING THE QUESTIONS

Now that you're familiar with the passage, you're ready to attack the questions. As we've noted, there are two broad types of GMAT Reading Comprehension questions: *global questions*, which ask about the passage as a whole, and *detail questions*, which require you to locate information in the passage to answer very specific questions.

Global Questions

Global questions, which account for about one quarter of all Reading Comprehension questions, most commonly ask about the main idea of a passage or about how it's put together. Because your reading of the passage was focused on understanding authorial intent—what the author is trying to convey and how he or she has set about accomplishing this—you should be ready to answer these questions without referring to the passage.

It's also helpful to note that wrong answer choices to global Reading Comp questions tend to follow classic patterns. Common wrong answer choices to global questions include those that:

- Are too specific, dealing with just one portion of the passage
- Are too broad, going outside the scope of the passage
- Contradict the passage
- Are too strongly worded; if an answer choice contains strong wording, ask yourself whether the wording is clearly supported by the passage (if not, it's wrong)

Note: If you're down to two answers, it pays to take the time to look for differences between them and, if necessary, to find something in the passage that will make one of the choices wrong.

KAPLAN)

Main Idea Questions

Now try to answer the main idea question from the passage you've just read and summarized. Refer to your own summary of the main idea and then attack the answer choices. You should be able to locate a paraphrase of your summary, or to eliminate wrong answer choices based on the above criteria.

1. The primary purpose of this passage is to

     (A) suggest that the National Forest System is plagued by many problems

     (B) argue that it is necessary to restructure the management of federal forest lands

     (C) insist that private corporations be allowed to manage the country's natural resources

     (D) discuss the role of private corporations in the management of the National Forest System

     (E) highlight the competing needs of public agencies managing national resources

Here, the main idea of the passage is clearly found in the first paragraph: Managing forests as public corporations would have several advantages over the present system. The closest paraphrase of this is (B), which mentions restructuring forest management.

Now let's look at the wrong answers. (A) is too specific, completely missing the main drift of the passage. The author mentions the problems referred to in (A), but the focus is the solution, not the problems. (C) and (D) refer to *private* corporations—never discussed in the passage. And (E) goes beyond the scope of the passage, referring to the competing needs of various agencies managing national resources while the passage discusses only the National Forest System.

Structure Questions

Other global questions ask about the structure or organization of the passage. Let's see whether you can answer the following based upon your initial reading of the passage.

2. Which of the following best describes the organization of the passage?

     (A) A proposal is made and then supporting arguments are set forth.

     (B) One claim is evaluated and then rejected in favor of another claim.

     (C) A point of view is stated and then evidence for and against it is evaluated.

     (D) A problem is outlined and then various solutions are discussed.

     (E) Opposing opinions are introduced and then debated.

This question type can often be answered by referring to your road map (i.e., the notes about the paragraphs you jotted down on the scratch paper as you read the passage), for example—paragraph 1: "*need better forest mgmt*"; paragraph 2: "*how pub corps work*"; and paragraph 3: "*advantages.*" In any case, the organization could be summarized as follows: a proposed solution, detailed explanation of solution, and finally some advantages. The closest paraphrase is (A), which mentions "proposal" and "support" for the proposals.

Note how each of the wrong answers has wording that makes it clearly wrong. The author evaluates a claim or proposal in (B), but never *rejects* it for another. (C) is off because the author never gives evidence against the proposal. Nor does the author mention other *solutions* (D), or *opposing opinions* (E).

Detail Questions

Most Reading Comprehension questions will ask you about specific details in the passage. On detail questions, you will often have to go back to the passage to research the answer. Once you've located information to answer the question, the correct answer will almost always be a paraphrase of what you've found.

Wrong answer choices to detail questions commonly do one of the following:

- Contradict the passage
- Use similar wording, but distort what's said in the passage
- Go beyond the scope of the passage, stating things that aren't said
- Paraphrase from the wrong part of the passage (in other words, they don't answer the question being asked)
- Use extreme wording

Take a look at the next question:

3. According to the passage, the present problems of federal forest lands derive mainly from

   (A) overuse by the population

   (B) inefficient organization

   (C) hostility from special interest groups

   (D) the corporate mentality of Congress

   (E) opposition to reform by government employees

In which paragraph would you find information pertaining to the sources of the present problems of federal forest lands? Sometimes you may be able to answer detail questions without referring back to the passage. More often, though, you will have to research the passage. You should be able to locate the relevant information to a detail question easily either by:

- The wording in the question, which will lead you to similar wording in the passage, or
- Your road map, which will help you to know where to look.

In this case, your work creating a road map and restating the main idea should have come in handy. You know the passage is about forest land management, and that the first paragraph discusses what has led to the need for reform. The main cause, says paragraph 1, is structural inefficiency. The correct answer, (B), should jump out at you as a paraphrase of the author's main criticism. Of the wrong answers, (A) public overuse, (D) the corporate mentality of Congress, and (E) opposition to reform by government workers, are never mentioned. (C) could be stretched to fit the idea of "political vulnerability" found in the last line, but it's too strongly worded ("hostility"), and even worse, it doesn't answer the question that was asked, which is about the source of present problems, not the problems per se.

Line Reference Questions

Sometimes the test maker is kind enough to tell you exactly where to look in the passage to research the answer. Take a look at the following:

4.   The author's attitude towards the "hierarchical structure" mentioned in line 4 can best be characterized as

   (A) resigned

   (B) admiring

   (C) skeptical

   (D) bitter

   (E) ambivalent

Questions that ask about the author's tone or attitude towards a subject may be either global or detail, as in this case. Since you are told exactly where to go in the passage, go ahead and reread the sentence containing the line reference. Try to formulate your own answer to the question before you look at the answer choices. Sometimes reading just the sentence that contains the line reference will not be sufficient; you may have to read a few lines before and after the reference to get a sense of the context.

By the way, questions that ask about the author's tone or attitude are gifts. You simply have to figure out whether the author's attitude to the subject at hand is positive or negative, and eliminate answers that go the wrong way. Then get rid of answer choices that are too extreme or that are otherwise off.

Paragraph 1 cites "hierarchical structure" as *the basic problem*. Thus, the answer here must be negative—strongly negative—but in keeping with the passage's unemotional tone. "Admiring" (B) is out, as is "bitter" (D), which sounds too emotional. The other negative answers are "resigned," "skeptical," and "ambivalent." (A) is out because the author is *not* resigned—he's *advocating* a change. "Ambivalent" (E) is wrong because it implies mixed feelings, some positive, some negative. The author never expresses any positive feelings towards the current hierarchy. Thus, the answer has to be "skeptical" (C), which is both negative and purposeful.

Inference Questions

Inference questions are also quite common on Reading Comprehension, and may be either global or detail. Any time you are asked to determine what a passage *suggests* or what can be *inferred* from a passage, you are being asked to draw an inference, rather than find what is explicitly stated in the passage.

Don't get carried away by this distinction, however. As we will discuss later in the Critical Reasoning chapter, the GMAT writers don't expect you to infer too much when they ask an inference question. While you may occasionally have to combine information from two parts of the passage or make a deduction, you don't want to go overboard in reading between the lines. In fact, the GMAT writers often invite you to over-think by making a detail question look like an inference question—for example asking what the passage *suggests* when the answer is, in fact, explicitly stated.

Here's what you need to know about this question type: The correct answer to an inference question is the one answer that *must be true* given what's stated in the passage. Consequently, common wrong answer choices on inference questions are those that:

- Contradict the passage
- Are too strongly worded
- Go beyond the scope of the passage, suggesting things that aren't said

Let's take a look:

5.   The author suggests that administrators of federal forest lands have been handicapped by which of the following?

   Ⓐ The public expectation that federal forest lands will remain undeveloped
   Ⓑ The failure of environmental experts to investigate the problems of federal forest lands
   Ⓒ The inability of the federal government to compete with private corporations for the services of skilled professionals
   Ⓓ The unwillingness of Congress to pass laws to protect federal forest lands from private developers
   Ⓔ The difficulty of persuading citizens to invest their capital in a government-run endeavor

Admittedly, the answer to this question is somewhat hard to locate because much of the passage talks directly or indirectly about forest management problems. Paragraph 1 mentions complexity, while paragraph 3 discusses inefficiency, personnel problems, and political issues, any of which could be the answer. (A), (B), (D), and (E) are never mentioned, while (C) corresponds to the personnel issue.

Note also that the correct answer does not require a major reach. The passage states, in reference to the proposed restructuring: "A positive program of advancement, more flexible job classifications, professional training, and above all, the ability to counter outside bids with higher salary, would enable a corporation to retain its best workers." Hence, it doesn't take much inferring to conclude that present administrators are hampered by the inability to compete with private corporations for the services of skilled professionals.

Special Question Formats

The GMAT writers also like to complicate matters from time to time with question formats that require an extra amount of effort. Let's take a look at these questions.

Roman Numeral Questions

Roman Numeral questions are quite popular on the GMAT, and are generally considered harder than average. This is because these questions require you to look for three pieces of information in the passage by which to evaluate the three enumerated options. We recommend that you consider each option one at a time and that you eliminate answer choices as you go along (sometimes you'll get lucky and you won't have to evaluate all three options). Try out the following:

6.   According to the passage, the responsibilities of a corporation authorized to manage a National Forest should include which of the following?

   I.   Establishing formal procedures for making official reports of the corporation's financial well-being

   II.   Earning at least a minimum return on the corporation's resources and assets

   III.   Achieving a maximum level of profits on the corporation's capital investments

   (A) I only
   (B) II only
   (C) III only
   (D) I and II only
   (E) I, II, and III

For starters, the question asks about how a public corporation should function, so you should know from your road map that paragraph 2 is where to research the answer. The first half of paragraph 2 deals with the legal authority of a public corporation, and the second half deals with its obligations, primarily financial.

It should be easy for you to affirm options I and II; paragraph 2 states that the responsibilities are to earn a minimum, "public utility" rate of return, and to report financial activities. Therefore, you should get rid of choices (A), (B), and (C). As to option III, paragraph 2 explicitly states that the primary goal is not "to maximize profit." Choice (D), options I and II only, is correct.

EXCEPT Questions

EXCEPT questions are considered the toughest of all Reading Comprehension questions. This is because these questions require you to go to the answer choices and find information in the passage that will corroborate all of the answer choices EXCEPT the correct one. In other words, you're looking for the one answer choice that's wrong. The good news about EXCEPT questions is that if you get one on the CAT, it means you must be doing well. Let's give one a try:

7.   According to the passage, all of the following are potential benefits of forming public corporations to manage federal forest lands *EXCEPT*

   (A) less turnover of personnel
   (B) more effective management of natural resources
   (C) the ability to offer competitive salaries
   (D) less vulnerability to special interest groups
   (E) expansion of federal forest land boundaries

Although some EXCEPT questions require hunting through the entire passage for the answer, this one is not so bad. Once again, your road map should have led you to research the final paragraph for the answer to this question. Paragraph 3 names three benefits: efficiency, stable personnel, and less vulnerability to politics. You're looking for something that's *not* one of these benefits, and (A), (B), (C), and (D) all paraphrase these benefits. Only (E), forest land *expansion*, was never mentioned.

As we've seen, the key to doing well on Reading Comprehension questions lies in knowing how to read for the gist of the passage, how to research the passage for answers to specific questions, and how to spot the correct answer or, alternatively, how to recognize and eliminate wrong answers. Now it's time for you to try some passages on your own.

PRACTICE QUESTIONS

Make sure to apply the Kaplan Four-Step Method for Reading Comprehension to the following questions. Also, try timing yourself and see if you can finish this practice set in less than 25 minutes (this may require you to alter the way you read some of the passages, as discussed earlier in this chapter). Remember that on the CAT you have to answer the questions in the order they're given, and earlier passages affect your score more than later passages. Keep this in mind and try to answer the questions in order as you go through this and other practice sets in this book.

The search for an explanation of the historically weak status of U.S. third-party movements is illuminated by examining the conditions that have favored the growth of a strong two-party system. Different interests and voting blocs predominate in different regions, creating a geographically fragmented electorate. This heterogeneity is comple-
(5)   mented by a federal political structure that forces the major parties to find voter support at state and local levels in separate regions. For example, the Democratic Party long sought and drew support simultaneously from northern black urban voters and from segregationists. Such pressures encourage the major parties to avoid political programs that are too narrowly or sharply defined. The nondoctrinal character of U.S. politics
(10)   means that important new issues and voting blocs tend to be initially ignored by the major parties. Such issues—opposition to immigration and the abolition of slavery are two historic examples—tend to gain political prominence through third parties.

Ironically, the same factors that lead to the emergence of third parties contribute to the explanation of their failure to gain national political power. Parties based on
(15)   narrow or ephemeral issues remain isolated or fade rapidly. At the same time, those that raise increasingly urgent social issues also face inherent limits to growth. Long before a third party can begin to broaden substantially its base of voter support, the major parties are able to move to attract the minority of voters that it represents. The Democratic Party, for instance, appropriated the agrarian platform of the
(20)   Populist Party in 1896, and enacted Socialist welfare proposals in the 1930s, in both cases winning much of the popular bases of these parties. Except for the Republican Party, which gained national prominence as the Whigs were declining in the 1850s,

no third party has ever achieved national major-party status. Only at state and local levels have a handful of third parties been sustained by a stable voting bloc that remains unrepresented by a major party.

1. The primary purpose of this passage is to

    (A) examine the appeal of U.S. national third parties to the electorate at state and local levels

    (B) trace the historical rise and decline of third-party movements in the United States

    (C) explain why most U.S. third-party movements have failed to gain major-party status

    (D) demonstrate that U.S. politics has traditionally been non-ideological in character

    (E) suggest a model to explain why certain U.S. third-party movements have succeeded while others have failed

2. Which of the following does the author suggest was an important factor in the establishment of the Republican Party as a major national party?

    (A) The polarization of national opinion at the time of a major social crisis

    (B) The unique appeal of its program to significant sectional interests

    (C) The acceptance of its program by a large bloc of voters unrepresented by a major party

    (D) The simultaneous decline of an established major party

    (E) The inability of the major parties of the era to appeal to all sectional interests

3. According to the author, the major factor responsible for the rise of third parties in the United States has been the

    (A) domination of major parties by powerful economic interests

    (B) inability of major parties to bring about broad consensus among a variety of voters and interest groups

    (C) slow response of major parties to new issues and voting groups

    (D) exclusion of immigrants and minorities from the mainstream of U.S. politics

    (E) variety of motivations held by voting blocs in different regions

Despite increasing enrollments of women in medical schools, feelings of isolation among women medical students persist. Women students still have to contend with the social stereotype of a male doctor. In addition, institutions themselves may uninten-tionally foster feelings of separateness. Comparatively few women are hired for faculty
(5)   positions, thus offering women students few role models. The pervasive sexual humor of male doctors and students further intensifies the woman students' alienation. Alienation, in turn, negatively affects individual self-perception.

As women enter medical study in increasing numbers, they may feel less at odds with their peers and the teaching establishment. Institutional bias will, no doubt,
(10)   also change in response to changing societal values. However, we should not wait

passively for gradual social processes to bring changes; schools must provide current students with support services designed to meet women's needs. In a recent study, 48 percent of the women questioned rated a student support group as the most important support service a school can provide.

4. The passage cites all of the following as causing psychological problems for women medical students *EXCEPT*

   (A) feelings of alienation from teachers and fellow students

   (B) prevailing societal conceptions about doctors

   (C) declining admissions of women to medical schools

   (D) expressions of sexism by peers and superiors

   (E) absence of positive female models for women students

5. The author of the passage would be most likely to agree with which of the following?

   (A) Medical schools practice widespread discrimination on the basis of sex.

   (B) Gender-based stereotyping encourages feelings of isolation among women medical students.

   (C) Some medical school policies are deliberately designed to make women students feel isolated.

   (D) Social norms must change before institutional bias can decline.

   (E) The majority of women medical students have a negative self-image.

6. The passage suggests that which of the following would be likely to reduce the isolation felt by women medical students?

   I.   An increased proportion of women in medical schools

   II. An increase in the number of women filling faculty positions in medical schools

   III. An increase in support services available to women students

   (A) I only

   (B) II only

   (C) I and II only

   (D) I and III only

   (E) I, II, and III

7. In terms of its tone and form, the passage is most appropriately described as

   (A) an impassioned polemic

   (B) an indignant protest

   (C) a reasoned appeal

   (D) a detached summary

   (E) a biased speculation

Shopping mall developers seek to attract large department stores that will act as "anchors"—high-traffic stores that will bring many customers into their complex. However, when a department store chain seeks to site a new store, it must take into consideration that the high level of customer traffic generated by the new store may be
(5)   exploited by nearby smaller retailers. It will decline to build if it is judged that the large store's "positive externality" will serve primarily to increase sales at nearby small competitors. Mall developers can circumvent this problem and retain a mixture of large and small retailers by internalizing the department store's externality—that is, by bringing some of the benefits associated with the department store back to the store itself.

(10)   The ability of malls to do so lies in the fact that their developers own the entire complex. They can charge rents that reflect not only the contribution that each store makes to the mall's overall revenues, but also the business that a store brings to the mall's other tenants. Recent studies of malls in the American Midwest show that in a mall with two or three department stores, a small shoe store or restaurant might pay rent per square
(15)   foot that is five times the rate charged to department stores in the complex, while a jeweler in a mall with four or five department stores could pay twenty times the rate paid by the mall's anchors.

The partiality shown department stores increases with mall size, even though the study shows that department stores in different-sized complexes usually generate about
(20)   the same sales per square foot. The disparity in the rents charged between department stores and small retailers cannot be explained simply by the fact that small stores make greater sales per square foot of floor space; rather, the smaller stores are willing to subsidize the department stores for the sales that department stores generate for them, and the greater the traffic, the more they are willing to pay.

8.   The author's primary purpose in writing this passage is to

(A) indicate the competitive advantages that malls have over traditional shopping districts

(B) introduce the concept of positive externality and explain its relevance to shopping malls located in the American Midwest

(C) argue that mall owners exploit small stores by manipulating their rents so that large store owners benefit

(D) explain how mall developers attempt to increase customer traffic for a mall by varying rental rates for different kinds of stores

(E) demonstrate how mall developers maximize the number of retailers in their malls by internalizing the benefits of positive externality

9. Which of the following can be inferred from the passage?

   (A) Jewelers in small malls pay more rent per square foot than do shoe stores in large malls.

   (B) Department store chains consider more than potential sales per square foot when determining where to locate stores.

   (C) If mall developers were to charge the same rent per square foot for every store, malls would likely experience a surplus of department stores and a shortage of smaller retailers.

   (D) Positive externality is a greater problem for small stores than for larger department stores.

   (E) If not for the phenomenon of positive externality, malls would not be able to attract large department stores as tenants.

10. Which of the following statements about large malls and small malls can be logically inferred from the passage?

   (A) Department stores in large malls generate more sales per square foot than do department stores in small malls.

   (B) Small malls tend to attract more specialized stores than large malls, and therefore do not need as many anchor stores.

   (C) The disparity in rent per square foot between small retailers and anchor stores is greater in larger malls than smaller malls.

   (D) Small retailers in large malls often resent paying higher rent than anchor stores, and eventually move to smaller malls where the disparity is less pronounced.

   (E) Because larger malls are normally assumed to attract an upscale clientele, they can charge small retailers more rent per square foot than smaller malls can.

(5)

For many years, the observation that certain intensely bright young stars are concentrated along the spiral arms of disk-shaped galaxies remained unexplained. But recent research suggests both a solution to the puzzle of these "O-stars," which are a million times brighter than the sun, and a mechanism that may partially explain the process of star formation in general.

(10)

Astronomers have long been aware that stars are made up of interstellar gas and dust, but until recently the specific sequence of events that signaled their birth was a mystery. Today, however, the stars in spiral arms of disk-shaped galaxies are thought to result from density waves induced by gravitational fluctuations at the galactic center. These waves appear to function as the lines along which scattered clouds of interstellar gas and dust collect into much larger clouds, which then coalesce into clumps of high concentration, out of which different types of stars, including O-stars, eventually emerge. Extensive mapping of these cloud complexes, or nebulas, has established a correlation between these complexes and O-stars—a coincidence too striking, in view of the expanse

(15)

of empty space within galaxies, to be the result of chance.

Since they produce a red florescence, O-stars are usually found in glowing nebulas that astronomers have labeled H II regions. O-stars cannot migrate out of these regions because their lifespans are too short. Therefore, astronomers have studied H II regions to determine how clouds and O-stars interact.

(20)

These observations suggest that the interaction between clouds and O-stars is a self-perpetuating cycle in which stars will be produced until the cloud material is used up. O-stars consume their fuel rapidly and release huge amounts of energy. Moreover, O-star radiation contributes to driving a shock wave into these clouds, compressing gas and dust there. Out of this tremendous compression of gas and dust arises a second

(25)

generation of young stars, among them new O-stars.

11. Which of the following best describes the organization of the passage?

    (A) A puzzle is presented and then two possible scientific solutions are discussed.

    (B) A new phenomenon is described and then the scientific methods used to study it are discussed.

    (C) Recent scientific research is described and then applied to solve an existing problem.

    (D) A previously known phenomenon is described and then explained by scientific observations.

    (E) A number of scientific hypotheses are discussed and then observations concerning their validity are described.

12. The passage states all of the following about O-stars *EXCEPT*:

    (A) They consume their fuel quickly.

    (B) They are found in glowing nebulas.

    (C) They are much bigger than the sun.

    (D) They emit large amounts of radiation.

    (E) They cannot migrate out of H II regions.

13. According to the passage, interstellar gas and dust coalesce into "clumps of high concentration" (lines 11–12)

    (A) only in H II regions of space

    (B) because of gravitational fluctuations in galactic arms

    (C) when O-stars migrate out of H II regions

    (D) after releasing huge amounts of energy

    (E) before new stars are formed

14. The author mentions "O-star radiation" (lines 22–23) in order to

    (A) explain why O-stars have short lifespans

    (B) outline the role of O-stars in star formation

    (C) emphasize the reddish glow of certain nebulas

    (D) prove that O-stars interact with cloud complexes

    (E) predict the rate at which nebulas use up their gas and dust

ANSWERS AND EXPLANATIONS

1.	C	6.	E	11.	D
2.	D	7.	C	12.	C
3.	C	8.	D	13.	E
4.	C	9.	B	14.	B
5.	B	10.	C		

1. Choice (C) is correct.

Here the "primary purpose" is fairly clearly articulated in the very first sentence of the passage: "The search for an explanation of the historically weak status of U.S. third-party movements is illuminated by examining the conditions that have favored the growth of a strong two-party system." In other words, the purpose of the passage is to explain why most U.S. third party movements have failed to gain major party status (C).

A quick vertical scan of the verbs knocks out a few answer choices. GMAT passages are never comprehensive enough to "trace the historical rise and decline" (B) or "demonstrate" (D) anything exhaustively—(D) is also out because it doesn't mention third-party movements, clearly the topic of this passage. (A) is out because the passage is primarily concerned with the failure of third parties to rise above the state and local levels, not their success there. Finally, (E) is out because no "model" is given to explain the success of some third-party movements; again, the passage is about the general failure of third-party movements nationally.

2. Choice (D) is correct.

This is a detail question, so you just have to scan the passage to find where the Republican Party is mentioned, near the end of the passage. The exact line states: "Except for the Republican Party, which gained national prominence as the Whigs were declining in the 1850s, no third party has ever achieved national major-party status." Clearly, it doesn't take much to infer that the party's establishment was facilitated by the "simultaneous decline of an established major party."

Because this is a detail question, answers from the wrong part of the passage can be counted out, including (C), an irrelevant detail from the second paragraph. (A) is nowhere mentioned, nor is (B) or (E). *Note*: Just because the question uses the word *suggest*, don't overthink it; just locate the information in the passage—the correct answer will still very often be almost a paraphrase of what you locate.

3. Choice (C) is correct.

You're looking for factors to explain the rise of third parties, not their ultimate failure, so you want to research the first paragraph. There it states: "important new issues and voting blocs tend to be initially ignored by the major parties. Such issues . . . tend to gain political prominence through third parties." (C) represents a close paraphrase of this thought.

(A) is out; "powerful economic interests" are nowhere mentioned. (B) is off base; as a general rule major parties are able to bring about broad consensus. And (D) is out; if minorities were excluded from the mainstream of U.S. politics, black urban voters would not be a significant voting bloc of the Democratic Party. Finally, (E) is out; major parties generally deal successfully with the variety of motivations held by voting blocs in different regions by avoiding narrowly defined political programs.

4. Choice (C) is correct.

We're looking for the one answer not cited by the passage. According to sentence 1, enrollments of women in medical schools are increasing, not declining.

Choice (A) is the major problem mentioned in the passage, described variously as feelings of "isolation," "separateness," and "alienation" (sentences 1, 3, and 5) from "peers and the teaching establishment" (paragraph 2). Choices (B), (D), and (E) all contribute to this major problem.

5. Choice (B) is correct.

This is one form of inference question, but as we know, on the GMAT, you aren't expected to infer too much. Sentence 3 mentions "the social stereotype of a male doctor." Since this comes right after the reference to "feelings of isolation" in sentence 1, we can infer that the author thinks gender-based stereotypes are one cause of such feelings (B).

Of the wrong answers, (A) is not supported; enrollments of women are increasing, though there are still few women faculty members—at worst there's a mixed picture, and nothing in the passage supports the idea of "widespread discrimination." (C) contradicts sentence 4, which says institutional policies may "unintentionally" foster feelings of separateness. (D) distorts sentence 2 in the second paragraph; to say changing values will cause institutional bias to decline is not to say that social norms *must* change before bias will decline. (E) exaggerates the last sentence in paragraph 1; we can infer that some women medical students have a negative self-perception, but not that they are the majority.

6. Choice (E) is correct.

This is a fairly easy Roman Numeral question. Option I is supported by the first sentence of paragraph 2. As women increasingly enter medical schools, they "may feel less at odds with their peers and the teaching establishment." Option II is supported by paragraph 1, which states that the lack of women in faculty positions results in a lack of role models, inferably a source of feelings of isolation. Finally, the author argues that schools should "provide . . . support services designed to meet women's needs." Their "needs" inferably relate to their feelings of isolation. Thus, III is correct as well.

7. Choice (C) is correct.

The question asks about both tone and content. The *tone* of the passage is quiet; the author summarizes facts, cites a statistic, and does not yell or scream. The *content*, however, is not disinterested; the author definitely advocates changes—medical schools should not "wait passively" for society to change but should do more to address the problems of "current students." (C) is the choice that best fits this combination of a quiet, persuasive tone and clear-cut advocacy. "Impassioned" and "indignant" in (A) and (B) are both too shrill; and the passage is not really a "polemic" (a sharply phrased argument directed against some person or position) or a "protest" (the author is *for* certain changes, but that's not the same thing). "Detached" (D) misses the author's involvement in the subject—this author *cares*; and "summary" misses his or her advocacy. In (E), some persons might feel the author is "biased," but the passage is not primarily a "speculation," but a plea for changes, or an "appeal," as in correct choice (C).

8. Choice (D) is correct.

The primary purpose is set up in the first paragraph: Mall developers seek department stores because they bring a lot of customers to the malls; however, in order to get those department stores, they have to make it worthwhile for them. The next two paragraphs explain how developers solve this problem by varying rents to compensate the department stores. So, the primary purpose is concisely stated in choice (D), to explain how mall developers attempt to increase customer traffic by varying rental rates for different kinds of stores. Choices (A) and (E) state ideas that are not present in the passage: a comparison with other shopping districts is not made; and maximizing the number of retailers is not discussed. Choice (C) is way too strongly worded and contrary to the tone of the passage; it is never suggested that small stores are exploited, and in any event hiking rents on small stores is not the main point of the passage. Choice (B) may be tempting, because the concept of positive externality clearly is important to the passage, but it's too specific, referring only to the American Midwest. The studies of Midwestern malls are brought up only to support the author's argument.

9. Choice (B) is correct.

The question provides no clues as to where to look in the passage for the answer, so we have to work from the answer choices. Choice (B) is correct because the passage states that department store chains will decline to build in a mall if their presence will "primarily" benefit other stores. Therefore, it can't be just their own sales that concern them: They also consider the benefit they provide to other stores. (B) is also a fairly softly worded answer choice, which we love to see as the answer to an inference question. (A) goes too far; although we are told that jewelers sometimes pay more per square foot than shoe stores in large malls, we can't infer that the same is true of small malls. (C) states the opposite of what the passage implies. Department stores demand lower rents per square foot to compensate for their "positive externalities," so a developer offering the same rates to all stores would have a dearth of department stores. (D) likewise contradicts the passage; smaller stores are never said to have "positive externalities," only department stores. Even if smaller stores have that "problem," nothing in the passage implies that smaller stores suffer more from that problem than do larger ones. Finally, (E) gets it wrong because the passage never suggests that positive externality is what attracts department stores to malls. The developers want the department stores for their "positive externalities," not vice versa.

10. Choice (C) is correct.

(A) is contradicted by the passage, which says that sales per square foot for department stores are about the same for large and small malls. (B) is nowhere suggested by the passage; differences between the mix of stores in large and small malls are never discussed. (C) is a winner. The passage states that "the partiality in rent shown department stores increases with mall size," which is equivalent to saying that the disparity in rent between anchor (department) stores and small stores is greater for larger malls than smaller malls. (D) is way off base. Resentment never comes up in the passage, nor does the feelings of developers or store owners. (E) makes a claim about "upscale clientele," which is not supported by the passage; the passage explains rental rates based on only customer traffic, not on how chic the store is. Remember to stick closely to the text on inference questions.

11. Choice (D) is correct.

The good news about "hard" science passages is that you don't actually have to understand the science to get the correct answer. This global question asks about the organization of the passage, so after quickly reading through the passage, attack the answer choices aggressively. Paragraph 1 mentions a previously known phenomenon: the location of O-stars in the spiral arms of disk-shaped galaxies. The rest of the passage explains the why and the what of this phenomenon: why O-stars form there and what function they serve there.

The first part of (A) is okay: a "puzzle" is presented; but this choice hops the tracks when it mentions two solutions. This is one of those "half-right, half-wrong" choices that you should watch out for. No new phenomenon is described (B), nor are scientific methods ever discussed. This choice violates the scope of the passage. (C) has things backwards: In the passage, the problem comes before the research. Like (B), (E) violates the scope: The author doesn't discuss a "number of scientific hypotheses."

12. Choice (C) is correct.

The only comparison made between O-stars and the sun appears in lines 3–4, which say that O-stars are brighter than the sun, not that they're bigger. Line 22 says that O-stars "consume their fuel rapidly" (A) and "release huge amounts of energy" (D); line 16 indicates that they're "usually found in glowing nebulas" (B) and "cannot migrate out of" H II regions (E). Note that in EXCEPT questions you're looking for the choice that is not true. Use process of elimination to throw out true choices.

13. Choice (E) is correct.

Since the question stem sends you back to lines 11–12, the answer is to be found in the middle of the second paragraph. The third sentence of this paragraph explicitly states that gas and dust are concentrated into dense clumps prior to the birth of stars, which is what (E) says. (A) and (C) refer to the wrong part of the passage: the third paragraph; moreover, (C) flatly contradicts information in that paragraph. (D) also refers to the wrong part of the passage, the fourth paragraph, and, besides, pertains to O-stars, not interstellar gas and dust. Finally, (B) gets the paragraph right, but, like (C), flatly contradicts the passage.

14. Choice (B) is correct.

Lines 22–23 say that O-star radiation "contributes to driving a shock wave" that compresses gas and dust in clouds. The following lines go on to say that new stars emerge out of this compressed gas and dust.

The short lifespans of O-stars (A) and the reddish glow of "certain nebulas" (C) are brought up in paragraph 3, but aren't linked to O-star radiation. (D) misrepresents the author's purpose: he's not out to "prove that O-stars interact with cloud complexes," he's out to explain how the two interact. (E) also misrepresents the author's purpose: he doesn't "predict" anything. Note that most questions to "hard" science passages tend to be very specific detail questions, in which either a line reference will be provided or the wording in the question will help you to locate the relevant information in the passage. Even if you don't fully understand the passage, you can often get these questions right.

Chapter 5: **GMAT Critical Reasoning**

We hope you're in a contentious mood, because people who love to argue are likely to do well in Critical Reasoning, our last Verbal question type. This is because Critical Reasoning is all about arguments, and your ability to break them apart, identify their weak spots, attack them, defend them—do what you will with them.

"Why are arguments so darn important?" you may well ask. Good question: This means you're not taking things lying down. This means you're getting in a mood to argue! The answer is that the ability to argue persuasively—to understand the logic of an argument, evaluate its merits, and be able to respond to its strengths and weaknesses—requires the critical thinking skills that any good business manager should have. Business managers need to be able to evaluate arguments and proposals with a critical eye. After all, not all business proposals are created equal!

The 41-question Verbal Section contains about 12 or 13 Critical Reasoning questions, so Critical Reasoning will account for about 30 percent of your Verbal score. We will show you how to evaluate Critical Reasoning arguments soon, but the first thing you need to do is familiarize yourself with this question type.

ANATOMY OF A CRITICAL REASONING QUESTION

Let's start by looking at the various parts of a typical Critical Reasoning question.

The Directions

The directions for this question type are short and sweet:

Directions: For each question, select the best of the answer choices given.

The directions are straightforward, but note once again that they ask you for the best answer—not the perfect answer.

The Stimulus

Above every question you'll find what we at Kaplan call the *stimulus*:

1.   A recent study has concluded that, contrary to the claims of those trying to ban cigarette advertisements altogether, cigarette ads placed on billboards and in magazines have little to no effect on the smoking habits of the smokers who view the ads. The study, which surveyed more than 20,000 smokers and solicited their reasons for continuing to smoke, found that practically no one in the survey felt that these advertisements influenced their decision to smoke.

This is a short passage, typically in the form of an argument, which may be drawn from many possible areas, including the natural sciences, the humanities, business, and even casual conversation. Even if the subject matter seems strange, relax. All the information you need to answer the question is on the screen. You don't need to bring in any outside knowledge.

The Question and Answer Choices

Here's the question:

The study's conclusion is based upon which of the following assumptions?

Read this first! Here's where you find out your task. You may need to identify an argument's assumption or flaw; you may need to determine what would strengthen or weaken the argument; or you may be asked to make a deduction. Pay close attention here: If you misinterpret the question, all your other work will go to waste.

- (A) People do not switch cigarette brands based on their exposure to cigarette ads on billboards and in magazines.
- (B) Cigarette ads on billboards and in magazines do not encourage nonsmokers to take up the habit.
- (C) Banning cigarette ads altogether will encourage people to give up smoking.
- (D) People are consciously aware of all the reasons they choose to smoke.
- (E) People who decide to smoke do so for rational reasons.

And these are the answer choices. As you no doubt know by now, the test makers have set up one (and only one) of these choices to be correct. If you understand the question and are able to follow the argument, you should be able to zero in on the correct answer quickly. Wrong answer choices usually distort the text, misrepresent its scope, or are the opposite of what you're looking for. You now know the basics of the Kaplan method for Critical Reasoning.

THE KAPLAN FOUR-STEP METHOD FOR CRITICAL REASONING

Here's our four-step method for handling this question type:

1. Read the question first.

You should always read the question before you look at the stimulus, because how you read and attack the stimulus will vary depending upon the task. If you know what you're supposed to do to the stimulus, you'll be able to focus your reading on the task ahead.

2. Read the stimulus.

Once you know your task, read the stimulus, paraphrasing as you go. Most, but not all, Critical Reasoning questions will require you to identify the parts of an argument. The key is to read actively and critically. Get a sense of how strong or weak the argument is.

3. Try to prephrase an answer.

Sometimes, if you've read the stimulus critically enough, you'll know the answer without even looking at the answer choices. Other times, you'll just have a general idea of the answer may say. Either way, you'll have an easier time finding the correct answer if you have a sense of what you're looking for.

4. Attack the answer choices.

If you were able to prephrase an answer, skim the choices looking for a match. If you couldn't come up with a prephrase, read and evaluate the answer choices. You can always eliminate answer choices that stray beyond the scope of the stimulus. Other eliminating strategies will vary depending upon the question asked. Once you've settled on an answer, you may want to reread the question quickly to confirm that you've answered the question that was asked.

BREAKING DOWN AN ARGUMENT

As noted, the typical Critical Reasoning stimulus is in the form of an argument, and the typical Critical Reasoning question will require you to understand the argument, which involves being able to identify its component parts. But just what do we mean by "argument" on the GMAT? What we do *not* mean is a disagreement involving loud and abusive language, sometimes requiring intervention by the police.

On the GMAT, an argument is an attempt at a reasoned appeal—it's a piece of text in which an author puts forth a claim and tries to support it. Thus, every GMAT argument contains the following parts:

- The conclusion (the author's claim; the point he or she is trying to make)
- The evidence (the support the author offers for the conclusion)

Identifying the Conclusion and Evidence

For starters, you don't want to make the mistake of thinking that the *conclusion* must come at the *end* of the stimulus. A conclusion could be the first sentence, followed by the evidence, or it could be the last sentence, with the evidence preceding it. Since doing well on Critical Reasoning requires being able to identify an argument's component parts, we must have a way to distinguish the argument's conclusion from its evidence. Fortunately, there are several.

Keywords

In chapter 3, we discussed the concept of Keywords, the structural clues that authors use to signal logical connections between ideas. Luckily, there are distinct Conclusion Keywords and distinct Evidence Keywords, and even luckier still, the GMAT writers use these Keywords frequently. Here are the most important ones to watch out for:

Conclusion Keywords: *Therefore   Thus   As a result   Hence   Clearly   So   Consequently*

Evidence Keywords: *because   since   for*

Note: If a sentence contains an Evidence Keyword, the part with the Evidence Keyword contains evidence; the rest of the sentence contains the conclusion.

But what if the structure of the argument isn't handed to you on a platter? Sometimes, there are no explicit Keyword signals in the argument. Fortunately, there are other ways to skin an argument.

The "One Sentence" Test

As already noted, an argument's conclusion is the author's main point. It's the belief the author wants the reader to adopt, or the actions she wants him to take. Evidence, on the other hand, is just there to support the conclusion; a piece of evidence tends to sound like an undisputed fact rather than a strongly held view.

Therefore, if no obvious Keyword points the way to the conclusion, give the stimulus the One Sentence Test: Ask yourself what statement the author would make if limited to a single sentence. The statement you come up with (which may sound like a recommendation or an order) should be the conclusion.

The "What" versus "Why" Test

There's one last technique that can help you to distinguish between evidence and conclusion. It's based on the fact that the evidence and the conclusion answer two different types of questions, as you can see:

This part:	Answers the question:
Conclusion	What does the author believe (should be done)?
Evidence	Why does the author believe this?

So if you're unsure whether a particular statement is evidence or a conclusion, ask yourself: Does this sentence express what the author believes? Or, does it explain why the author believes it?

Identify the conclusions in the following arguments:

1. *Get Going* magazine surveyed its readers and found that three out of every four people who want to visit the Andaman Islands wish to do so on a package tour provided by a tour operator. Since tour operators currently in business can provide tours for only 60 percent of those who wish to visit the Andaman Islands, setting up a travel company that offers tours to the Andaman Islands is a relatively risk-free way to make money.

2. In a recently published study, researchers concluded that steady chromium intake, even in small doses, can significantly lower the life expectancy of some primates. In the study, 250 chimpanzees were reared in a laboratory and given small but constant doses of chromium. Within 17 years, all of the chimps had died. Moreover, their average lifespan was just over 11 years, whereas the average lifespan for untreated chimps in the wild is approximately 40 years.

Once you locate the conclusion, the rest of the stimulus should be evidence that supports the conclusion. We'll see whether you've properly identified the conclusions in a bit. But there's a third crucial component to every GMAT argument. Did you find the evidence in the above arguments strong enough to convince you of the conclusions? Or, did you find that additional evidence would be necessary for the argument to be convincing? This additional evidence—facts that need to be, but haven't been, established or mentioned—has a special name.

Assumptions

There are very few vocabulary words you need to know for the GMAT, but here's one of them:

Assumptions act as additional, unstated evidence. They are statements that must be true for the argument to be valid.

To find assumptions, compare the terms in the conclusion with the terms in the evidence. Then ask yourself: "What's missing?" Almost every GMAT argument contains a logical gap between the evidence and the conclusion. The author's assumptions are what fills that gap. With practice, as you read a GMAT argument, the author's assumptions should start to jump right out at you. This is because the same types of assumptions appear over and over again on GMAT arguments.

Let's see how well you do at spotting assumptions. Take another look at the two arguments you just analyzed. Weigh the conclusions you identified against the evidence, and ask yourself what's missing. Remember to read critically. Put the author's assumptions in your own words and then see whether you identified the same assumptions (and conclusions) that we did.

1. The Andaman Islands Argument.

The author assumes that _____

_____

_____

2. The Chromium Chimps Argument.

The author assumes that _____

_____

_____

Answers and Explanations

1. *The Andaman Islands Argument*: We hope you located the conclusion in the last sentence, namely: "[S]etting up a travel company that offers tours to the Andaman Islands is a relatively risk-free way to make money." This conclusion is based on a survey by *Get Going* magazine, which found that 75 percent of those who want to visit Andaman Islands would like to do so on a package tour, whereas package tour providers at present can provide such tours for only 60 percent of those wishing to visit the islands. Here are some assumptions we found:

   - The author assumes that everyone who *wishes* to visit the Andaman Islands will in fact *do* so. If some of the people who wish to visit the islands won't actually do so, then the present tour providers may be more than sufficient to handle the numbers wanting package tours who actually will visit the islands.

   - The author also assumes that the survey is not biased. What if *Get Going* magazine specializes in reviewing package tours and its readership is much more likely to prefer package tours than your average tourist? If the survey is not representative, then the conclusion is not valid.

2. *The Chromium Chimps Argument*: Here the conclusion was found in the first sentence: "[S]teady chromium intake, even in small doses, can significantly lower the life expectancy of some primates." This conclusion was based on the study in which chimps given small but constant doses of chromium in a laboratory had average lifespans of 11 years, compared with average lifespans of chimps in the wild of about 40 years. This is a classic causal argument and here are some assumptions we found:

   - The author assumes that chimps raised in a lab and chimps in the wild would normally have similar life expectancies.

   - Even more important, the author assumes that there wasn't something else that caused the chimps in the study to die prematurely. Who knows? Maybe most of the chimps succumbed to a sudden outbreak of Ebola virus. The point is that in a causal argument, it's always assumed that there's not another plausible explanation for what happened.

Let's recap what we've learned about the structure of arguments.

Evidence + (*Assumption*) → Conclusion

These are the components of an argument. When you break down an argument on the GMAT, you should begin by identifying the author's conclusion (what the author wants you to believe) and the evidence (why the author thinks you should accept the conclusion). From there you should be able to identify the missing steps or gaps between the evidence and the conclusion. These are the author's assumptions.

Spotting the author's assumptions will obviously help you to answer questions that ask about assumptions. But uncovering an argument's assumptions is also key to handling many other types of questions. It's time to examine the types of questions that commonly appear on Critical Reasoning.

COMMON CRITICAL REASONING QUESTION TYPES

Now that you know how to identify the parts of an argument, let's look at how to apply the Kaplan Four-Step Method to the most common Critical Reasoning question types.

Assumption Questions

Let's take another look at the question with which we began this chapter:

1. A recent study has concluded that, contrary to the claims of those trying to ban cigarette advertisements altogether, cigarette ads placed on billboards and in magazines have little to no effect on the smoking habits of the smokers who view the ads. The study, which surveyed more than 20,000 smokers and solicited their reasons for continuing to smoke, found that practically no one in the survey felt that these advertisements influenced their decision to smoke.

    The study's conclusion is based upon which of the following assumptions?

    (A) People do not switch cigarette brands based on their exposure to cigarette ads on billboards and in magazines.

    (B) Cigarette ads on billboards and in magazines do not encourage nonsmokers to take up the habit.

    (C) Banning cigarette ads altogether will encourage people to give up smoking.

    (D) People are consciously aware of all the reasons they choose to smoke.

    (E) People who decide to smoke do so for rational reasons.

To answer an Assumption question, begin by identifying the conclusion and evidence in the stimulus, and then try to spot the author's key assumption. This should make it easy for you to locate the correct answer. But in case you run into any trouble, note that wrong answers to Assumption questions commonly do one of the following:

- They go beyond the scope of argument. Each argument is written within narrow parameters. Wrong answer choices will typically go outside the terms of the author's debate.

- They use language that's too extreme, once again going beyond what the author is attempting to claim.

- They do not support the argument. Remember that an assumption must *support* the argument. Even more than that, it *must be true* for the argument to be valid.

That final point deserves extra emphasis. In fact, to prove that you've actually located the answer choice that contains the assumption, you can always employ the *Denial Test*. Here's how it works: Simply deny or negate the statement and see if the argument falls apart. If it does, you've located a necessary assumption. If, on the other hand, the argument is unaffected, the choice is wrong.

Now let's see if you found the correct answer to the above question.

The argument concludes that cigarette ads placed on billboards and in magazines have little to no effect on the smoking habits of the smokers who view the ads. This conclusion is based upon survey of 20,000 smokers which found that practically none of them felt that these ads influenced their decision to smoke. Choice (D) identifies the key assumption here. If people aren't consciously aware of all of the reasons they choose to smoke, then the fact that those surveyed don't *feel* that the ads influence their decision to smoke does not prove that these ads don't affect their smoking habits.

Now let's look at the other choices:

> (A) People do not switch cigarette brands based on their exposure to cigarette ads on billboards and in magazines.

This statement goes outside the scope of the argument. The argument concerns smokers' decision to smoke, not which brands they choose once they've decided to smoke.

> (B) Cigarette ads on billboards and in magazines do not encourage nonsmokers to take up the habit.

This choice is again outside the scope of the argument. We're concerned with the smoking habits of smokers who view the ads. How nonsmokers react to the ads is of no concern to us.

> (C) Banning cigarette ads altogether will encourage people to give up smoking.

This choice contradicts the argument, which is the opposite of what we're looking for. An assumption should *support* the conclusion.

> (E) People who decide to smoke do so for rational reasons.

This choice goes too far. There's nothing in the argument that implies that people who decide to smoke do so for *rational* reasons.

You'll probably see a couple of Assumption questions in your Verbal Section. Here are some other ways that an Assumption question could be phrased on the test:

- Which of the following is assumed by the author?
- Which of the following, if added to the passage, would make the conclusion valid?
- The validity of the argument depends on which of the following?
- The argument presupposes which of the following?

Now let's look at some other questions that also require you to identify the author's assumptions.

Strengthen and Weaken Questions

By far the most common Critical Reasoning question type will ask you either to strengthen or to weaken the argument. About half the questions in your Verbal Section will ask you to do one or the other. Strengthen/Weaken questions are usually pretty self-explanatory; here's how they might be worded:

Strengthen:

- Which of the following, if true, would most strengthen the argument above?
- Which of the following, if true, would provide the most support for the argument above?
- The argument above would be more persuasive if which one of the following were found to be true?

Weaken:

- Which of the following, if true, would most weaken the argument above?
- Which of the following, if true, would most seriously damage the argument above?
- Which of the following, if true, casts the most doubt on the argument above?

When you're asked to strengthen or weaken an argument, once again you want to break apart the argument by first identifying the evidence and conclusion, and then finding the author's key assumptions. Here's why:

- To strengthen an argument, you want to pick the choice that fills in a key assumption.
- To weaken an argument, you want to pick the choice that denies or undercuts a key assumption.

If you're having trouble spotting a key assumption, look for the answer choice that either reinforces or undermines (depending upon the question) the validity of the author's conclusion. It also pays to know that wrong answers to Strengthen/Weaken questions commonly do one of the following:

- They go outside the scope of the argument. Even though these questions ask for new information that, if true, would strengthen or weaken the argument, this information still has to be consistent with the terms and logic of the argument.
- They introduce irrelevant comparisons.
- They do the opposite of what they're supposed to—that is, they weaken the argument when they're supposed to strengthen it, or vice versa.

Note, however, that strong wording is *not* an eliminator on Strengthen/Weaken questions. In fact, if the wording to a Strengthen/Weaken answer choice is too qualified (containing words like *some*, *occasionally*, or *possibly*), you should ask yourself whether the statement is truly strong enough to affect the argument.

Try this one out for size. Afterwards you can compare your work to ours.

2. Whitney Hospital's much publicized increase in emergency room efficiency, which its spokespeople credit to new procedures for handling trauma patients, does not withstand careful analysis. The average time before treatment for all patients is nearly 40 minutes— the highest in the city. And for trauma victims, who are the specific target of the guidelines, the situation is even worse: The average time before treatment is nearly half an hour— more than twice the city average.

Which of the following, if true, would most seriously weaken the author's conclusion about the value of the new procedures?

(A) The city hospitals with the most efficient emergency rooms utilize the same procedures for handling trauma patients as does Whitney Hospital.

(B) After the new procedures went into effect, Whitney's average time before treatment for trauma patients and patients in general dropped by nearly 35 percent.

(C) Because trauma patients account for a large percentage of emergency room patients, procedures that hasten their treatment will likely increase overall emergency room efficiency.

(D) Due to differences in location and size of staff, not all emergency rooms can be expected to reach similar levels of efficiency.

(E) The recently hired administrators who instituted the new procedures also increased Whitney's emergency room staff by nearly 15 percent.

The author concludes that, contrary to publicized reports touting its new procedures for handling trauma patients, Whitney Hospital's ER is no more efficient than before. As evidence the author points out that Whitney's ER waiting periods for patients, and for trauma patients in particular, are the highest in the city. But does this evidence truly support the conclusion? Not really. Just because Whitney's ER is the slowest in the city, that doesn't mean that its efficiency hasn't grown by leaps and bounds. Evidence comparing Whitney to other hospitals (which is all the author presents) is irrelevant. What matters is how Whitney's present efficiency compares to its previous efficiency. If (B) is true, then Whitney's efficiency is up, likely due to the new procedures. Even though it's still the slowest ER around, it's improved markedly.

As for the other choices:

(A) The city hospitals with the most efficient emergency rooms utilize the same procedures for handling trauma patients as does Whitney Hospital.

This choice introduces an irrelevant comparison. The fact that these procedures are used in the best ERs proves nothing. First, the other ERs could be fast for reasons other than the procedures. Second, even if the procedures generally increase efficiency, Whitney's staff could be so incompetent that the procedures are ineffective. We need information about Whitney's past ER efficiency, not information about other hospitals.

(C) Because trauma patients account for a large percentage of emergency room patients, procedures that hasten their treatment will likely increase overall emergency room efficiency.

This choice is too weak to affect the argument; even if the procedures are intended to speed the treatment of trauma victims (that's not actually said, you notice), there's no reason to assume that they worked at Whitney.

> (D) Due to differences in location and size of staff, not all emergency rooms can be expected to reach similar levels of efficiency.

This might excuse Whitney for offering below-average care, but it gives us no reason to think that Whitney's care has improved, which is what we need.

> (E) The recently hired administrators who instituted the new procedures also increased Whitney's emergency room staff by nearly 15 percent.

This choice, if anything, strengthens the conclusion, because it gives us another plausible explanation for any possible increases in ER efficiency. Even more problematic, this choice provides no reason to believe that there has been an increase in efficiency, which is what we need to weaken the argument.

Flaw Questions

Flaw questions are less common than Strengthen/Weaken or Assumption questions, but you could well see one on Test Day. It could be phrased in various ways:

- The argument above is flawed in that it ignores the possibility that . . .
- Which of the following points to the most serious logical flaw in the argument above?
- Which of the following would reveal most the absurdity of the conclusion drawn above?

Don't confuse these questions with Weaken questions. On a Weaken question, you're supposed to find additional information that, if true, would weaken the argument, whereas on a Flaw question, you know the evidence doesn't support the conclusion very well at all, and it's up to you to explain why.

You should begin by breaking down the argument as usual, and then pick the answer choice that explains why the evidence falls short. It should also be fairly easily to eliminate wrong answer choices on this question type. You can simply get rid of any answer choice that misrepresents the argument.

Try out this strategy here, and then compare your work to ours.

3. It doesn't surprise me that the critic on our local radio station went off on another tirade today about the city men's choir. This is not the first time that he has criticized the choir. But this time his criticisms were simply inaccurate and unjustified. For ten minutes, he spoke of nothing but the choir's lack of expressiveness. As a professional vocal instructor, I have met with these singers individually; I can state with complete confidence that each of the members of the choir has quite an expressive voice.

Which of the following indicates the most serious flaw in the author's reasoning?

(A) He directs his argument against the critic's character rather than against his claims.

(B) He ignores evidence that the critic's remarks might in fact be justified.

(C) He cites his own professional expertise as the sole explanation for his defense of the choir.

(D) He assumes that a group will have a given attribute if each of its parts has that attribute.

(E) He attempts to conclude the truth of a general situation from evidence about one specific situation.

The evidence here is that each member of the choir *individually* has an expressive voice. But the conclusion is that the choir as a *whole* is expressive. But just because each voice is expressive alone doesn't mean that all the voices will be expressive together. (D) points out this flaw in the author's reasoning.

As for the wrong answer choices:

(A) He directs his argument against the critic's character rather than against his claims.

Although the author is rather vehement in disputing the critic's claims, he doesn't address the critic's *character*.

(B) He ignores evidence that the critic's remarks might in fact be justified.

There is no evidence provided in support of the critic's remarks; the flaw is not that the author ignores evidence that might hurt his argument, but that he uses evidence that doesn't really prove anything.

(C) He cites his own professional expertise as the sole explanation for his defense of the choir.

This choice is a little tougher because the author does provide his own opinion as his only explanation. Yet he is a professional vocal instructor, and we have no reason to doubt his qualifications.

(E) He attempts to conclude the truth of a general situation from evidence about one specific situation.

This choice doesn't make any sense. There's no attempt made to generalize from a specific situation here. The author limits his conclusion to attacking, with a specific observation, the radio critic's very specific critique.

All the Critical Reasoning questions that we've looked at so far have required us to identify the component parts of an argument. But this is not always the case, as we shall now see.

Inference Questions

You're likely to see a few Inference questions on the GMAT. On these questions, it's no longer necessary for you to distinguish between the evidence and the conclusion when you read the stimulus. In fact, if anything, you can treat the entire stimulus as evidence and draw your own conclusion. There are many ways that an Inference question could be worded, including the following:

- The facts above best support which of the following conclusions?
- Which of the following conclusions can be properly drawn from the information above?
- If the statements above are all true, which of the following can be properly inferred on the basis of them?
- If the statements above are true, which of the following must be true?

We just noted that an Inference question asks you to treat the entire passage as evidence and then form your own conclusion. But, as we mentioned in the Reading Comprehension chapter, you are never supposed to infer *too much* on the GMAT. In fact, the key to answering an Inference question is to *pick the choice that must be true* without bringing in anything from outside of the passage. If a choice needs any assumptions in order to work, then that choice is wrong.

Consequently, wrong answers to an Inference question typically:

- Go outside the scope of the passage
- Are too extreme (be wary of words such as *never, always, must,* etc.)

Pay particularly close attention to the wording of the answer choices. Only one choice will be an absolutely safe deduction from the passage. To see how this works, try answering the following question. Look for the proper inference, and then compare your work with ours.

4.   When parents allow their children to spend a large amount of time watching television, those children see many more images of violence than do children who watch very little television. The more violent images a child sees, the more violent that child will become. The more violent a child is, the more likely the child is to commit crimes as an adult.

If the statements in the passage above are true, which of the following must also be true?

(A) With an increase in the number of acts of violence committed by children, one can expect to find a concurrent increase in the amount of television watched by children.

(B) If parents did not allow their children to watch television, juvenile delinquency would be unlikely.

(C) No child will develop an aversion to violence if he or she is permitted to watch television.

(D) The more parents try to discourage their children from watching television, the more likely those children are to become criminals.

(E) If a child sees more images of violence on television, the likelihood of that child committing crimes as an adult increases.

The point of the passage is that the more television a child sees, the more images of violence he is likely to see, and thus the greater the chances of his becoming violent and then engaging in criminality as an adult. So TV viewing is being set up as sufficient to bring about an increase in violence and criminality. It is not, however, set up as necessary to an increase in violence and criminality. The argument leaves open the possibility that other factors can effect an increase in violence. Once we grasp this distinction we can go about eliminating answer choices.

(A) With an increase in the number of acts of violence committed by children, one can expect to find a concurrent increase in the amount of television watched by children.

This choice infers that with an increase in child violence one should expect an increase in children's television viewing. Not necessarily. As we just said, other factors could account for an increase in child violence.

(B) If parents did not allow their children to watch television, juvenile delinquency would be unlikely.

This choice infers that delinquency is unlikely if children's TV viewing is prohibited. Not necessarily. Other factors may also make delinquency likely.

(C) No child will develop an aversion to violence if he or she is permitted to watch television.

This choice is *way* too strongly worded. The passage merely claims that more TV violence leads to more violent children, not that *no* child who is permitted to watch TV will develop an aversion to violence.

(D) The more parents try to discourage their children from watching television, the more likely those children are to become criminals.

This choice directly contradicts the stimulus. The stimulus says that *allowing*, not *discouraging*, children to view TV will make them more likely to become criminals.

(E) If a child sees more images of violence on television, the likelihood of that child committing crimes as an adult increases.

Finally, we have a valid deduction. The stimulus says that children who see more violent images on TV become more violent, and thus, more likely to commit crimes as adults. This choice, the correct answer, merely omits the middle term (become more violent) and moves from the violent images straight to the increased likelihood of criminality.

Note: In this example, the correct answer was the logical conclusion to which the author appeared to be heading. This will not always be the case. Sometimes an inference will logically complete an argument; other times, the proper inference may be a trivial point that could easily be dismissed. Just make sure you pick the one choice that *must* be true.

Explain Questions

"Explain" questions are the final common Critical Reasoning question type. These questions are different from all the others we've seen; this is because the stimulus to an Explain question does not present an argument at all, but rather describes a situation with two or more seemingly contradictory facts. Your job is to explain away this seeming contradiction. You're likely to see at least one Explain question on Test Day.

Explain questions may be worded many ways, including the following:

- Which of the following, if true, would explain the discrepancy described above?
- Which of the following, if true, contributes most to an explanation for the apparent contradiction noted above?
- Which of the following, if true, best helps to resolve the paradox outlined above?

These questions ask you to explain how two or more seemingly contradictory facts can simultaneously be true. Before attempting to find an explanation, make sure you have a good grasp of the situation that needs explaining. Only one answer choice will address all of the facts in dispute. Wrong answer choices, on the other hand, usually:

- Touch upon only one of the facts in dispute
- Deepen the mystery
- Make an irrelevant comparison
- Misrepresent the scope of the situation

Give the following a try, and then compare your work to ours:

5.   The number of applicants applying to top graduate programs has declined by more than 10 percent since the mid-1990s. However, the number of students admitted to these same programs has not decreased commensurately, and the caliber of the students admitted, as measured by their undergraduate GPAs and standardized test scores, has actually improved markedly.

Which of the following, if true, best explains the seemingly contradictory trends described above?

(A) The number of applicants applying to second- and third-tier graduate programs has also declined by more than 10 percent since the mid-1990s.

(B) Many potential graduate school applicants are put off by the ever-increasing cost of a graduate education.

(C) Because of improved economic opportunities, general interest in leaving the work-force to go to graduate school has waned in recent years.

(D) The greater premium awarded to degrees from top graduate programs has made the applicant pool increasingly competitive, discouraging those with less impressive academic records from applying.

(E) The number of women applying to top graduate programs has increased since the mid-1990s, while at the same time the number of men applying to top graduate programs has declined.

The passage sets up the following contradictory facts to be resolved:

- The number of applicants applying to top graduate programs has declined by more than 10 percent since the mid-1990s.
- The number of students admitted to these same programs has not decreased commensurately, and the caliber of the students admitted, as measured by their undergraduate GPAs and standardized test scores, has actually improved markedly.

Choice (D) alone addresses both sides of the contradiction, explaining that these programs have become increasingly competitive due the higher premium placed on getting a graduate degree from these institutions, and that this in turn has discouraged those with less impressive records from even bothering to apply.

Now let's look at the wrong answer choices:

(A) The number of applicants applying to second- and third-tier graduate programs has also declined by more than 10 percent since the mid-1990s.

This choice is outside the scope of the situation to be addressed. We are not interested in the trends in graduate programs other than the top ones.

(B) Many potential graduate school applicants are put off by the ever-increasing cost of a graduate education.

This choice addresses only one side of the contradiction. The ever-increasing cost of graduate school may help explain why the number of applicants to top schools has gone down, but it does nothing to address why the caliber of those applying has nonetheless improved.

(C) Because of improved economic opportunities, general interest in leaving the work-force to go to graduate school has waned in recent years.

This choice likewise addresses only the first side of the contradiction. Nowhere does it explain why the caliber of the remaining applicants has improved.

(E) The number of women applying to top graduate programs has increased since the mid-1990s, while at the same time the number of men applying to top graduate programs has declined.

Finally, this choice introduces an irrelevant comparison. The fact that more women and fewer men are applying to top graduate programs does nothing to address either side of the contradiction.

PRACTICE QUESTIONS

Now that we've examined how to apply the Kaplan Four-Step Method to all the most common Critical Reasoning questions, you should be ready to try out what you've learned on the following practice questions. If you encounter a question type you haven't seen before, fear not. Identifying the conclusion, evidence, and underlying assumptions of the argument will most likely be the key to solving the question. If you can't ascertain the correct answer, eliminate as many wrong answer choices as you can, make your best guess, and move on.

1. Enrollment in graduate and professional programs tends to be high in a strong economy and much lower during recessions. The perceived likelihood of future job availability, therefore, affects people's willingness to pass up immediate earning potential in order to invest in career-related training.

    The argument above assumes that

    (A) the perceived likelihood of job availability has decreased in recent years

    (B) all those who avoid graduate and professional school during an economic slump do so because of the perceived lack of future jobs

    (C) perceptions of the likelihood of job availability are related to the state of the economy

    (D) those who enroll in graduate and professional schools during a strong economy help increase the economy's strength

    (E) graduate and professional programs admit fewer students during recessions

2. **The university's decision to scale back significantly its teaching of the literary and philosophical classics of the Western Tradition is misguided.** Proponents of the move argue that today's students are not interested in these works and desire more practical business-related courses that will help them in their future careers. But any student lacking a sufficient grounding in the thought and tradition that underlie the present civilization cannot be said to be fully educated. **The classics are the primary vehicle for instilling such knowledge.**

    Which of the following best expresses the relationship between the two bolded statements above?

    (A) The first statement offers a hypothesis and the second statement offers conflicting evidence.

    (B) The first statement suggests an alternative explanation for the phenomenon described in the second statement.

    (C) The second statement provides evidence for a conclusion drawn in the first statement.

    (D) The second statement must be true for the first statement to be true.

    (E) The second statement is an inference drawn from the first statement.

KAPLAN

3. Due to a string of dismal performances, a touring band has begun to lose its audience. News of the disappointing concerts has traveled quickly via cable stations and the Internet, and has negatively influenced ticket sales for future performances. Due to the poor ticket sales, a number of promoters have canceled the band's upcoming shows, forcing the band to attempt to recoup its touring and recording expenses from fewer total performances.

   Which of the following, if true, taken together with the information above, best supports the prediction that more of the band's shows will be canceled?

   (A) The promoters who canceled shows did so with the promise that they would monitor the band's reception in other cities before deciding whether or not to reschedule the canceled shows.

   (B) The pressure to restore its diminishing fan base and recoup its overall expenses from a decreased number of performing opportunities is likely to cause the band to perform poorly in future concerts.

   (C) Because of the canceled shows, it will be impossible for the band to earn a profit on the current tour.

   (D) If the band cannot salvage the tour, its next CD will likely fail economically unless the band can restore its image through music videos.

   (E) It is impossible for the management of a rock band to predict accurately the success of a tour because fans of rock bands are notoriously fickle in their tastes.

4. Over the past several years, Running River Water Park has experienced a serious decline in attendance and sales despite the addition of several state-of-the-art water slides. This year, the Board of Directors lowered the park's weekday admission prices in order to attract more customers. Attendance during the first two months of this year's season has been 30 percent higher than the attendance during the same two months last year. Clearly, the price cut has had the desired effect.

   Each of the following, if true, weakens the conclusion above *EXCEPT*

   (A) Nationwide, the number of people attending amusement parks has increased by 30 percent this year over last year.

   (B) Grand Excursions Amusement Park, located ten miles from Running River, has been closed during most of this year's season due to unexpected equipment problems.

   (C) The most popular movie released this summer, *The Big Chase*, features a long action sequence that was filmed at Running River.

   (D) Several large businesses relocated near Running River during the past year bringing with them many employees and their families.

   (E) Most amusement park visitors are aware of the admission prices before they arrive at an amusement park.

5. Staff members at the Willard Detention Center typically oversee students' schedules and make all final decisions regarding the required activities in which students participate. Students are permitted, however, to make their own decisions regarding how they spend their free time. Therefore, students should be permitted to make their own decisions regarding the elective courses that they wish to take.

   The conclusion above would be more reasonably drawn if which of the following were inserted into the argument as an additional premise?

   (A) Decisions regarding required activities are more important than decisions regarding the elective courses that students take.

   (B) Students are more willing to take elective courses than to participate in required Center activities.

   (C) Required activities contribute more to the students' rehabilitation than do their free-time activities.

   (D) Staff members at Willard have found that elective courses are more beneficial for students than the available free-time activities.

   (E) When compared for decision-making purposes, elective courses are more like free-time activities than required activities.

6. The average math score on a state-wide proficiency exam for students attending Middlebury High School last year was 20 points higher than the average math score for students attending nearby Ellingsford High School. Therefore, any student at Ellingsford High School wishing to achieve a better math score on next September's proficiency exam should transfer to Middlebury High School over the summer.

   Which of the following statements, if true, would most significantly strengthen the conclusion drawn in the passage?

   (A) Middlebury High School offers its students a unique, week-long course just before they take the proficiency exam that has consistently proven effective in raising student scores.

   (B) One third of all the students who have transferred to Middlebury High School the summer before taking the test got scores that are at least 20 points higher than the average score at Ellingsford High School.

   (C) Middlebury High School students who transfer to Ellingsford High School in the summer before they take the proficiency exam get average scores that are comparable to the average scores of students who remain at Middlebury.

   (D) In the past five years, the average score at Ellingsford High School has been rising at a faster rate than has the average score at Middlebury High School.

   (E) Students wanting better proficiency-exam scores are transferring to Middlebury High School at a high rate, which will ultimately result in a lowering of the school's average score.

7.   A study found that last year roughly 6,000 homeless people in the United States were admitted to hospitals because of malnutrition. In the same year, a little more than 10,000 nonhomeless people were admitted to hospitals for the same reason. These findings clearly show that the nonhomeless are more likely to suffer from malnutrition than are the homeless.

The answer to which of the following questions would be most likely to point out the illogical nature of the conclusion drawn above?

(A) What is the relative level of severity of the malnutrition suffered by each group cited in the study?

(B) To what extent, on average, are the nonhomeless better off financially than the homeless?

(C) To what extent are the causes of malnutrition in the nonhomeless related to ignorance of proper dietary habits?

(D) What percentage of each group cited in the study suffered from malnutrition last year?

(E) What effect would a large increase in the number of homeless shelters have on the incidence of malnutrition among the homeless?

8.   History has shown that severe and sudden political instability strikes the Republic of Balanda roughly once every 50 years. The most recent example was the attempt on the president's life in 1992. The reaction of average investors in Balanda to crisis situations in the country cannot be predicted in advance. The government's fiscal affairs department has introduced an electronic protection mechanism into the market in the hopes of avoiding a prolonged large-scale selloff. The mechanism is triggered in specific instances based on estimations of how average investors will react to changes in corporate data and economic indicators.

If the statements above are true, which of the following conclusions can be drawn regarding the electronic protection mechanism?

(A) Sometime within the next 50 years severe and sudden political instability in Balanda will trigger the protection mechanism.

(B) Whether the protection mechanism will function appropriately in response to a sudden political event depends on whether the event is seen by investors as positive or negative.

(C) It is unclear how well the protection mechanism would work in the event of a sudden political coup if such an event were partially or wholly unrelated to changes in corporate data and economic indicators.

(D) There would be no way for the protection mechanism to differentiate between market fluctuations resulting from economic factors and those that are caused by political instability.

(E) The protection mechanism would be purposely destroyed by political insurgents if they were able to infiltrate the government's fiscal affairs department.

9. Country X complains that Country Y's high tariffs on imported goods have artificially inflated the price of cars imported from Country X into Country Y, and that this is the reason that few of Country X's cars are sold in Country Y. On the other hand, Country X's very low tariffs allow Country Y to sell many cars there at relatively low prices. Country X says that if Country Y would lower its tariffs, then Country X's cars would be able to compete in Country Y and an equitable balance of trade would be achieved.

   Which of the following, if true, would most undermine the validity of Country X's explanation for the poor sales of its cars in Country Y?

   (A) In places where the tariffs on goods from both countries are equal, Country Y's cars far outsell cars from Country X.

   (B) Cars imported from Country Z sell poorly in Country Y.

   (C) In countries where tariffs on imported goods are higher than in Country Y, Country X sells more cars than does Country Y.

   (D) Other goods from Country X sell poorly in Country Y.

   (E) Sales of Country Y's cars are high even in countries that have higher tariffs on imported goods than does Country X.

10. Many adults, no matter what their age, respond to adversity by seeking advice only from their parents. Consciously or not, they regress to a psychological state of childhood dependence in which the parent is seen as the only source of wisdom and comfort. Adults who do not regress to this childhood mode turn for advice in adversity only to other loved ones—a spouse or a best friend—whom they perceive and relate to as peers.

    If all of the above statements are true, which of the following must also be true?

    (A) One's parents offer more wisdom in adversity than those whom one perceives as peers.

    (B) Adults who do not suffer adversity look only to their parents for advice.

    (C) No adults seek advice in adversity from total strangers.

    (D) Adults who seek advice in adversity from their parents do not expect to receive wisdom and comfort.

    (E) Adults who regress to a state of childhood dependence lose touch with their peers.

11. Recent experiments in the Southern Ocean offer the promise of controlling the threat of global warming by creating organic "sponges" for carbon dioxide, which is widely considered the main culprit for rising global temperatures. Scientists were able to grow a lush strip of phytoplankton 150 kilometers long by fertilizing a patch of the ocean with hundreds of kilograms of an iron compound. Phytoplankton presently accounts for over half of the photosynthesis on Earth, the process by which carbon dioxide is absorbed and converted into oxygen. A major limiting factor in the production of phytoplankton is lack of iron, but by fertilizing oceans with iron compounds scientists hope to be able to reduce carbon dioxide levels and reverse the greenhouse effect.

Which of the following, if true, casts the most serious doubt upon the advisability of using the fertilization method described above to control carbon dioxide levels?

(A) In some oceans, the growth of phytoplankton is also limited by how much nitrogen, phosphorus, and silicon are available.

(B) The cost of fertilizing the oceans with sufficient quantities of iron to reverse the greenhouse effect is likely to be very high.

(C) Iron naturally reaches the seas in the form of wind-blown mineral dust, which becomes more or less abundant as conditions on land change.

(D) Fertilization efforts will do nothing to curb the production of more carbon dioxide emissions.

(E) The oceans are a complex system, and the long-term consequences of ocean fertilization may be the opposite of what is predicted.

12. University systems that use graduation rates to determine which campuses are allotted additional funds are acting counter to their stated goals. The universities say they are trying to raise academic standards, yet they are actually encouraging campuses to graduate students regardless of achievement.

Which of the following statements, if true, would help to validate the approach taken by the university systems mentioned above?

(A) Graduation rates for university systems with this policy are among the highest in the nation, but the graduates from these systems score poorly on tests of basic skills.

(B) The campuses that need the additional funds the most are the ones that have the lowest graduation rates.

(C) The new funds will be allotted for facility upgrades, not new faculty positions or staff pay increases.

(D) Graduation examinations currently exist that require every graduate at each university to demonstrate a minimum level of achievement.

(E) An opposing plan focuses on providing extra funding based not on graduation rates, but on the percent of students that pass basic skills tests.

ANSWERS AND EXPLANATIONS

1. C	5. E	9. A
2. C	6. A	10. C
3. B	7. D	11. E
4. E	8. C	12. D

1.   Choice (C) is correct.

We're asked to find an assumption. The argument involves a question of cause and effect. Since enrollment in graduate and professional programs tends to be high when the economy is strong and low when it is weak, the reason must be, according to the author, a matter of people's perceptions of job availability. Sounds reasonable, but do all the terms match up with those in this conclusion? We know from the question stem that they do not. What's missing? Well, the evidence pertains to the state of the economy. But the conclusion strays into the area of psychology—people's perceptions. Are these the same things? The author treats them as such by arguing from evidence regarding the state of the economy to a conclusion based on people's *perceptions* of the economy. The author takes the relationship between these for granted, but technically, in order for the argument to work, this must be established. (C) reveals this basic assumption.

2.   Choice (C) is correct

Questions such as this one, which ask about the functions played by the bolded sentences in an argument, have become increasingly popular on the GMAT—so there's a good chance you'll see one on Test Day. Once again, your primary task is to break down the argument and identify its parts. Here the conclusion is in fact the first sentence of the passage; the rest of the passage goes on to explain why the university's decision is misguided. The first sentence, when it is phrased as an assertion, as here, is often the conclusion of the passage. So why is the university's decision misguided? (1) Students lacking a certain grounding cannot be considered fully educated. (2) The classics are the primary vehicle for instilling such knowledge. So the final sentence (second statement) provides evidence for the conclusion drawn in the first sentence (first statement), which is exactly what (C) says. You can also use the process of elimination. (A) is out because the second statement offers no *conflicting* evidence. (B) is out because the second statement does not describe a *phenomenon* and the first statement suggests no *alternative* explanation. (D) is out because the second statement does not have to be true in order for the first statement to be true, nor is the second statement an inference, or logically drawn conclusion, of the first statement, as (E) states.

3.   Choice (B) is correct.

This question is a little unusual in that the conclusion—more of the band's shows will be canceled—appears in the actual question. You already know the argument's conclusion, so read the passage carefully and follow the flow of the evidence presented. Dismal performances led to a drop in ticket sales for future concerts, which in turn led concert promoters to cancel concerts, putting additional pressure on the band to make up the lost money from fewer shows. We're looking for the choice that leads to more canceled shows, and it's not easy to predict the answer here. But you can test each choice to see where it fits into this chain of events, if at all. Canceled concerts must now lead to a result that will trigger additional canceled concerts. What do you already know leads to canceled concerts? Dismal performances and lower ticket sales. Keep this in mind while testing out the choices. (B) works by turning the chain of events into a vicious cycle. If (B) were true, we would expect the events to follow the same course, culminating in the cancellation of more shows. Of the wrong choices, (A) indicates that some of the shows that have already been canceled might be rescheduled. Optimally, the band would get to perform the original number of shows, and at worst, the band will perform the current reduced number of concerts. But there is nothing here to indicate that even more shows will be canceled. (C) begins with the canceled concerts but then jumps beyond the scope of the argument to the issue of "profit." The impossibility of earning a profit under the current circumstances is an effect of the canceled shows—but it does nothing to suggest that more shows will be canceled. (D) discusses the long-term prospects for the band, but nothing here suggests that more shows on the current tour will be canceled. The effect that this tour ultimately has on the band's next CD does not directly influence what happens now. (E) goes beyond the scope of the evidence. The accuracy of the management's predictions is not at issue.

4.   Choice (E) is correct.

This is a Weaken "EXCEPT" question, so you're looking for the one choice that would *NOT* weaken the conclusion. This is a classic causal argument. The author concludes that the Water Park's admissions price cut is responsible for the increase in attendance over the same period last year. Of course, to weaken a causal argument, one needs only to point out another plausible explanation for the increase in attendance. (A), which notes an increase in park attendance nationally, (B), which notes the closing of a competitor, (C), which notes favorable publicity in a popular movie for the park, and (D), which notes an increase in the size and affluence of the local population, all offer other plausible reasons for the increase in attendance. Only (E), which notes that most people are aware of admission prices, would strengthen, rather than weaken, the conclusion, since public awareness of the price cut would be necessary for the price cut to have a positive effect on attendance.

5.   Choice (E) is correct.

The argument here is a simple one: Since students at the Willard Detention Center make their own decisions about free time, they should also make their own decisions about elective courses. The argument assumes that, for these students, decisions about what to do with free time are similar to decisions about what electives to take in school. Since we're looking for a premise to complete the argument, look for a choice that provides evidence that these things are similar. (E) provides the evidence we need. If it is true that elective courses are more akin to free time than to required activities, then the conclusion that students should be able to choose their own electives is more reasonable. You could have eliminated as follows: (A) is outside the scope of the argument; it's not the *importance* of the decision that's at issue here, it's who should have the power to make the decision. (B) is irrelevant: Students' relative willingness to take the different types of courses doesn't matter. The argument concerns only who should make the decisions regarding activities. (C) may explain why staff members oversee decisions about required activities, but it tells us nothing about why students should be allowed to choose their own elective courses. In fact, it doesn't refer to elective courses at all. (D) follows the same general pattern of the other wrong choices, focusing on an irrelevant issue (in this case, the relative benefits of electives versus free-time activities), rather than the issue at hand: who should make the decisions.

6.   Choice (A) is correct.

As you read the stem, you should have tried to identify the evidence and conclusion, and think about the possibility that an assumption glues the two together. An answer choice that validates that assumption will strengthen the author's argument. The author argues that since Middlebury High School students tend to get better math scores on the test, Ellingsford High School students who want better math scores should transfer to Middlebury the summer before they take the test. Think about the time frame employed here: The author assumes that former Ellingsford High School students will learn what they need to improve their math scores almost immediately after transferring to Middlebury. The correct answer will most likely offer a plausible reason why this might not be the case. (A) provides a plausible reason to expect that students who transfer to Middlebury during the summer can significantly benefit before taking the test in September by taking advantage of the unique, week-long course offered just before test day. If (A) is true, then a major stumbling block to the potential efficacy of the proposal is removed, and the argument would be strengthened.

As to the wrong choices: (B) tells us nothing. The average score of only part of a group cannot be fairly compared to the average score of an entire group. A third of the students who remained at Ellingsford High School may also have scored at least 20 points higher than their school's average. (C) weakens the argument's conclusion. If Middlebury students who transfer to Ellingsford during the summer before they take the test still get higher math scores, then the notion that transferring the summer before is a cure-all seems less plausible. (D) presents an irrelevant comparison. The scores at Ellingsford High School may be rising faster than those at Middlebury High School, but the average score at Middlebury is still 20 points higher than the average score at Ellingsford. (E) goes beyond the scope of the argument because the argument does not concern itself with what will happen *ultimately*. The main issue is whether Ellingsford students can raise their scores by transferring. Even if (E) is true, and many students transfer and Middlebury's test score average drops, it's impossible for us to tell whether the transferees' scores are higher or lower than they would have been had they remained at Ellingsford.

7. Choice (D) is correct.

The question stem reveals that the argument in the stimulus is fatally flawed. As you read the passage, identify the evidence and conclusion, and watch for a questionable assumption or some other flaw along the way. The argument is based on numbers: Since only 6,000 homeless people suffering from malnutrition were admitted to U.S. hospitals last year, compared to 10,000 nonhomeless people, the nonhomeless must be more likely to suffer from malnutrition. But *total numbers* mean *nothing*! We cannot figure the odds of suffering from malnutrition solely from the number of malnourished people in each group. We need to know the *percentage* of homeless people suffering from malnutrition versus the *percentage* of nonhomeless people suffering from malnutrition. Clearly there are far more nonhomeless people than homeless people in the United States, so the argument contains a ludicrous assumption: that the two groups are comparably sized. The correct answer to the question will somehow point this out. (D) provides the question whose answer would provide the information we need to correctly understand the odds. It allows us to see how the raw numbers cited do not support the author's counterintuitive conclusion that the nonhomeless are more susceptible to malnutrition than are the homeless. As to the wrong answers, (A) goes beyond the scope of the argument. The argument involves the likelihood of suffering from malnutrition, not the relative levels of severity. (B) also introduces a new issue—finances. No matter how much people with homes are better off financially than the homeless, the fact remains that more nonhomeless were hospitalized for malnutrition than homeless. (C) introduces another new issue. The argument draws no conclusion about the causes of malnutrition within these groups, only about the likelihood of malnutrition. (E) is irrelevant to the argument as presented: The future possibility of remedying homelessness to some degree does not impact upon these numbers and this particular conclusion drawn from them.

8. **Choice (C) is correct.**

You must draw an inference in this question—so you are looking for a softly worded answer that must be true given the statements in the argument. It's difficult to predict the correct answer here, so your best bet is to test the choices rigorously, looking for the one that absolutely *must be true*. (C) draws a reasonable conclusion based on the evidence. If political instability involves changes in corporate data and economic indicators, then the mechanism should work the way it is designed to work. But if the incident does not involve those elements, then how the mechanism will work becomes unclear, because the behavior of investors will be unpredictable. Of the wrong answers, (A) goes too far when it infers that a severe and sudden political instability will occur within 50 years. The 1992 attempt was only an example of the political instability that occurs roughly every 50 years, and the 50-year period was an average, not an absolute limit. Furthermore, even if there is an attempt on the president's life, it is unclear how investors will react because their behavior in such situations cannot be predicted in advance. (B) goes beyond the scope of the argument. Whether investors perceive sudden political events positively or negatively isn't mentioned in the stimulus, so we can't infer that that perception makes any difference to the accuracy of the mechanism. (D) takes its inference too far. The mechanism might be able to differentiate between various types of market fluctuations, even though it might not be able to trigger appropriate responses to some of them. And (E) takes the argument far beyond its original scope. Nothing in the stimulus leads to a prediction of what might happen to the protection mechanism in the event of political instability.

9. **Choice (A) is correct.**

Find the author's conclusion and evidence, and the assumption linking them. Weaken the argument by invalidating that assumption. The argument develops from evidence that Y's high tariffs make X's cars relatively expensive, but X's low tariffs make Y's cars relatively cheap. The argument concludes that if Y lowers its tariffs, then real competition and an equitable balance of trade would result. Country X assumes that Y sells more cars in X than X sells in Y because of the price difference created by the different tariffs. This suggests a classic case of ignored alternatives. Look for a choice that suggests that there might be an alternative explanation besides the difference in tariffs that could explain the weakness of X's car sales relative to Y's. (A) weakens country X's argument by illustrating that the effect (more Y cars sold than X cars) is possible without the supposed cause (a tariff imbalance favoring Y). This implies that something other than tariffs—the reason offered by X for its poor performance in the car market—could very well explain the difference in sales (maybe X's car's are no good).

10. **Choice (C) is correct.**

The question stem sends us searching for a valid inference that can be drawn from the statements in the passage. You're looking for a conclusion *that must be true* based upon the statements in this argument. Reading the passage, you learn that adults can be divided into two groups: adults who seek advice in adversity only from their parents, and the remainder, who seek that advice only from other loved ones. There is not much room here for argument. All adults fall into one or the other of these categories, but not both. If these statements are true, then adults must turn either to parents or to other loved ones in times of adversity, and to no one else. (C) is a valid inference, given the evidence above. Adults seek advice from parents or other loved ones—not from strangers. Of the wrong answers, (A) introduces a concept foreign to the evidence. The passage tells us nothing about the relative wisdom of parents and peers. (For all we know, everyone gives terrible advice.) (B) introduces another concept foreign to the evidence. The passage tells us nothing about what people do for advice when they are not in adversity. (D) goes beyond the scope of the evidence. Expectations are not discussed in the passage. The issue here is where people in trouble go for advice—not what they expect to find. And (E) goes too far. Adults who regress will seek advice from parents if they face adverse circumstances and wish to get advice. This doesn't mean they will necessarily lose touch with peers.

11. Choice (E) is correct.

We're looking for the answer that does the best job at weakening the argument. This is a causal argument, which concludes that a plan to fertilize the oceans with iron compounds will be able to reverse the greenhouse effect. The chain of reasoning goes like this: By fertilizing the oceans to iron compounds, phytoplankton will grow, creating organic "sponges" to soak up carbon dioxide, widely believed to be responsible for global warming. We're looking for an answer that weakens this chain of causality. (E), which notes oceans are a complex system, and consequences of fertilization could be the *opposite* of what's predicted, does a good job of this. What if the plan ends up exacerbating the greenhouse effect? That would certainly cast doubt upon the advisability of the plan!

Of the wrong answers, (A), which discusses *some* oceans, is too weak to affect the argument. There's nothing in the argument to suggest that *all* the oceans need to be fertilized. (B), which mentions the high cost of the plan, is beyond the scope of the argument. The argument does not suggest the cost is a factor; after all, we're discussing a plan to save the planet! (C) is completely irrelevant to the issue at hand. Who cares about how iron naturally reaches the sea? And finally, (D) does nothing to invalidate the plan. Sure, emission-reduction plans may also be in order, but that doesn't mean we shouldn't try to reduce present carbon dioxide levels.

12. Choice (D) is correct.

The trickiest part of this question is understanding whose position we're trying to validate and whose we're trying to attack (it gets confusing when the argument involves opposing positions, as here). Here we're trying to validate the approach taken by the university systems, which the author argues is flawed; so, in other words, we're trying to weaken the author's critique. So what is the approach taken by the university systems? And what is the author's critique? The systems use graduation rates to determine which universities are awarded extra funds. This, the author argues, encourages campuses to graduate everyone, *regardless of achievement*. (D), which notes that exams exist that require every graduate to prove a minimum level of achievement, attacks the author's contention that the approach will lead to people graduating regardless of achievement.

Of the wrong answers, (A) strengthens the author's argument, as it agrees with his contention that achievement standards are being disregarded. (B) argues against the university systems' approach, although not for the same reasons as the author. (C) makes a completely irrelevant point. What's at issue is not how the money is *spent* by schools, but how it is *allotted* to them. And (E) doesn't validate the approach taken by the university systems, but in fact hints that there may be a fairer approach out there.

PART THREE

Practice Sets

SENTENCE CORRECTION PRACTICE SET ONE

Time: 25 Minutes/22 Questions

Directions: The following questions consist of sentences that are either partly or entirely underlined. Below each sentence are five versions of the underlined portion of the sentence. The first of these, choice (A), duplicates the original version. The four other versions revise the underlined portion of the sentence. Read the sentence and the five choices carefully, and select the best version. If the original seems better than any of the revisions, select choice (A). If not, choose one of the revisions.

These questions test your recognition of correct grammatical usage and your sense of clear and economical writing style. Choose answers according to the norms of standard written English for grammar, word choice, and sentence construction. Your selected answer should express the intended meaning of the original sentence as clearly and precisely as possible, while avoiding ambiguous, awkward, or unnecessarily wordy constructions.

1. To be a leading producer in the computer industry, a company must be international, achieve a turnover that makes efficient large-scale production possible, <u>and secure information about technical advances</u>.

    (A) and secure information about technical advances

    (B) and securing information about technical advances

    (C) while secure information about technical advances

    (D) and secure information of how to technically advance

    (E) and secure information in regards to technical advances

2. Of the people who brought about the Reformation, the religious revolution that grew out of objections to the doctrines of the medieval church, <u>Martin Luther is the best known of them</u>.

    (A) Martin Luther is the best known of them

    (B) the best known is Martin Luther

    (C) the better known of them was Martin Luther

    (D) Martin Luther is better known

    (E) the best known one was Martin Luther

3. Declining enrollments are forcing smaller private colleges to choose <u>between raising tuition and reduction of the staff</u>.

    (A) between raising tuition and reduction of the staff

    (B) among raising tuition and reducing staff

    (C) between raising tuition or reducing staff

    (D) between raising tuition and reducing staff

    (E) between the rise of tuition and the reduction of the staff

4. The bylaws of a corporation specify how the directors of the corporation are to be elected, whether the existing stockholders will have first right to buy any new stock issued by the firm, <u>as well as duties of management committees</u>.

    (A) as well as duties of management committees

    (B) as well as the duties that the management committees have

    (C) and that the management committees have duties

    (D) and the management committees have duties too

    (E) and what the duties of management committees will be

KAPLAN

5. Although it is conceivable that certain electronic devices implanted in the brain may someday correct blindness caused by nerve damage, there is now no clear evidence <u>of their ability to do it</u>.

   (A) of their ability to do it

   (B) of their doing that

   (C) that they can do so

   (D) that they might one day be able to do it

   (E) to do so

6. Setting up a corporation requires more paperwork and legal provision <u>than to establish either a proprietorship or a partnership</u>.

   (A) than to establish either a proprietorship or a partnership

   (B) than what it requires to establish either a proprietorship or a partnership

   (C) than to either establish a proprietorship or a partnership

   (D) than establishing either a proprietorship or a partnership

   (E) than establishing proprietorships and partnerships

7. The Minnesota Multiphasic Personality Inventory, a test developed in the 1930s to assess character, attitudes, and behavior, <u>is finally being revised, after many attacks recently as dated and culturally biased</u>.

   (A) is finally being revised, after many attacks recently as dated and culturally biased

   (B) has recently been attacked as dated and culturally biased and is finally being revised

   (C) is finally under revision for receiving much recent attack as dated and culturally biased

   (D) was finally revised recently because it is being attacked as dated and culturally biased

   (E) is finally to be revised after recent attacks as dated and culturally biased

8. In the Champagne region of France, <u>wine growers still harvest grapes as they have done</u> for centuries, by carefully handpicking their crop and storing their precious fruit in specially aged casks.

   (A) wine growers still harvest grapes as they have done

   (B) the wine grower still harvests grapes as he has

   (C) wine growers still harvest grapes as was done

   (D) wine growers still harvest grapes as has been done

   (E) wine growers still harvest grapes as they did

9. A new generation of <u>sophisticated copy machines, capable of unprecedented detail and accuracy, are</u> prompting the development of more complex currency designs to prevent counterfeiting.

   (A) sophisticated copy machines, capable of unprecedented detail and accuracy, are

   (B) sophisticated copy machines, capable for unprecedented detail and accuracy, is

   (C) sophisticated copy machines, capable of unprecedented detail and accuracy, is

   (D) sophisticated copy machines, capable for unprecedented detail and accuracy, are

   (E) sophisticated copy machines that are capable of unprecedented detail and accuracy are

10. In an unusual move for a Republican, the <u>president's directive established price controls</u>.

   (A) the president's directive established price controls

   (B) the president's directive was to establish price controls

   (C) the president was successful in the establishment of controls on prices

   (D) the president had instituted controls on prices

   (E) the president established price controls

11. The United Automobile Workers returned to the A.F.L.-C.I.O. because <u>of the wish of both groups to strengthen labor's role not only in politics but also industry.</u>

   (A) of the wish of both groups to strengthen labor's role not only in politics but also industry

   (B) both groups wished to strengthen labor's role in politics as well as in industry

   (C) the strengthening of labor's role in politics as well as industry was wished for by both groups

   (D) it was wished by both groups to strengthen labor's role in politics and industry as well

   (E) both groups wished to strengthen labor's role in both of the two areas of politics and industry

12. Of all the countries contiguous to China, <u>the Soviet Union's borders were most strongly defended.</u>

   (A) the Soviet Union's borders were most strongly defended

   (B) the borders of the Soviet Union were defended more strongly than any of the others

   (C) the Soviet Union's borders stood out for the strength of their defensive capability

   (D) the Soviet Union had the most strongly defended borders

   (E) the Soviet Union's were the most strongly defended borders

13. Unlike <u>the people whom settled the Western states after the passage of the Homestead Act of 1862, the hope of the prospectors and adventurers who came to California during the gold rush was</u> to get rich quickly.

   (A) the people whom settled the Western states after the passage of the Homestead Act of 1862, the hope of the prospectors and adventurers who came to California during the gold rush was

   (B) the people who settled the Western states after the passage of the Homestead Act of 1862, the hope of the prospectors and adventurers who came to California during the gold rush was

   (C) that of the people who settled the Western states after the passage of the Homestead Act of 1862, the prospectors and adventurers who came to California during the gold rush hoped

   (D) that of the people whom settled the Western states after the passage of the Homestead Act of 1862, the hope of the prospectors and adventurers who came to California during the gold rush was

   (E) the people who settled the Western states after the passage of the Homestead Act of 1862, the prospectors and adventurers who came to California during the gold rush hoped

14. <u>Before George Eliot became the popular and respected novelist known as George Eliot, she was</u> an anonymous translator and essayist of formidably far-ranging scholarship.

   (A) Before George Eliot became the popular and respected novelist known as George Eliot, she was

   (B) Before she had been the popular and respected novelist, George Eliot, she was

   (C) George Eliot has been the popular and respected novelist, George Eliot, after such time as she was

   (D) Before George Eliot became the popular and respected novelist, George Eliot, she was

   (E) George Eliot, before she was the popular and respected novelist, George Eliot, had been

KAPLAN

15. <u>Just like Congress is the legislative branch of the Federal government of the United States, so</u> Parliament is the legislative body of the United Kingdom of Great Britain and Northern Ireland.

   Ⓐ Just like Congress is the legislative branch of the Federal government of the United States, so

   Ⓑ As Congress is the legislative branch of the Federal government of the United States,

   Ⓒ As Congress is the legislative branch of the Federal government of the United States, in the same way

   Ⓓ Just as Congress is the legislative branch of the Federal government of the United States, so

   Ⓔ Just as the Federal government of the United States' legislative branch is Congress,

16. <u>The reason Frances Willard founded the Women's Christian Temperance Union was because she believed that national prohibition of alcohol will empty the poorhouses, jails, and asylums of the United States.</u>

   Ⓐ The reason Frances Willard founded the Women's Christian Temperance Union was because she believed that national prohibition of alcohol will empty the poorhouses, jails, and asylums of the United States

   Ⓑ Frances Willard founded the Women's Christian Temperance Union, the reason being that she believed that national prohibition of alcohol will empty the poorhouses, jails, and asylums of the United States

   Ⓒ The reason Frances Willard founded the Women's Christian Temperance Union was she believed that national prohibition of alcohol will empty the poorhouses, jails, and asylums of the United States

   Ⓓ Because she believed that national prohibition of alcohol would empty the poorhouses, jails, and asylums of the United States, so Frances Willard founded the Women's Christian Temperance Union

   Ⓔ Frances Willard founded the Women's Christian Temperance Union because she believed that national prohibition of alcohol would empty the poorhouses, jails, and asylums of the United States

17. The combination of technical expertise, commercial enterprise, and <u>that the government backs them judiciously should ensure Italian firms continuing</u> to innovate and gain competitively in world markets.

   Ⓐ that the government backs them judiciously should ensure Italian firms continuing

   Ⓑ the government backing them judiciously should ensure Italian firms of being about to continue

   Ⓒ judicious government backing should ensure that Italian firms will continue

   Ⓓ the government's judicious backing should ensure Italian firms that they will continue

   Ⓔ the government to back them judiciously should ensure Italian firms of continuing

18. The sloth, <u>which is a South American mammal related to armadillos and anteaters, live in tropical forests where they travel</u> through the trees upside down.

   Ⓐ which is a South American mammal related to armadillos and anteaters, live in tropical forests where they travel

   Ⓑ a South American mammal related to armadillos and anteaters, live in tropical forests where they travel

   Ⓒ a South American mammal related to the armadillo and the anteater, lives in tropical forests where it travels

   Ⓓ a South American mammal related to the armadillo and the anteater, lives in tropical forests where they travel

   Ⓔ a South American mammal in relation to the armadillo and the anteater, lives in tropical forests where it travels

19. Early derisive reactions from art critics and established painters <u>did not discourage the Primitivist painter Henri Rousseau to exhibit repeatedly, despite him completely lacking formal training and starting late</u> as a professional artist.

    (A) did not discourage the Primitivist painter Henri Rousseau to exhibit repeatedly, despite him completely lacking formal training and starting late

    (B) did not discourage the Primitivist painter Henri Rousseau exhibiting repeatedly, completely lacking formal training though he was, and starting late

    (C) did not discourage the Primitivist painter Henri Rousseau to exhibit repeatedly, despite their complete lack of formal training and late start

    (D) did not discourage the Primitivist painter Henri Rousseau in exhibiting repeatedly, despite his complete lack of formal training and late start

    (E) did not discourage the Primitivist painter Henri Rousseau from exhibiting repeatedly, despite his complete lack of formal training and late start

20. The poll taxes enacted in the Southern states between 1889 <u>and 1910 disenfranchised many citizens, since</u> payment of the tax was a prerequisite for voting.

    (A) and 1910 disenfranchised many citizens, since

    (B) to 1910 disenfranchised many citizens, since

    (C) and 1910 have disenfranchised many citizens since

    (D) to 1910 has been disenfranchising many citizens because

    (E) and 1910 had the effect of disenfranchising many citizens, inasmuch as

21. <u>With a population equal to Kansas in an area one three-hundredth its size, Singapore is the most densely populated nation in the world, averaging</u> almost ten thousand people per square mile.

    (A) With a population equal to Kansas in an area one three-hundredth its size, Singapore is the most densely populated nation in the world, averaging

    (B) With a population equal to that of Kansas in an area one three-hundredth its size, Singapore is the most densely populated nation in the world, averaging

    (C) With Kansas's population in one three-hundredth of its area, the densest population in the world is that of Singapore, with an average of

    (D) Singapore has the same population as Kansas but only one three-hundredth of its area, and makes it the most densely populated nation in the world, averaging

    (E) Singapore is the most densely populated nation in the world, with Kansas's population in one three-hundredth of its area, or an average of

22. Many medical schools are now offering courses in the ethics of treating terminal patients, partly to alert students about the legal implications involved in such treatment, <u>but primarily to prepare students, through discussion and forethought, to make responsible decisions that respect terminal patients' dignity</u>.

    (A) but primarily to prepare students, through discussion and forethought, to make responsible decisions that respect terminal patients' dignity

    (B) but primarily so as to prepare students, by discussing and by thinking ahead, for responsible decision making that respects terminal patients' dignity

    (C) but primarily for the purpose of preparing them, with discussion and forethought, to make responsible decisions that respect terminal patients' dignity

    (D) but primarily for preparing them, through discussion and forethought, for deciding responsibly so that they respect terminal patients' dignity

    (E) but primarily to prepare them, by discussing and thinking ahead, to responsibly decide so as to respect the dignity of terminal patients

KAPLAN

ANSWERS AND EXPLANATIONS

1. A
2. B
3. D
4. E
5. C
6. D
7. B
8. A
9. C
10. E
11. B
12. D
13. E
14. A
15. D
16. E
17. C
18. C
19. E
20. A
21. B
22. A

1. A

All items in a list must be in parallel form. The word "secure" is used in its secondary meaning of "to make safe." "Secure" is in the same form as "be" and "achieve," so (A) is fine as is. (D) and (E) also use the correct form of "secure," but they contain unidiomatic phrases.

2. B

After you read the sentence, always scan the choices quickly to spot differences. Two choices here use "better," three use "best." "Better" is used when you compare two people or things. "Best" is used when you compare one person or thing to a whole group. Since you're comparing Martin Luther to *ALL* the people who brought about the Reformation, you have to use "best." "Them" and "one" in (A) and (E) are ambiguous and unnecessary.

3. D

Words linked by "and" must be in similar grammatical form. (A) is wrong because "and" links "raising" and "reduction." We're discussing two things, so we need "between," not "among" in (B). (C) uses "or" when it should use "and." (You choose between X and Y not X or Y.) In (E), colleges aren't choosing "the rise."

4. E

Elements in a list must be in similar form. In (A), there's a list of three things specified in the corporation's bylaws: "how . . . ," "whether . . . ," and "as well as . . . ." "As well as" doesn't fit, does it? "What," in (E), is in the same form as "how" and "whether."

5. C

On a question as short as this, you don't have to worry as much about scanning for differences. Just read quickly through the answer choices and you should be able to "hear" which one's best. In (C), "doing so" is an academic-sounding but correct usage that can pop up on the GMAT. Watch out for it and other bookish-sounding phrases typical of GMAT style. If you can't use your ear for correct English, use logic and process of elimination. (E) is short. That might be a reason to prefer it. But if you plug in (E), you see it makes the sentence say that "evidence" is doing something. In (A), (B), and (D), "it" and "that" are ambiguous. That is, they don't clearly refer to one and only one noun.

6. D

"Than" must compare grammatically similar terms: *Cooking chickens* is different from *cooking eggs*, not *cooking chickens* is different from eggs. Since "setting" is not underlined, you'll have to make the underlined portion agree with it. So let's look for an "-ing" form. That narrows it down to (D) and (E). "Corporation" is singular, so we have to compare it to singular nouns: A proprietorship or a partnership, in (D).

7. B

Listen for things that sound funny in the original sentence, and find the choice that's most precise. In (A), "attacks recently" is illogical and awkward-sounding. The test isn't under revision "for receiving attack," in (C). It's under revision *after* receiving attack. In (D), it seems as though the attack happens before and after the revision. In (E), it's not clear that it's the test that's being attacked. (B) makes the sequence of events clear: The test has recently been attacked and is finally being revised.

8. A

If you can't spot an error in the original, scan the choices and look for reasons to cross some out. Then guess from the rest. (B) uses the singular "wine grower," but you need the plural to go with "their crop" and "their fruit" in the nonunderlined part of the sentence. (C) and (D) make the sentence switch from active ("harvest") to passive ("as was done", "as has been done") for no good reason. Avoid the passive if possible. In (E), "did" implies that the wine growers have stopped harvesting. Growers still harvest, so you need "have done" in (A) to indicate continuing action.

9. C

Like many GMAT sentences, this one is complex, but contains a predictable, relatively simple error. If you familiarize yourself with commonly tested errors and learn how to correct them, sentence corrections can be a breeze. As soon as you see a subject ("a generation") followed by a long phrase ("of sophisticated copy machines capable of unprecedented detail and accuracy") beware! GMAT sentence corrections often contain subjects and verbs that are separated. The verb "are" here is separated from the subject "generation," but they still need to agree. *Generation* is singular, so it should be "a new generation is prompting." In (B), it's unidiomatic to say "capable for." You need to say "capable of" detail.

10. E

What should an introductory phrase followed by a comma prompt you to do? Check to see if the phrase correctly modifies what follows it. You can't say that a directive is making "an unusual move for a Republican." No, it's a person, the president, that's making the move. (E) says what the author of the sentence wants to say, clearly and simply. That's preferable on the GMAT.

11. B

Connectors like "as well as" or "not only . . . but also" must link like terms. So if you say "in politics," you have to say "in industry." (E) is unnecessarily wordy.

12. D

This question contains the same type of recognizable error as number 9 does. "Of all the countries contiguous to China" can't modify "the Soviet Union's borders," "the Soviet Union's," or "the borders of the Soviet Union." It has to modify "the Soviet Union."

13. E

"Like" or "unlike" signal comparisons, one of the test makers' favorite places to introduce errors. So when you see a sentence like this, which hits you with "unlike" first thing, make sure that the sentence compares similar things, things that can be logically compared and things that are in the same grammatical form. Here, "the people whom settled the Western states . . ." and "the hope of the prospectors . . ." are both nouns, but they can't be logically compared. You can't compare people to "hope," a feeling. You have to compare people to people, and that's what choice (E) does. In (E), "the people who settled the Western states" are compared to "the prospectors and adventurers." Also note that you need "who" instead of "whom." For more on this distinction, see the Grammar Reference Guide in the appendix.

14. A

Don't hypercorrect. About one fifth of sentence corrections will be correct as is. Many of these sound like something you'd never say or write unless you were writing a term paper. George Eliot didn't become George Eliot, as (B), (C), (D), and (E) have it. She became known as George Eliot. The word "before" determines the sequence of events in the sentence. Hence, "Before George Eliot became . . . *she was . . . .*"

15. D

Be on the lookout for connectors like "as," "just as," and "like." Here you have to decide which one to use. In everyday speech, this distinction isn't so important, but on the GMAT it is. If you're a native speaker of English, you should be able to use your sense of correct English to tell that "just as . . . so" is correct. Otherwise, jot down this and other commonly used GMAT idioms as you come across them, and learn them.

16. E

It's fine to skip a few long, heavily underlined sentences if you get bogged down on them. Sentences like this one can be intimidating, but they don't have to be if you can spot the error quickly. Phrases like "the reason . . . was because" are too wordy to be correct on the GMAT. Practice so you can quickly recognize and reject them. (D) would be okay if "so" were eliminated. As it is, stick with the most economical and logical phrase: "Willard . . . founded the . . . Union because . . . ."

17. C

When you see a list or series, ask yourself, "Are all the listed items similar grammatically and logically?" The phrase that matches "technical expertise" and "commercial enterprise" is "judicious government backing," in (C). (D) is close but it's not as compact, and GMAT often rewards compact language. Also, (D)'s "ensure Italian firms that they will" is unclear.

18. C

Every pronoun must CLEARLY and LOGICALLY refer to ONE specific noun, and agree with that noun. You're talking about the sloth here. That's singular. To be GMAT correct, you have to compare the sloth to the armadillo and the anteater. That knocks out (A) and (B). (D) uses "they." "They" can't stand for "sloth." It can stand for only the plural noun "forests," which makes no sense. If you were working quickly, you might think it's okay to substitute "they" for "the sloth." But GMAT English is picky. If the noun "sloth" is singular, its pronoun must be singular too. (E) is wrong because the phrase "in relation to" is unidiomatic. You say "X is related to Y," not "X is in relation to Y."

19. E

The correct idiom is "discourage from exhibiting." You can't say "despite him completely lacking." You have to say "despite his complete lack of."

20. A

Here's another connector you should know: Between . . . and (as in "Between me and you . . . "). When you scan the choices, quickly narrow down the possibilities by picking out incorrect idioms like "between . . . to." In (C), you could use "have" only if you were talking about continuing action. You say "the recent poll taxes have disenfranchised many citizens," but if you're talking about action that started and finished in the past, you simply say "the taxes disenfranchised many citizens." In (E), "had the effect of" and "inasmuch as" are wordy and therefore wrong.

21. B

Be sensitive to the small variations in answer choices. They allow you to zero in on subtle errors like the one in this sentence. When you got to the answer choices here, you may have noticed that each one plays with the wording of "population equal to Kansas." You can compare only like terms. You can't say "a population equal to Kansas," because you can compare a population only to another population; you can't compare a population to a state. In (B), "that of" should have sounded really good to you; "that" stands for "population." "With a population equal to that of Kansas" is just a shorter and more elegant way of saying "With a population equal to the population of Kansas." In (C), the population isn't "with an average" of ten thousand people per square mile.

22. A

In (A), "but" connects two similar phrases: "To alert . . . " and "to prepare." Answers (B), "so as to prepare," (C), "for the purpose of preparing," and (D), "for preparing," break this parallel construction. (E) has "to prepare," but the pronoun "them" is ambiguous, and "so as to" is too wordy.

SENTENCE CORRECTION PRACTICE SET TWO

Time: 25 Minutes/22 Questions

Directions: The following questions consist of sentences that are either partly or entirely underlined. Below each sentence are five versions of the underlined portion of the sentence. The first of these, choice (A), duplicates the original version. The four other versions revise the underlined portion of the sentence. Read the sentence and the five choices carefully, and select the best version. If the original seems better than any of the revisions, select choice (A). If not, choose one of the revisions.

These questions test your recognition of correct grammatical usage and your sense of clear and economical writing style. Choose answers according to the norms of standard written English for grammar, word choice, and sentence construction. Your selected answer should express the intended meaning of the original sentence as clearly and precisely as possible, while avoiding ambiguous, awkward, or unnecessarily wordy constructions.

1. The chairman of the board of directors <u>have decided that this year's profits will be used</u> for research and development, rather than for a shareholder dividend.

    (A) have decided that this year's profits will be used

    (B) has decided that this year's profits will be used

    (C) have decided on using this year's profits

    (D) has decided on using this year's profits

    (E) decided this year's profits will have been used

2. <u>Like most religions, the teachings of Sikhism are codified in</u> a book.

    (A) Like most religions, the teachings of Sikhism are codified in

    (B) Like most other religions, the teachings of Sikhism are codified in

    (C) Sikhism's teachings, like those of most other religions, are codified in

    (D) For their codification, like the teachings of most religions, Sikhism has

    (E) Like those of most religions, Sikhism has codified its teachings in

3. <u>Not only do deep-sea divers risk nitrogen narcosis, often called "raptures of the deep," if they descend below 200 feet, but</u> they also fall prey to decompression sickness, commonly known as "the bends," if they ascend too quickly.

    (A) Not only do deep-sea divers risk nitrogen narcosis, often called "raptures of the deep," if they descend below 200 feet, but

    (B) Deep-sea divers risk nitrogen narcosis, often called "raptures of the deep," if they descend below 200 feet, but

    (C) Nitrogen narcosis, often called "raptures of the deep," is risked by deep-sea divers if they descend below 200 feet, in addition

    (D) The descending of deep-sea divers to below 200 feet causes them risking nitrogen narcosis, often called "raptures of the deep," and

    (E) Not only does a deep-sea diver risk nitrogen narcosis, often called "raptures of the deep," if they descend below 200 feet, but

4. <u>A 32 percent wage hike, working four days a week, and above all a higher standard of factory safety is a demand</u> that management must meet if it wishes to avoid a crippling strike.

   Ⓐ A 32 percent wage hike, working four days a week, and above all a higher standard of factory safety is a demand

   Ⓑ A 32 percent wage hike, a four-day work-week, and above all a higher standard of factory safety is a demand

   Ⓒ A 32 percent wage hike, a four-day work-week, and above all a higher standard of safety in the factory are demands

   Ⓓ A 32 percent wage hike, working four days a week, and above all a higher standard of factory safety are demands

   Ⓔ Hiking wages 32 percent, working four days a week, and above all heighten the standard of factory safety are demands

5. Although new farm subsidy legislation is presently being considered in the House of Representatives, <u>significant revision is to be expected if it is to be passed.</u>

   Ⓐ significant revision is to be expected if it is to be passed

   Ⓑ they do not expect it passing without significant revision

   Ⓒ they do not expect it passing without it being significantly revised

   Ⓓ it is not expected to pass without it being significantly revised

   Ⓔ it is not expected to pass without significant revision

6. At a recent conference, the Transit Authority <u>has stated that the provisions in the Clean Air Act fail</u> to promote mass transit as an alternative to private transportation.

   Ⓐ has stated that the provisions in the Clean Air Act fail

   Ⓑ stated that the provisions of the Clean Air Act fail

   Ⓒ has stated that the provisions of the Clean Air Act will fail

   Ⓓ stated that the provisions in the Clean Air Act are a failure

   Ⓔ has stated the provisions in the Clean Air Act failed

7. A revolution has taken place in medical science as a result of <u>the introduction of new methods of surgically implanting artificial and human organs.</u>

   Ⓐ the introduction of new methods of surgically implanting artificial and human organs

   Ⓑ the introduction of new surgical implantation methods of human and artificial organs

   Ⓒ the surgical introduction of new artificial and human organ implantation methods

   Ⓓ the introduction of implantation methods of new artificial and human organs

   Ⓔ the introduction of methods of surgically implanting new artificial and human organs

8. <u>Added to worries about budget cuts and cost of living increases,</u> the administrators of public healthcare facilities must contend with the possibility of a strike by employees.

   Ⓐ Added to worries about budget cuts and cost of living increases

   Ⓑ Added to budget cuts and increases in the cost of living

   Ⓒ In addition to worry about cuts in the budget and as the cost of living increases

   Ⓓ Added to their worrying about budget cuts and cost of living increases

   Ⓔ In addition to worrying about budget cuts and increases in the cost of living

9. Renaissance scientist Copernicus found that his rejection of the Ptolemaic system placed him at odds <u>not only with the Church and the scientific community of his day, but also with ship captains, who navigated according to a geocentric universe</u>.

   (A) not only with the Church and the scientific community of his day, but also with ship captains, who navigated according to a geocentric universe

   (B) opposing the Church and the scientific community of his day, and also the ship captains, who navigated according to a geocentric universe

   (C) not only in opposition to the Church and the scientific community of his day, but with ship captains, who navigated according to a geocentric universe

   (D) not only with the Church and the scientific community of his day, but with ship captains, who calculated their navigations on a geocentric basis

   (E) opposing not only churchmen and scientists, but the ship captains, who navigated according to a geocentric universe

10. Despite <u>them attempting to do it</u>, doctors have not yet found a cure for the common cold.

    (A) them attempting to do it

    (B) their attempts to do so

    (C) them attempting to do so

    (D) the fact that they have attempted to do it

    (E) their attempts to do it

11. Unlike the Pulitzer, which is given for a specific work, <u>an author receives the Nobel Prize for a lifetime's achievement in literature</u>.

    (A) an author receives the Nobel Prize for a lifetime's achievement in literature

    (B) an author's lifetime achievement in literature receives the Nobel Prize

    (C) the Nobel Prize is awarded to an author's lifetime's achievement in literature

    (D) the Nobel Prize is awarded for a lifetime of achievement in literature

    (E) the Nobel Prize is awarded for a lifetime of achievement in literature by an author

12. Medical researchers, who have identified a genetic abnormality in parents of children with Downs syndrome, <u>which they believe, instead of the age of the mother, may be</u> the cause of this congenital birth defect.

    (A) which they believe, instead of the age of the mother, may be

    (B) which, they believe, may be more important than the age of the mother as

    (C) believe this abnormality and not the age of the mother as being

    (D) believe that this abnormality, other than how old the mother is, may be

    (E) believe that this abnormality, rather than the age of the mother, may be

13. Unable to walk without assistance, <u>radio provided Franklin Roosevelt with a medium for conveying</u> a message of vigor and confidence that would have been belied by the visual image presented on television.

    (A) radio provided Franklin Roosevelt with a medium for conveying

    (B) Franklin Roosevelt conveyed in radio

    (C) Franklin Roosevelt used radio to convey

    (D) radio allowed Franklin Roosevelt to convey

    (E) through radio it was possible

KAPLAN

14. Modern inventions such as the pneumatic drill may seem to have improved the work conditions of manual laborers, but in fact, <u>have increased the incidence of health hazards such as silicosis because it has aggravated the dust hazard</u> involved in excavation and demolition.

    Ⓐ have increased the incidence of health hazards such as silicosis because it has aggravated the dust hazard

    Ⓑ has increased the incidence of health hazards such as silicosis because it has aggravated the dust hazard

    Ⓒ have increased the incidence of health hazards such as silicosis because they have aggravated the dust hazard

    Ⓓ increased the incidence of health hazards such as silicosis because they aggravated the dust hazard

    Ⓔ increased the incidence of health hazards such as silicosis because of aggravating the dust hazard

15. The Federal Reserve <u>Board assumes primary responsibility of the regulation for</u> this nation's commercial banks and savings institutions.

    Ⓐ Board assumes primary responsibility of the regulation for

    Ⓑ Board's assumption of primary responsibility for the regulation of

    Ⓒ Board's assuming primary responsibility to regulate

    Ⓓ Board assumes primary responsibility for the regulation of

    Ⓔ Board regulates primary responsibility for

16. The ground swell of public opinion made <u>it inevitable that the Senate would approve</u> the president's energy proposals.

    Ⓐ it inevitable that the Senate would approve

    Ⓑ it inevitable that the Senate had approved

    Ⓒ it inevitable of the Senate to approve

    Ⓓ inevitable the approval of the Senate of

    Ⓔ the approval of the Senate inevitable of

17. Though caterpillars transform large amounts of plant matter into animal tissue and wastes, and therefore hold an important place in the food chain, <u>they are so voracious that they have become an economic</u> threat to farmers whose crops they eat.

    Ⓐ they are so voracious that they have become an economic

    Ⓑ they are of such voracity, they have become an economical

    Ⓒ so voracious are they as to become an economical

    Ⓓ such is their voracity, they become an economic

    Ⓔ there is so much voracity that it has become an economical

18. The nations with nuclear capabilities have restrained the proliferation of nuclear weapons less by reaching military understandings than <u>by the refusal to sell</u> associated technologies.

    Ⓐ by the refusal to sell

    Ⓑ not selling

    Ⓒ the refusal to sell

    Ⓓ refusing to sell

    Ⓔ by refusing to sell

19. During and immediately after the California gold rush, the way for a merchant to generate the most profit was to move a limited amount of scarce goods to San Francisco as quickly as possible, rather than <u>to carry larger loads more slowly, determining</u> the design of the clipper ship.

    Ⓐ to carry larger loads more slowly, determining

    Ⓑ to carry larger loads more slowly, a situation that determined

    Ⓒ carry larger loads more slowly, which determined

    Ⓓ slowly carry larger loads which determined

    Ⓔ carrying larger loads more slowly, and this was a situation in determining

KAPLAN

20. The analyst suggested that traders pay more attention to a broader measure of the money supply, known as M2, <u>but still not to ignore</u> standard indicators.

    (A) but still not to ignore
    (B) and not to ignore any longer
    (C) but that they still not ignore
    (D) and not that they continue to ignore
    (E) but that they are still not ignoring

21. According to the teachings of the Buddhist and Hindu religions, <u>attaining nirvana is to enter</u> a state of supreme liberation, leaving behind the desires that perpetuate the cycle of death and rebirth.

    (A) attaining nirvana is to enter
    (B) to attain nirvana is entering
    (C) to attain nirvana is
    (D) to attain nirvana is to enter
    (E) attaining nirvana is to be entering

22. The principal has sought approval for her plan to grant promotions to only those seventh-grade students proficient in <u>reading without meeting with opposition.</u>

    (A) reading without meeting with opposition
    (B) reading, having met with no opposition
    (C) reading, without the opposition of others
    (D) reading, and has not met with opposition
    (E) reading without opposition

ANSWERS AND EXPLANATIONS

1. B
2. C
3. A
4. C
5. E
6. B
7. A
8. E
9. A
10. B
11. D
12. E
13. C
14. C
15. D
16. A
17. A
18. E
19. B
20. C
21. D
22. D

1.   B

GMAT likes to introduce errors by separating the subject and verb. Practice with Sentence Corrections, so you anticipate and ignore distracting phrases like "of the board of directors." "Have" has to agree with the singular subject "chairman," rather than with the plural "directors." (B) is right because the correct idiom is "decided that," not "decided on."

2.   C

When you see "like" or "unlike," watch out for faulty comparisons. You can't compare "most religions" to the "teachings of Sikhism." You have to find the choice that compares teachings to teachings or religions to religions. (C) uses "those" to stand for "teachings." But in (E), it's not clear what "those" stands for. A pronoun like "those" must refer to an already expressed noun, so "those" must follow "teachings." (D) also has an unclear pronoun, "their."

3.   A

"Not only . . . but also" must connect similar terms. "Deep-sea divers not only risk" and "but also fall prey" are correctly paralleled in (A). (B) would work if "and" was substituted for "but." There are two problems with (C): "nitrogen narcosis . . . is risked" and the fact that (C) is actually two complete sentences incorrectly linked with a comma. You'd need a period after "feet," and a capital "i" in "in." In (E), "they" doesn't refer clearly and unambiguously to one specific plural noun. In (A), "they" can mean only "divers." In (D), the beginning is a bit wordy, and "causes them risking . . . " sounds awkward. The infinitive "to risk" is needed in place of "risking."

4.   C

Whenever you see a list on the GMAT, check that the items in it are in grammatically similar form. If you quickly scan the choices, you see that only (B) and (C) put the three listed items in similar form: *wage hike, workweek,* and *standard*. The subject is plural. That is, the three things listed in the sentence *are* demands the management must meet. So (B) can't work.

5.   E

On GMAT Sentence Correction, the wrong choices often contain unnecessary words. That's why, if you're clueless, you should favor the shorter choices. Correct choice (E) is one of the shortest. So is (B), but in (B), "they do not expect it passing" is unidiomatic. You have to say "they do not expect it *to* pass."

6. B

When you scan the choices, notice you have to choose between three that begin with "has stated" and two that begin with "stated." Many GMAT Sentence Corrections exhibit this "3-2 split" answer choice pattern. Use this to your advantage. Begin by deciding which of the two forms, "has stated" or "stated," is correct. This is strategic: You deal with one small problem at a time, and narrow down your choices. The Transit Authority made their statement and it was over. The action didn't continue. So you should say "the Transit Authority *stated*." (B), "the provisions fail to promote mass transit," is more concise than (D), "the provisions are a failure to promote mass transit."

7. A

The original is long-winded and probably not the best one you've ever read. GMAT sentences don't have to be beautiful; they just have to be correct (about one fifth of the Sentence Corrections in each set *will be* correct as written in the stem). The wrong choices here are nonsensical. In (B), what's "methods of . . . organs"? There's no such thing. In (C), what's "surgical introduction of . . . methods"? (D) and (E) say that the artificial and human organs are new. But it's *the methods* that are new.

8. E

An intro phrase set off by a comma is your signal to watch out for modification errors. Simply put, that means make sure the sentence is logical. Here, you have a "3-2" pattern in the answer choices, so you can use this to quickly narrow down the possibilities. It's not *the administrators* that are added to worries, budget cuts, or worrying, so (A), (B), and (D) are out. (C) may seem to make sense, but look at it closely: "Worry" is wrong, and administrators are worrying about cuts in the budget *and* as the cost of living increases. "And" must link similar terms, but it doesn't in (C).

9. A

The correct phrase is "at odds with," not "at odds . . . opposing," in (B) and (E), or "at odds . . . in opposition," in (C). It's better to say "navigated according to a geocentric universe" than "calculated their navigations on a geocentric basis," in (D).

10. B

Here you have another "3-2 split," this time between "to do it" and "to do so," in the answer choice endings. "It" is an ambiguous pronoun. You might assume "it" stands for "cure," but if you substitute "cure" for "it" in the sentence, you get the unidiomatic "despite them attempting to do a cure." If you're not familiar with idiomatic expressions like "to do so," learn to recognize them. As you practice Sentence Correction, write down any usages that are correct but unfamiliar to you. "Doctors" is the subject. You use the pronoun "their," not "them," to stand for "doctors." For more discussion of pronouns, see the Grammar Reference Guide in appendix 1.

11. D

Like number 8, this question contains an intro phrase set off by a comma. This time you've got to rearrange the rest of the sentence to fit the intro. So what can correctly follow "Unlike the Pulitzer"? You can compare only similar things; the Pulitzer Prize must be compared to some other prize. In (C), the prize isn't awarded to an author's achievement, it's awarded to an author. In (E), "author" incorrectly follows "literature" ("literature by an author"), making it unclear who exactly is doing the achieving. In (D), "author" correctly goes with "lifetime" (in the phrase "an author who has had a lifetime of achievement"). (D) makes it clear whose achievement is being awarded.

12. E

To finish the Sentence Correction section on time, you have to cut through the wordiness of these questions. You can often do this by temporarily ignoring parts of the sentence that are set off by commas. Here, that's "who have identified . . . with Downs syndrome" and "instead of the age of the mother." The rest of the sentence should make sense and be complete without these. But in the original you get "Medical researchers . . . which they believe . . . may be the cause of this congenital birth defect." In (C), (D), and (E), the subject "medical researchers" has a verb, "believe." In (C), "believe . . . as being" is unidiomatic. ("Being" is wordy and often appears in wrong choices.) In (D), you need "rather" instead of "other," and "how old the mother is" isn't parallel to "abnormality."

13. C

You don't want to say that radio was unable to walk without assistance. You want to say that Franklin Roosevelt was So the noun "Franklin Roosevelt" must follow the intro phrase, as it does in (B) and (C). In (B), it's wrong and awkward to say that Roosevelt "conveyed in radio a message." (C) puts it best: Roosevelt "*used* radio to convey a message."

14. C

(A) has to be wrong, because "it" illogically refers to "silicosis." Actually, "modern inventions," plural, have "aggravated the dust hazard." So you need "they" to follow "because," as in (C) and (D). There's no reason to use the past, in (E), because the hazard is still happening.

15. D

You say "assumes responsibility for." You don't take responsibility *of* or *to* completing your work, you take responsibility *for* completing it. If you plug in (B), you get an incomplete sentence. You need a noun, "Board," and a verb, "assumes." In (E), the Board isn't regulating responsibility.

16. A

You can say, "It was inevitable that I would miss my bus." But you can't say, "It was inevitable of me to miss my bus." You need "that." (B) says that it's "inevitable" that the Senate had approved the proposals, past tense. But something that's already happened can't be said to be inevitable.

17. A

The wrong choices use illogical and unidiomatic phrases. In (B), caterpillars can't be "of such voracity." In (C), you can't say something is so voracious *as* to become a threat to farmers. In (E), there is no way to tell that the caterpillars are the ones being voracious.

18. E

The phrase "less by . . . than by" is another connector that must link similar terms. What follows the first "by"? "Reaching." So what must follow the second "by"? "Refusing." (D) won't work. It takes out the second "by," which you need to complete the comparison.

19. B

In this long sentence, the connector "rather than" should jump out at you right away. In the phrase "to move . . . rather than to carry," "to move" and "to carry" need to be kept in parallel form. That narrows the possibilities to (A) or (B). Think about what the sentence is saying. In (A), the way for a merchant to generate profit isn't determining the design of the clipper ship. The way for a merchant to generate profit is a *situation* determining the design of the clipper ship. (E) is too wordy.

20. C

Put similar parts of a sentence in similar form. The analyst suggested two things: That traders *pay* more attention to the M2, but that they *still* not *ignore* standard indicators.

21. D

"Attaining" and "to enter" must be parallel. (D) gives this to you, with "to attain" and "to enter."

22. D

The principal is doing two things: seeking approval for her plan, and not meeting with any opposition. These two things should be in grammatically similar form. Since "has sought" isn't underlined, you need to change "without meeting with," in (A), to "has not met with," in (D).

SENTENCE CORRECTION PRACTICE SET THREE

Time: 25 Minutes/22 Questions

Directions: The following questions consist of sentences that are either partly or entirely underlined. Below each sentence are five versions of the underlined portion of the sentence. The first of these, choice (A), duplicates the original version. The four other versions revise the underlined portion of the sentence. Read the sentence and the five choices carefully, and select the best version. If the original seems better than any of the revisions, select choice (A). If not, choose one of the revisions.

These questions test your recognition of correct grammatical usage and your sense of clear and economical writing style. Choose answers according to the norms of standard written English for grammar, word choice, and sentence construction. Your selected answer should express the intended meaning of the original sentence as clearly and precisely as possible, while avoiding ambiguous, awkward, or unnecessarily wordy constructions.

1. One student at the school was not yet fifteen, yet he was already a <u>master in both chess and in bridge</u>.

    A   master in both chess and in bridge
    B   master of both chess and in bridge
    C   master of both chess and of bridge
    D   master both chess and bridge
    E   master of both chess and bridge

2. It has been demonstrated that individuals who participated in competitive sports <u>when they are in college tend towards remaining</u> physically active in their later years.

    A   when they are in college tend towards remaining
    B   when they were in college are likely to be
    C   when they were in college were apt to be
    D   when they are in college are apt to be
    E   when they were in college were liable to be

3. <u>Unlike the Puritan ethic, extolling hard work as the supreme virtue, many modern psychologists focus on the goals of inner peace and self-discovery</u>.

    A   Unlike the Puritan ethic, extolling hard work as the supreme virtue, many modern psychologists focus on the goals of inner peace and self-discovery
    B   Unlike believers in the Puritan ethic, which extols as the supreme virtue hard work, the goals of inner peace and self-discovery are focused on by many modern psychologists
    C   Unlike the Puritan ethic, which extols hard work as the supreme virtue, the focus of the doctrines of many modern psychologists are the goals of inner peace and self-discovery
    D   Unlike the Puritan ethic, which extols hard work as the supreme virtue, the doctrines of many modern psychologists focus on the goals of inner peace and self-discovery
    E   Unlike those of the Puritans, who extol hard work as the supreme virtue, many modern psychologists focus on the goals of inner peace and self-discovery

KAPLAN

4. The customer will not be responsible for
transactions made with lost or stolen credit cards
after issuing replacement cards.

   (A) The customer will not be responsible for
   transactions made with lost or stolen credit
   cards after issuing replacement cards

   (B) No customer will be responsible for transactions made with lost or stolen credit cards
   after they are issued replacement cards

   (C) The customer will not be responsible for
   transactions made with lost or stolen credit
   cards after replacement cards have been
   issued

   (D) Responsibility for transactions made with lost
   or stolen credit cards will not be the customer's
   after he is issued replacement cards

   (E) The customer will not be responsible for
   transactions made with lost or stolen credit
   cards after such time as they will have been
   issued replacement cards

5. Despite that they were able to calculate faster
than ever before possible, the earliest computers,
built with tubes instead of transistors, were too
bulky, expensive, and unreliable to be useful to
businesses.

   (A) Despite that they were able to calculate faster
   than ever before possible

   (B) Even though it could calculate faster than
   previously possible

   (C) Although faster in its calculating than ever
   before possible

   (D) Despite their calculations being faster than
   ever before possible

   (E) Despite their unprecedented speed of
   calculation

6. As genetics researchers achieve greater success
in their attempt to map the exact locations and
functions of human genes, the close connection
between genes and birth defects has become
increasingly clear.

   (A) close connection between genes and birth
   defects has become

   (B) closeness of the connection between genes
   and birth defects has become

   (C) close connection genes have with birth
   defects has been becoming

   (D) close connection between genes and birth
   defects has been becoming

   (E) close connection between genes and birth
   defects becomes

7. At Agincourt, Charles D'Albret's battle plan was
thwarted as a direct result of the irrepressible desire
the French nobility had to charge headlong into
any enemy offering a challenge.

   (A) as a direct result of the irrepressible desire the
   French nobility had to

   (B) because the French nobility had an irrepressible
   desire to

   (C) insofar as the French nobility desired to

   (D) because the French nobility would have an
   irrepressible desire to

   (E) by the French nobility's desire to irrepressibly

8. At their birthday party, the twins were eager to
begin opening their presents, but finishing was
hard for them.

   (A) finishing was hard for them

   (B) reluctant to finish

   (C) finishing them reluctant

   (D) were reluctant after finishing

   (E) their finishing reluctant

9. <u>That young girls score as well if not better than young boys on standardized tests disprove</u> one prevalent male-supremacy myth.

    Ⓐ That young girls score as well if not better than young boys on standardized tests disprove

    Ⓑ That young girls score as well if not better than young boys on standardized tests disproves

    Ⓒ That young girls score as well as if not better than young boys on standardized tests disproves

    Ⓓ That young girls score so well as if not better than young boys on standardized tests disprove

    Ⓔ The fact of young girls' scoring as well if not better than young boys on standardized tests disprove

10. During her testimony, the witness referred to facts about the defendant that had been ruled inadmissible as evidence, so the judge ordered that her remarks <u>were stricken from the record.</u>

    Ⓐ were stricken from the record

    Ⓑ are stricken from the record

    Ⓒ be stricken from the record

    Ⓓ are not recorded

    Ⓔ will not be recorded

11. To restore fishing grounds damaged by pollution, marine engineers can create an artificial reef by towing old barges to an offshore location <u>and sinking</u> to the sandy bottom.

    Ⓐ and sinking

    Ⓑ and sinking them

    Ⓒ and sinking it

    Ⓓ where it sinks

    Ⓔ having sunk them

12. Popular child psychologists have advocated that parents discipline male children <u>similarly to the fashion in which they discipline</u> daughters.

    Ⓐ similarly to the fashion in which they discipline

    Ⓑ in the same manner that they would use with

    Ⓒ like they would handle

    Ⓓ as they discipline

    Ⓔ as they would

13. In the Middle Ages, philosophers, <u>were so devoted to Aristotle that they neglected</u> the evidence of their own senses and accepted whatever he wrote.

    Ⓐ were so devoted to Aristotle that they neglected

    Ⓑ were so devoted to Aristotle as to neglect

    Ⓒ were devoted to Aristotle to such a degree that they were to neglect

    Ⓓ were so devoted to Aristotle that they had to neglect

    Ⓔ were as devoted to Aristotle as to neglect

14. <u>To rely on anecdotal evidence of social phenomena is ignoring</u> decades of increasing sophistication in the use of statistics in sociology.

    Ⓐ To rely on anecdotal evidence of social phenomena is ignoring

    Ⓑ To rely on anecdotal evidence of social phenomena is to ignore

    Ⓒ To rely on anecdotes for demonstration of social phenomena is ignoring

    Ⓓ Relying on anecdotal evidence of social phenomena is to ignore

    Ⓔ Relying on anecdotal evidence of social phenomena amounts to the ignoring of

KAPLAN)

15. The team streamed into the locker room, donned their uniforms, <u>and, before commencing its first practice, they joined in a brief strategy session</u>.

    Ⓐ and, before commencing its first practice, they joined in a brief strategy session

    Ⓑ and its first practice was preceded by a brief strategy session

    Ⓒ and a brief strategy session preceded its first practice

    Ⓓ and, before commencing their first practice, they joined in a brief strategy session

    Ⓔ and, before commencing their first practice, joined in a brief strategy session

16. Records of the first 736 British convicts deported to Australia reveal <u>convictions for crimes against property in all cases and they ranged</u> from highway robbery to forgery.

    Ⓐ convictions for crimes against property in all cases and they ranged

    Ⓑ convictions in all cases were for crimes against property and ranging

    Ⓒ the ranging of convictions for crimes against property in all cases

    Ⓓ that all were convicted of crimes against property ranging

    Ⓔ that all of them had convictions for crimes that were against property; the range was

17. A turning point in U.S. labor history was reached when most of the nation's air traffic controllers supported their union's strike and ignored President Reagan's demand <u>that they go back to work</u>.

    Ⓐ that they go back to work

    Ⓑ that these people go back to work

    Ⓒ for them to go back to work

    Ⓓ that they would go back to work

    Ⓔ they should go back to work

18. One of the informants eventually professed <u>ignorant of the crime, having</u> fear that his testimony would lead to reprisals against him by his former confederates.

    Ⓐ ignorant of the crime, having

    Ⓑ ignorantly to the crime, with

    Ⓒ ignorance of the crime, since

    Ⓓ ignorance of the crime, for

    Ⓔ to have ignorance of the crime, since

19. The nineteenth-century Russian composers known as "The Five" <u>were united by their holding</u> an ideal of a national music based on folk melodies and themes.

    Ⓐ were united by their holding

    Ⓑ had as their uniting ideal

    Ⓒ united each other with

    Ⓓ united based on

    Ⓔ were united with

20. The symphonies of Mahler are characterized by <u>a much freer use of dissonance than Haydn</u>.

    Ⓐ a much freer use of dissonance than Haydn

    Ⓑ a much freer usage than Haydn of dissonance

    Ⓒ a much freer use of dissonance than are those of Haydn

    Ⓓ a usage much freer than the dissonance of Haydn

    Ⓔ a use of dissonance that is much freer than Haydn

21. King James I of England tried unsuccessfully to merge the legislature of Scotland—his original kingdom—<u>with England</u>.

    Ⓐ with England

    Ⓑ and England

    Ⓒ with that of England

    Ⓓ and England's

    Ⓔ and England's legislature

22. In a convincing test of Newtonian physics, <u>it was anomalies in the orbit of Uranus that</u> led astronomers to predict the discovery of Neptune.

    Ⓐ it was anomalies in the orbit of Uranus that

    Ⓑ it was the orbit of Uranus showing anomalies that

    Ⓒ the orbit of Uranus showing anomalies was what

    Ⓓ the orbit of Uranus being anomalous was what

    Ⓔ anomalies in the orbit of Uranus

ANSWERS AND EXPLANATIONS

1. E
2. B
3. D
4. C
5. E
6. E
7. B
8. B
9. C
10. C
11. B
12. E
13. A
14. B
15. E
16. D
17. A
18. D
19. D
20. C
21. C
22. E

1. E

When you use the "both . . . and" formula, the things being linked have to be grammatically parallel. If you say "*both* of chess," you have to follow it with "*and* of bridge." If you say "of *both* chess," you have to follow it with "*and* bridge." And idiomatically, one speaks of a master of chess or bridge, not a master *in* chess or bridge. So (E) is the best answer.

2. B

The main differences in the answer choices have to do with verb tense. Notice that "participated," which is not underlined, is in the simple past tense. Since the people in question participated in sports while in college, we need the past tense "were," not the present tense "are," which eliminates (A) and (D). The next question is whether the next verb should be past or present: were or are? Well, the sentence seems to be describing a general truth, rather than merely facts about specific individuals in the past, and general truths are usually expressed in the present tense.

3. D

This sentence makes a comparison, so we have to make sure it's logical. You can't compare "the Puritan ethic" with "many modern psychologists" as in (A), nor with "the focus of the doctrines of many modern psychologists," as in (C). You can't compare "believers in the Puritan ethic" with "the goals of inner peace and self-discovery" in (B). You can't compare "those of the Puritans" (those what?) with "many modern psychologists," in (E). Only (D) makes a logical comparison, between "the Puritan ethic" and "the doctrines of many modern psychologists."

4. C

The problem here has to do with modification. Who or what will issue replacement cards? Not the customer, certainly, but that's what (A) seems to be saying. Choices (B) and (E) have a pronoun reference problem: The plural "they" refers to the singular "customer." "Responsibility . . . will not be the customer's" in (D) is more awkward than "the customer will not be responsible."

5. E

This question presents problems of idiom. "Despite that" in (A) is unidiomatic, and "than ever before possible" in (A), (C), and (D) is awkward. Choice (B) has a clear pronoun reference problem: The singular "it" is used to refer to the plural "computers."

KAPLAN

6. E

Logically, both things must be going on in the present. The genetics researchers are achieving success and the connection between genes and birth defects is becoming clear. So there's no need to switch to the past "has become" or "has been becoming" as (A), (B), (C), and (D) do.

7. B

This question presents problems of style. There is no reason to say "as a direct result of" when "by" will do, so (A) is out. "Insofar" in (C) does not make the logical connection between the parts of the sentence clear enough. There is no reason to use "would have" in (D). Finally, "irrepressibly charge," in (E), makes less sense than "irrepressible desire," in (B).

8. B

Here, we want an answer that's grammatically parallel to "were eager to begin."

9. C

This question tests your knowledge of a common idiom. The correct expression is "as well as . . . if not better than." Choices (A), (B), and (E) lack the "as." Choice (D) turns "as well as" into "so well as."

10. C

This question tests your understanding of the subjunctive of requirement. "Ordered that" should be followed by "be stricken," which is the simple form of the verb, the infinitive without the word "to."

11. B

A good place to start is with pronoun reference. First, let's be clear that you do need some pronoun in the answer to serve as the object of "sinking"; (A) seems to say that it is the engineers who sink to the bottom. The pronoun must refer to barges, which is plural; we need "them," not "it," so (C) and (D) can be eliminated. "Having sunk," in (E), illogically suggests that the engineers sunk the barges before towing them into position. The correct answer is (B).

12. E

Here, the main things to look for are clarity and brevity. The shortest choice, (E), is best: None of the other, longer,

choices are any clearer. In (A), "discipline male children" is parallel to "discipline female children," but the word "discipline" need not be repeated. Choices (A) and (B) use other, wordier, grammatical constructions. Choice (C) uses "like" instead of "as." You use "like" when there's no verb, implied or stated, in the second half of the comparison. You say "He acts *like* me," but "He is *as* tall *as* I (am)." (D) changes the sentence's meaning.

13. A

What's needed here is the "so . . . that" construction. Choice (A) provides that. "So . . . as to" in (B) and "as . . . as to" in (E) are unidiomatic. "To such a degree that they were to neglect" in (C) and "they had to neglect" in (D) introduce unnecessary verbiage.

14. B

The rule that's being tested here is the one that says that things joined by "is" have to be parallel. You can join an infinitive (to rely) with an infinitive (to ignore), or a participle (relying) with a participle (ignoring), but not a participle with an infinitive or an infinitive with a participle. Hence, choice (B) is correct.

15. E

The question tests parallelism: The three things that the team did have to be expressed in the same form. To match "streamed" and "donned," you need "joined." This eliminates (B) and (C). You just say "the team streamed, donned, and joined . . . ." There's no need to say "and they joined," in (A) and (D). This leaves (E) as the correct answer. Notice, by the way, that the team, though technically singular, is construed as plural in the part of the sentence that's not underlined; it must be construed in the same way throughout the sentence, and this is another reason why (A), (B), and (C) are wrong.

16. D

If you have the option, it's usually more concise to put a modifying idea in a phrase instead of in a clause. Here you really don't need the clause "and they ranged." Strongly suspect that there will be a more efficient choice than this. A scan of the tail ends shows that only (D) works. In (B), "and ranging" is needlessly wordy, made worse by the fact that (B) also uses "in all cases" where (D) has the more concise "all." In (E), "the range was" is too verbose, and its wordiness is compounded by the use of "that were against property" where "against property" would do just fine. (C) uses the awkward, wordy phrase "the ranging of convictions." After eliminating everything else, select (D).

17. A

This question tests your knowledge of the subjunctive of requirement, used after a word like "demand," and employing the word "that," a subject, and the infinitive form of a verb without the "to." The choice that uses this form correctly is (A). Actually, (B) uses it correctly too, but "they" is much more concise than "these people."

18. D

Here we have another question of idiom. You profess "ignorance," not ignorant or ignorantly; this eliminates (A) and (B). "To have ignorance," in (E), is unnecessarily wordy. Finally, before a noun like "fear," we need a preposition like "for," not a conjunction like "since."

19. D

You don't say people were "united by their holding," so (A) is wrong (B) unnecessarily repeats "ideal." In (C), what does it mean to say the composers "united each other"? This makes no sense. In (E), the composers didn't unite *with* the ideal. (D) is the only choice that makes sense. On GMAT Sentence Correction, favor compact answer choices.

20. C

The two previous examples illustrate how the GMAT tests you on eliminating unnecessary words. But as your instructor and the course material have made clear, finding the most effective expression is not as simple as just going for the shortest choice. You must distinguish between necessary and unnecessary omissions, and you must be careful not to eliminate *necessary* words. In this sentence, the word "than" indicates a comparison, so make sure that like things are being compared. Here Mahler's symphonies are compared to "Haydn." That's no good. Eliminate (A).

(E) repeats the mistake of (A). (B) and (D) contain the unGMAT-like "usage" where "use" would do just fine. (D) actually is neither parallel nor logical, since "usage" is said to be "freer" than the "dissonance of Haydn." (B) contains the misplaced modifier "of dissonance," which should come after "usage." After the eliminations, only (C) is left standing.

21. C

Here's another example of how you have to distinguish between necessary and unnecessary omissions. You need to compare legislature to legislature. So don't go for the shortest choice. You need "that of" to complete the comparison. Also, the correct idiom is "merge . . . with." You don't merge one thing and another—you merge one thing *with* another. Eliminate (A).

Select (C). If you only knew one of the two things tested here, you could still have eliminated two or three choices. The need to compare likes eliminates (A) and (B), while the need to use proper idiom eliminates (B), (D), and (E).

22. E

"It was anomalies" should jump out at you as bad style for the GMAT. Look for more concise versions in the choices. There are only three ways to begin this clause, so if you don't like the original "it was anomalies," see whether "the orbit," in (C) and (D), or "anomalies," in (E), works out any better. "The orbit" didn't lead to the discovery (the anomalies did), so (C) and (D) can't be right. The answer has to be (E), because it is much more concise than (A).

PASSAGE 1—THE NORTON AND RHEE MODEL

The relevance of formal economic models to real-world policy has been a topic of some dispute. The economists R. D. Norton and S. Y. Rhee achieved some success in

(5) applying such a model retrospectively to the Korean economy over a fourteen-year period; the model's figures for output, prices, and other variables closely matched real statistics. The model's value in policy terms, however,

(10) proved less clear-cut. Norton and Rhee performed simulations in which, keeping long-term factors constant, they tried to pinpoint the effect of short-term policy changes. Their model indicated that rising prices for imported

(15) oil would increase inflation; reducing exports by five percent would lower Gross Domestic Product and increase inflation; and slowing the growth of the money supply would result in slightly higher inflation.

(20) These findings are somewhat startling. Many economists have argued that reducing exports will lessen, not increase, inflation.

And while most view escalating oil costs as inflationary, few would think the same of

(25) slower monetary growth. The Norton-Rhee model can perhaps be viewed as indicating the pitfalls of a formalist approach that stresses statistical "goodness of fit" at the expense of genuine policy relevance.

1. The author is primarily concerned with

   (A) proposing a new type of economic analysis

   (B) criticizing an overly formal economic model

   (C) advocating the use of statistical models in determining economic policy

   (D) suggesting an explanation for Korean inflation

   (E) determining the accuracy of Norton and Rhee's analysis

2. The author mentions "a fourteen-year period" (line 6) in order to

   (A) indicate how far into the future Norton and Rhee's model can make accurate predictions

   (B) acknowledge the accuracy of Norton and Rhee's model in accounting for past events

   (C) explain the effect of reducing exports on inflation

   (D) demonstrate the startling nature of Norton and Rhee's findings

   (E) expose the flaws in Norton and Rhee's model

3. The most significant criticism leveled against Norton and Rhee's model is that it

   (A) excludes key statistical variables

   (B) is too abstract to be useful in policy making

   (C) fails to adjust for Korea's high rate of inflation

   (D) underestimates the importance of economic growth

   (E) fails to consider the effect of short-term variations in the economy

4. It can be inferred that the most surprising finding of the Norton-Rhee study is that

    Ⓐ reducing exports would reduce inflation

    Ⓑ high oil prices worsen inflation

    Ⓒ an increase in exports can slow the rate of growth

    Ⓓ slower monetary expansion would worsen inflation

    Ⓔ long-term factors do not affect economic growth

PASSAGE 2—ECOLOGY

A basic principle of ecology is that population size is partly a reflection of available food resources. Recent experiments suggest that the relationship is more complex than for-
(5) merly thought. Specifically, the browsing of certain rodents appears to trigger chemical reactions in food plants that, in turn, affect the size of the rodent populations. Two examples of such regulation have been reported.

(10) Berger has demonstrated the power of a naturally occurring chemical called 6-MBOA to stimulate reproductive behavior in the mountain vole, a small mouselike rodent. 6-MBOA forms in young grass in response to browsing
(15) by voles. Berger experimented by feeding oats coated with 6-MBOA to nonbreeding winter populations of voles. After three weeks, she found a high incidence of pregnancy among females. Since the timing of reproduction is
(20) crucial to the short-lived vole in an environment in which the onset of vegetative growth may be considerably delayed, the phytochemical triggering of reproductive behavior represents a significant biological adaptation.

(25) In an example reported by Bryant, plants appear to have developed a phytochemical defense against the depredations of snowshoe

hares in Canada. Every ten years, for reasons that are unclear, the hare population swells.
(30) The result is overbrowsing of certain deciduous trees and shrubs. Bryant found that trees favored by the hare produce young shoots high in terpene and phenolic resins, which discourage hare browsing. After treating non-
(35) resinous willow twigs with resinous extracts and placing treated and untreated samples at hare feeding stations, Bryant found that samples containing at least half of the resin concentration of natural twigs were untouched.
(40) The avoidance of resinous shoots, he concludes, may play a role in the decline of the hare population to normal levels.

Both of these reports suggest areas for further research. For example, data should be
(45) reviewed to determine if periodic population explosions among lemmings (another small rodent living in a northern environment) occur during years in which there is an early onset of vegetative growth; if so, a triggering
(50) mechanism similar to that prompted by the vole may be involved.

5. The author provides specific information to answer which of the following questions?

    Ⓐ What factors other than food supply affect the population size of rodents?

    Ⓑ Why is the timing of the voles' reproductive effort important?

    Ⓒ Are phytochemical reactions found only in northern environments?

    Ⓓ How does 6-MBOA trigger reproductive activity in the mountain vole?

    Ⓔ What are the causes of the periodic increase in the snowshoe hare population?

6. The passage describes the effect of 6-MBOA on voles as a "significant biological adaptation" (line 24) because it

   Ⓐ limits reproductive behavior in times of food scarcity

   Ⓑ prompts the vole population to seek new food sources

   Ⓒ supports species survival during periods of fluctuating food supply

   Ⓓ maximizes the number of offspring in individual litters

   Ⓔ minimizes territorial competition

7. Which of the following statements can be inferred about plant shoots containing large amounts of terpene and phenolic resins?

   I. They serve as a form of natural defense.

   II. Their growth is stimulated by increases in the hare population.

   III. They are unappetizing to hares.

   Ⓐ I only

   Ⓑ II only

   Ⓒ III only

   Ⓓ I and III only

   Ⓔ I, II, and III

8. It can be inferred that the study of lemmings proposed by the author would probably

   Ⓐ strengthen the conclusions of Bryant

   Ⓑ cast doubt on the conclusions of Bryant

   Ⓒ support the specific findings of Berger

   Ⓓ provide evidence as to whether Berger's conclusions can be generalized

   Ⓔ disprove common beliefs about the relationship between population size and food supply

9. The author of the passage is primarily concerned with

   Ⓐ reviewing findings about phytochemical regulation of rodent populations

   Ⓑ outlining the role of 6-MBOA in regulating population size

   Ⓒ summarizing knowledge on population size of rodents

   Ⓓ explaining why earlier studies of population size were wrong

   Ⓔ describing mechanisms used by plants to protect themselves

10. Bryant's interpretation of the results of his experiment (lines 37–39) depends on which of the following assumptions?

    Ⓐ The response of hares to resinous substances may be different in nature than under experimental conditions.

    Ⓑ The periodic rise in the hare population is triggered by an unknown phytochemical response.

    Ⓒ Many hares will starve to death rather than eat resinous shoots.

    Ⓓ Hares alter their breeding behavior in response to the declining availability of food.

    Ⓔ Significant numbers of hares die from ingesting the resins in shoots.

11. The experiments described in the passage did each of the following *EXCEPT*

    Ⓐ measure changes in the behavior of test animals

    Ⓑ measure changes in the populations of experimental animals

    Ⓒ simulate a hypothesized phytochemical effect in nature

    Ⓓ measure the consumption of foods by test animals

    Ⓔ analyze the effects of food on breeding behavior

KAPLAN

PASSAGE 3—CIVIL RIGHTS LAW

There is an intriguing note to the current call upon civil rights law to help remedy the undervaluation of women's work. Until fairly recently, government was not expected to
(5) solve workers' economic grievances, however valid they might be. Many assumed that the responsibility lay with workers themselves. Collective bargaining was the preferred instrument for pursuing pay equity for women.
(10) Rather than call upon the law to regulate the market from the outside, one could try to reshape or otherwise influence the market so that women themselves would be better able to address the problem. This could be done
(15) by raising absolute wage levels in low-paying, predominantly female industries (such as retail clothing) or by changing the pay relationship between largely female and largely male occupations within a single industry,
(20) such as auto manufacturing. Through union representation, employees in traditionally female jobs in an industry could identify the actual degree of underpayment of their work and then, as a group, pressure their employer
(25) to remedy it. In addition, this process would encourage those affected—men and women alike—to be sensitive to the limits of available resources, to be pragmatic about the pace at which the wage structure could be revised.

(30) I do not mean to suggest that collective bargaining is a foolproof means for closing the gender gap in wages. To the extent that the problem involves the undervaluation of non-union female occupations in an otherwise
(35) unionized industry, political hurdles will discourage unionized employees from supporting revisions in the wage structure. And to the extent that the problem is the concentration of women in low-paying industries—textiles,
(40) for example—the product market imposes serious economic constraints on a substantial closing of the wage gap.

Despite the imperfections of tools like collective bargaining for redressing wage dispari-
(45) ties between men and women, a reliance on law or government is favorable for neither individual firms nor our economy as a whole. Nonetheless, although opponents of mandatory public remedies may correctly fear
(50) those remedies as being a cure worse than the disease, they are wrong when they imply that the current system of wage determination by business management is perfectly healthy.

12. In line 14, "this" most likely refers to

   (A) increasing the wages of women and men in a single industry

   (B) bringing about changes in market conditions

   (C) changing the dynamic of collective bargaining

   (D) relying on civil rights law to remedy economic grievances

   (E) applying group pressure on an employer

13. According to the author, the process of unionization and collective bargaining could do all of the following EXCEPT

   (A) overcome market pressures that keep wages in some industries lower than in others

   (B) encourage worker flexibility in adjusting a new pay scale to economic conditions

   (C) help workers to apply group pressure on employers

   (D) aid in determining the degree to which women are being underpaid

   (E) sensitize workers to the limits of their industry's ability to institute change

14. Which of the following best summarizes the author's main point?

    Ⓐ Pay inequity for women exists because of the lack of unionization in traditionally female occupations.

    Ⓑ Government regulation of industry to achieve pay equity for women is unnecessary because management has the power to effectively determine wages.

    Ⓒ Unionization would solve all industry problems relating to the valuation of women's work.

    Ⓓ Government regulation of women's wages is necessary only in those industries where collective bargaining is ineffective.

    Ⓔ Collective bargaining is preferable to government actions in redressing the under-valuation of women's work.

15. The author mentions textiles (line 40) in order to

    Ⓐ demonstrate the potential harm of govern-ment regulation of industry

    Ⓑ outline a strategy for achieving pay equity for women

    Ⓒ indicate how quickly employees can reason-ably expect to achieve pay equity

    Ⓓ give an example of a situation in which collective bargaining may be ineffective

    Ⓔ show why civil rights laws are the most important tool for increasing women's wages

16. It can be inferred that the author's attitude towards opponents of government regulation of wage determination mentioned in the last paragraph is characterized by which of the following?

    I. Distrust of their motives

    II. Sympathy with some of their concerns

    III. Disagreement with some of their assumptions

    IV. Opposition to their political principles

    Ⓐ I only

    Ⓑ III only

    Ⓒ I and II only

    Ⓓ II and III only

    Ⓔ I, II, and IV

17. In the final paragraph, the author addresses "opponents of mandatory public remedies" (lines 49–50) by

    Ⓐ arguing that those remedies would benefit the economy

    Ⓑ implying that alternative methods of correcting wage disparities would be worse

    Ⓒ asserting that the present approach to setting wages is flawed

    Ⓓ defending civil rights legislation as a solution to social problems

    Ⓔ insisting that those remedies are a viable means of correcting wage disparities

18. The passage refers to which of the following as reasons for preferring collective bargaining to legislation as a method of ending the undervaluation of women's work?

    I. The greater responsiveness of collective bargaining to existing conditions that affect wage levels

    II. The general desirability of using private rather than public remedies

    III. The potential of collective bargaining for achieving a uniform national solution to the problem of gender wage disparities

    Ⓐ I only

    Ⓑ III only

    Ⓒ I and II only

    Ⓓ II and III only

    Ⓔ I, II, and III

KAPLAN

ANSWERS AND EXPLANATIONS

1. B
2. B
3. B
4. D
5. B
6. C
7. D
8. D
9. A
10. C
11. E
12. B
13. A
14. E
15. D
16. D
17. C
18. C

PASSAGE 1—THE NORTON AND RHEE MODEL

Topic and Scope: A discussion of the relevance of formal economic models to real-world policy. The author uses the model applied to Korea by Norton and Rhee to show shortcomings of such models.

Purpose and Main Idea: Author wants to reveal the shortcomings of formal economic models.

Paragraph Structure: Paragraph 1 describes the Norton and Rhee model. Paragraph 2 shows how the results of the application contradict the general trends of real-world economic policy.

1.   B

The passage begins by posing the question of how useful formal models are, and concludes by calling Norton and Rhee's model an example of the "pitfalls" of formalism. (B) captures this critical approach, though it misses the broader implications hinted at in the opening sentence. There's nothing that indicates that Norton and Rhee's method of analysis was "new," (A), nor is the author "proposing" it; on the other hand, she doesn't propose any *other* approach. (C) is what the author is very skeptical about; certainly she doesn't "advocate" using such models. (D) is a mess. Norton and Rhee were not trying to explain Korean inflation as a whole, but to see how various economic factors would affect inflation; and the author is not even trying to do that, but to discuss Norton and Rhee's work. (E) is something the author does do, but it is incidental to the broader purpose of criticizing "formalism."

2.   B

The passage says that Norton and Rhee "achieved some success in applying such a model retrospectively to the Korean economy over a fourteen-year period." In other words, the model is fairly effective in analyzing past events, as (B) suggests.

Since the "fourteen-year period" refers to the past, not the future, (A) is clearly wrong; in fact, one of the main points of the passage is that Norton and Rhee's model is not particularly useful for predicting the future. Choices (C), (D), and (E) refer to matters discussed later in the passage.

3. B

The whole passage is critical of Norton and Rhee, but the last sentence offers the only explicit criticism: Their approach is "formalist" (or abstract) and lacks "policy relevance." (B) paraphrases this criticism. The only economic factors specifically excluded from the model, (A), are the long-term factors mentioned in the middle of paragraph 1; there is no suggestion that Norton and Rhee should be criticized for this procedure. (C) is something that the model does do, since it is aimed at finding the effect of various factors on inflation. The "importance" of economic growth, (D), is not discussed at all and certainly not underestimated. (E) is contradicted by paragraph 1: These are exactly the factors Norton and Rhee *did* consider.

4. D

The last paragraph calls Norton and Rhee's findings "startling," and then cites other economists' views on three points discussed in the preceding paragraph. The most surprising finding is the one "few" economists would agree with; the *least* surprising is the one "most" economists would agree with; and the one that "many" economists dispute lies somewhere in between. The finding "few" economists would agree with, that slower monetary growth is inflationary, is summarized in correct choice (D). (B) refers to the least controversial point, that rising oil costs are inflationary (Norton and Rhee share the orthodox view on this question). Choices (A) and (C) refer to the "in between" finding, on the effects of reduced exports, and are wrong for this reason. In addition, they distort the finding. Norton and Rhee contended that reduced exports would *increase* inflation (the choice paraphrases the "orthodox" view). And they argued that lower (not higher) exports would lower GDP, (C)—no finding about higher exports is implied. Lastly, keeping the long-term factors constant, (E), does not mean that they don't affect growth, simply that Norton and Rhee were not examining their effects on growth.

PASSAGE 2—ECOLOGY

Topic and Scope: A basic scientific principle: "Population size is partly a reflection of available food resources." Specifically, author uses two experiments (one by Berger, one by Bryant) to illustrate how changes in food supply can dramatically affect the size of rodent populations.

Purpose and Main Idea: Author wants to demonstrate that the relationship between population and food supply "is more complex than formerly thought."

Paragraph Structure: In paragraph 1, the second sentence is key: "Recent experiments suggest that the relationship is more complex than formerly thought." *You can guess from these words that the passage will go on to discuss these experiments*. The next sentence identifies the nature of the complexity—rodent browsing affects plant chemicals, which in turn affect the rodents. Paragraph 2 details Berger's experiment, which studied how plant chemicals *trigger reproductive activity among voles*. Paragraph 3 details Bryant's experiment, which studied the effect of plant chemicals on *declining populations of snowshoe hares*. Paragraph 4 discusses possible future research involving lemmings, another rodent with fluctuating populations.

5. B

With a question like this, you need to check each choice against the passage. A faster way to eliminate choices is to remember that the right answer often fits with the main idea, here the food-population relationship. Thus, (A) is wrong because it ventures away from this. (B) looks excellent, because the author devotes several lines at the end of paragraph 2 to explaining the importance of timing for vole reproduction. (C) is simply never covered. (D) is wrong because the author discusses the significance of 6-MBOA, but not its biologic mechanism. With (E), why the hares overpopulate is dismissed in the third paragraph with the words "for reasons that are unclear." The answer is (B).

6. C

This question asks about a detail from paragraph 2. The cited sentence says that timing is crucial because voles are short-lived and the timing of plant growth is unpredictable. You can infer that the plant-rodent relationship increases the vole population at times when food is more plentiful. The best restatement of this inference is (C). (A) goes the wrong way; 6-MBOA triggers breeding—it doesn't discourage it. (B), (D), and (E) are never mentioned anywhere.

7. D

The resinous shoots are discussed in the third paragraph. There, we are told that these shoots function as part of "a phytochemical defense against the depredations of snowshoe hares in Canada." This means that statement I is correct. We are also told the resins in these shoots "discourage hare browsing," and that hares avoid shoots artificially treated with these resins. This means that statement III must also appear in the correct answer. But the passage does not say that increases in the hare population cause plants to produce more resinous shoots, so statement II is not supported by the passage. Therefore, the answer is (D).

8.   D

The lemmings are mentioned in the last paragraph, which speculates that lemmings might, like voles, be affected by a plant trigger for breeding behavior. Some answer choices mention Berger and some mention Bryant. The lemmings are likened to voles, so Berger is the pertinent researcher here. This eliminates (A) and (B). (E) conflicts with the main idea. The author wants to prove something, not disprove it.

That leaves (C), supporting Berger's specific findings, and (D), indicating whether Berger's findings can be generalized. The paragraph doesn't talk about proving Berger's specific results with the voles; those are accepted as given. It does say that the lemmings, like voles, may be affected by a plant trigger. This implies (D), that Berger's findings may be applicable to other animals.

9.   A

The answer to this global question has to focus on something about the complex relationship between food and population size, including the rodent examples; it should also encompass the entire passage. Thus, the best answer is (A). (B) is a detail appearing only in the second paragraph, while (E) appears only in paragraph 3. (C) is too general, and (D) mentions a topic the author never covers.

10.   C

When you read about the hares, notice that Bryant's conclusion is pure speculation. He sees that the hares don't eat resinous shoots, and concludes that this "may play a role" in population decline. The assumption is that there's a connection between not eating the plants and a population reduction. Choice (C) corresponds: The avoidance of plants would lead to starvation, and population decline.

(A), if true, would *weaken*, not strengthen, Bryant's conclusion. (B) is irrelevant—the cause of the rise is unknown and doesn't concern Bryant; it's the decline that interests him. (D) mixes up the hares with the voles and

their breeding behavior. The hare experiment has nothing to do with breeding and reproduction. Finally, (E) is never suggested. Bryant concluded that the population decline was caused by *avoiding* the shoots, not by *eating* them.

11.   E

For this question, you need to eliminate each choice that was part of *both* experiments. Choice (A) was part of both: Berger measured how voles changed breeding behavior and Bryant measured how hares changed eating behavior. (B) also appears in both: Berger measured the rise and fall of vole populations, while Bryant measured hare populations. (C) and (D) apply to both experiments, since both scientists fed the animals chemically treated foods and noted consumption. (E) is correct: Only Berger's experiment dealt with the effect of food on breeding behavior. Bryant's hare experiment dealt with the effect of food on *eating* behavior.

PASSAGE 3—CIVIL RIGHTS LAW

Topic and Scope: Unfair differences between women's and men's wages; specifically, how to remedy such pay inequities.

Purpose and Main Idea: The author argues that collective bargaining is a more desirable way of solving wage disparities than are government-sponsored remedies such as civil rights laws.

Paragraph Structure: Paragraph 1 cites the use of civil rights law for remedying women's pay inequities, but immediately jumps to the topic of collective bargaining, asserting that it's a better alternative. A number of reasons are then given. Paragraph 2 acknowledges that collective bargaining is not foolproof and explains why. Paragraph 3 confirms the author's preference for collective bargaining. Note the conclusion: While the author agrees with opponents of "public remedies," she also issues a warning: That "the current system of wage determination" is far from "perfectly healthy."

12.   B

Since "This" is the first word in the sentence, you have to check the previous sentence to determine its meaning. The previous sentence says that instead of invoking civil rights law, one could try to influence the market so that women could address their own problems. The correct answer will paraphrase "influence the market," (B).

(A) and (E) appear after "This," and thus cannot be what the pronoun refers to. (C) mentions collective bargaining, but "changing its dynamic" is never discussed. (D) goes against the main idea, by favoring use of civil rights law over collective bargaining.

13. A

Figuring out where in the passage to look for an answer is vital! For something that collective bargaining *can't* do, you look at paragraph 2, which lists the shortcomings. There the author states that "the product market imposes serious economic constraints on a substantial closing of the wage gap," which makes (A) correct. Choices (B), (C), (D), and (E) are identified in paragraph 1 as things that collective bargaining *can* accomplish.

14. E

The bold and efficient approach here is to restate the main idea in your own words and then look for an equivalent. Here, (E) is close to the idea we came up with earlier: Collective bargaining isn't perfect, but it's preferable to civil rights law for addressing women's labor issues. (E) "jumps out."

With the wrong answers, (A) offers a detail. (B) distorts the passage—the author believes that government regulation is bad, but not that management should have unlimited power to set wages. (C) is a sweeping generalization—a negative sign in itself. Correct choices seldom use absolute words such as "all," "never," "always," and "every." And the passage explicitly states that unionization doesn't solve all problems. (D) runs counter to the author's attitude: The author never endorses any type of government remedy.

15. D

The textile industry is mentioned in the course of the author's admission that collective bargaining is not "foolproof." The passage says that "the concentration of women in low-paying industries" raises problems that are not easily resolved by collective bargaining. Thus, (D) is the best answer.

Choice (A) is wrong, because the second paragraph is not where the author makes a case against government

regulation. Choices (B) and (C) refer to matters discussed earlier in the passage. And (E) contradicts the author's argument.

16. D

The answer to this question is in the last paragraph, where the author refers to the "opponents" of government regulation. The author says that they aren't right about everything, although they are right about the evils of government intervention. This confirms options II and III—the author is sympathetic, but disagrees with part of their argument. Since only (D) includes both II and III, it must be the correct answer.

Statements I and IV suggest that the author's hostile to the opponents. The author generally agrees with them! The author takes issue with one point only.

17. C

Questions are sometimes consistent with each other! You examined the last paragraph in the previous question and found that the author agrees with the conclusion that public remedies are bad, but sharply questions the assumption that the present system is fine just the way it is. (C) restates this latter point. The four wrong choices run counter to the author's argument—at no point does the author endorse any form of government regulation or civil rights law.

18. C

As always, knowing where to look is crucial. The answer to this question will appear in the first paragraph, which lists all the reasons collective bargaining is good. Option I is implied at the end of the paragraph with "sensitive to the limits." Option II occurs at the beginning of the paragraph, which endorses self-help over civil rights law. Option III, however, is not found here. In fact, option III appears in the discussion of the weaknesses of collective bargaining in paragraph 2.

READING COMPREHENSION PRACTICE SET TWO

Time: 25 Minutes/18 Questions

Directions: Each passage in this section is followed by several questions. After reading the passage, choose the best response to each question and mark it on your answer sheet. Your replies are to be based on what is actually stated or implied in the passage, and not on your own knowledge. You may refer to the passage while answering the questions.

PASSAGE 1—DEBT CRISIS

The debt crisis affecting many developing countries has had three causes: imprudent management and borrowing by debtor countries; imprudent lending by banks; and rising
(5) interest rates. The rise in real interest rates to about 6 percent by 1982 increased the burden on borrowers and completely changed the nature of the debt problem. Such an increase had not been seen previously. In past debt
(10) crises, when loans were made at fixed rates, real interest rates rose with deflation. But once price levels stabilized, the interest bur-
den would be higher only to the extent of the proportional decline in price levels. And it
(15) remained quite possible that inflation would eventually reduce the burden. In this crisis, though, the real interest rate has risen and stayed high, and inflation has brought no relief.

(20) During the 1980s, fear of financial loss led U.S. commercial banks to sharply curtail their lending activity in debtor countries. In 1982, nine large banks had over 250 percent of their capital in loans to developing countries; by
(25) mid-1986, the nine banks had reduced their activities to the point where they had sufficient

equity and reserves to withstand potential losses. Although banks have stabilized their positions, many continue to carry devel-
(30) oping-country debt at face value.

Present bank strategies deal with the debt crisis by extending the effective maturity of loans. Although any method that reduces the flow of resources from debtor countries will
(35) help in the short run, further lending prom-
ises little relief to the debt problem. So long as real interest rates remain high, developing countries will remain in debt. There are two choices. Either the piecemeal approach con-
(40) tinues, or some form of debt relief occurs. For years, developing countries have paid the price of low growth and significant falls in real wages while making cash transfers to service their debt. Citizens of developing coun-
(45) tries are kept at low levels of income for the sake of capital gains for banks and their shareholders. With sensible debt relief, developing countries and lending institutions can begin to formulate growth-oriented development
(50) policies. This should be possible without increasing burdens on taxpayers in lender countries.

1. The primary purpose of this passage is to discuss

   (A) the causes of the debt crisis and potential solutions to it

   (B) the effects of rising interest rates

   (C) American banking in the 1980s

   (D) the future of banking in the United States

   (E) economic conditions in developing countries

2. The passage provides information that helps to answer which of the following questions?

   I. Did errors of economic management by developing countries contribute to the debt crisis?

   II. Are steps currently being taken to alleviate the debt crisis?

   III. Do taxpayers in lending countries support the notion of debt relief?

   (A) I only

   (B) II only

   (C) I and II only

   (D) II and III only

   (E) I, II, and III

3. Which of the following characterized responses to the debt crisis in the 1980s?

   (A) Increased pressure on debtor countries to pay interest due on loans

   (B) An increase in the percentage of their total capital large banks devoted to foreign loans

   (C) A decrease in the funds designated by banks to cover potential losses

   (D) Reliance by banks on inflationary pressure to reduce debt levels

   (E) A decline in bank lending and an increase in capital reserves

4. The author suggests that methods currently in place for dealing with the debt crisis are inadequate because they

   (A) increase the upward pressure on real interest rates without allowing any opportunity for reduction

   (B) allow real wages to rise at the expense of economic growth in debtor countries

   (C) fail to address problems of mismanagement in debtor and creditor countries

   (D) lessen the immediate burden of debt service but do not promote long-term growth

   (E) sacrifice a reduction of real interest rates for a short-term increase in loan maturity

5. In the passage, the author identifies all of the following as contributing to the current debt crisis *EXCEPT*

   (A) self-interest on the part of commercial banks

   (B) sustained high real interest rates

   (C) unwillingness of banks to extend the maturation periods of loans

   (D) unwise decisions made by commercial lending institutions

   (E) failure of inflation to reduce the interest burden

6. If the passage were to continue, the next topic the author would logically discuss would most likely be

   (A) possible steps that might bring about effective debt relief

   (B) options other than debt relief that might alleviate the debt crisis

   (C) current attitudes of bankers towards international lending

   (D) measures currently taken by debtor countries to reduce inflation

   (E) the effects of 1980s banking activities on debtor countries

PASSAGE 2—DESERT PLANTS

Desert plant populations have evolved sophisticated physiological behavioral traits that aid survival in arid conditions. Some send out long, unusually deep taproots; others
(5) utilize shallow but widespread roots, which allow them to absorb large, intermittent flows of water. Certain plants protect their access to water. The creosote bush produces a potent root toxin which inhibits the growth of com-
(10) peting root systems. Daytime closure of stomata exemplifies a further genetic adaptation; guard cells work to minimize daytime water loss, later allowing the stomata to open when conditions are more favorable to gas exchange
(15) with the environment.

Certain adaptations reflect the principle that a large surface area facilitates water and gas exchange. Most plants have small leaves, modified leaves (spines), or no leaves at all.
(20) The main food-producing organ is not the leaf but the stem, which is often green and non-woody. Thick, waxy stems and cuticles, seen in succulents such as cacti and agaves, also help conserve water. Spines and thorns
(25) (modified branches) protect against predators and also minimize water loss.

7. The passage refers to the spines and thorns of desert plants as

   I. genetically evolved structural adaptations that protect against predation

   II. genetic modifications that aid in the reduction of water loss

   III. structures that do not participate directly in food production

   (A) I only
   (B) III only
   (C) I and II only
   (D) II and III only
   (E) I, II, and III

8. The author suggests that the guard cells of desert plants act to do which of the following?

   I. Facilitate gas and water exchange between the plants and their surroundings

   II. Cause the stomata of desert plants to remain closed during daytime hours

   III. Respond to sudden, heavy rainfalls by forcing the plants' stomata to open

   (A) I only
   (B) II only
   (C) III only
   (D) I and II only
   (E) I, II, and III

9. The passage suggests that which of the following weather-related conditions would most benefit plants with shallow root systems?

   (A) An unusually prolonged drought
   (B) A windstorm
   (C) A flash flood
   (D) A light spring rain
   (E) A winter snowfall

10. The adaptations of desert plants to their environment would tend to support the statement that

    (A) the rate of genetic evolution is greater in the desert than in more temperate surroundings
    (B) structures in a plant that usually perform one function may, under certain conditions, perform different functions
    (C) while the amount of leaf surface area is critical for a desert plant, it is much less so for plants in most other environments
    (D) desert plants do not have many physiological and behavioral traits in common with other plants
    (E) desert plants could probably adapt to life in a variety of harsh ecosystems

11. All of the following are mentioned as examples of adaptation by desert plants *EXCEPT*

    (A) deep roots
    (B) shallow roots
    (C) poisonous roots
    (D) food-producing leaves
    (E) spines and thorns

12. The passage suggests that the adaptations of desert plants function to do all of the following *EXCEPT*

    (A) protect the plants' access to water
    (B) prevent the loss of water during the day
    (C) maximize the water and gas exchange
    (D) shield the plants from daytime heat
    (E) guard against predators

KAPLAN

PASSAGE 3—MIGRATION

The great migration of European intellectuals to the United States in the second quarter of the twentieth century prompted a transformation in the character of Western
(5) social thought. The influx of Continental thinkers fleeing fascist regimes had a great impact on American academic circles, leading to new developments in such diverse fields as linguistics and theology. But the greatest
(10) impact was on the emigrés themselves. This "migration experience" led expatriates to reexamine the supposedly self-evident premises inherited from the Continental intellectual tradition. The result, according to
(15) H. Stuart Hughes in *The Sea-Change*, was an increased sophistication and deprovincialization in social theory.

One problem facing newly arrived emigrés in the U.S. was the spirit of anti-intellectual-
(20) ism in much of the country. The empirical orientation of American academic circles, moreover, led to the conscious tempering by many European thinkers of their own tendencies towards speculative idealism. In addition,
(25) reports of oppression in Europe shook many Old World intellectuals from a stance of moral isolation. Many great European social theorists had regarded their work as separate from all moral considerations. The migration
(30) experience proved to many intellectuals of the following generations that such notions of moral seclusion were unrealistic, even irresponsible.

This transformation of social thought is
(35) perhaps best exemplified in the career of the German theologian Paul Tillich. Migration confronted Tillich with an ideological as well as a cultural dichotomy. Hughes points out that Tillich's thought was "suspended
(40) between philosophy and theology, Marxism

and political conformity, theism and disbelief." Comparable to the fusion by other expatriate intellectuals of their own idealist traditions with the Anglo-American empiricist
(45) tradition was Tillich's synthesis of German Romantic religiosity with the existentialism born of the twentieth-century war experience. Tillich's basic goal, according to Hughes, was to move secular individuals by making
(50) religious symbols more accessible to them. Forced to make his ethical orientation explicit in the context of American attitudes, Tillich avoided the esoteric academic posture of many Old World scholars, and was able to
(55) find a wide and sympathetic audience for his sometimes difficult theology. In this way, his experience in America, in his own words, "deprovincialized" his thought.

13. The author's main concern in the passage is to

   (A) characterize the effects of migration on U.S. history

   (B) show how Paul Tillich's career was representative of the migration experience

   (C) discuss the effects of the great migration on modern social thought

   (D) reveal the increased sophistication of post-migration thought

   (E) contrast European social thought with that of the United States

14. The author probably mentions H. Stuart Hughes (line 15) in order to

   (A) give an example of a European intellectual who migrated to America

   (B) cite an important source of information about the migration experience

   (C) demonstrate how one American academic was influenced by European scholars

   (D) pay tribute to Americans who provided European thinkers with a refuge from fascism

   (E) name a leading disciple of Paul Tillich

15. Which of the following statements describe Tillich's achievement?

    I.   He elucidated religious symbols in a secular context without sacrificing their impact.

    II. He shunned the esotericism of much theological scholarship.

    III. He adapted a traditional religiosity to the temper of the modern world.

    (A) I only

    (B) II only

    (C) I and II only

    (D) II and III only

    (E) I, II, and III

16. According to the passage, "reports of oppression in Europe" (line 25) affected social thinkers by forcing them to

    (A) rethink their moral responsibilities

    (B) reexamine the morality of European leaders

    (C) analyze the effects of migration on morality

    (D) reconsider their antisocial behavior

    (E) justify the moral value of social thought

17. It can be inferred that postmigration social thought is distinguished from premigration thought by its

    (A) less secular nature

    (B) greater social consciousness

    (C) more difficult theology

    (D) diminished accessibility

    (E) more theoretical nature

18. The passage suggests that the migration experience

    (A) had little major effect on American academic circles

    (B) led to the abandonment of the idealist philosophical tradition

    (C) made American intellectuals sensitive to oppression in Europe

    (D) caused emigré social thinkers to question certain of their beliefs

    (E) negated Tillich's influence on modern social thought

ANSWERS AND EXPLANATIONS

1. A
2. C
3. E
4. D
5. C
6. A
7. E
8. D
9. C
10. B
11. D
12. D
13. C
14. B
15. E
16. A
17. B
18. D

PASSAGE 1—DEBT CRISIS

Topic and Scope: The debt crisis; specifically, the causes of the debt crisis and the strategies for dealing with it.

Purpose and Main Idea: The author's purpose is to discuss both the causes of the debt crisis and the strategies for handling it. This is a descriptive passage, so there really isn't a very focused main idea. The author does say, however, that debt relief is a better way to deal with the debt problem than current bank strategies.

Paragraph Structure: The first paragraph lists the causes of the debt crisis and goes on to amplify the third cause, rising interest rates. The second paragraph outlines bank strategies for dealing with the debt crisis in the 1980s. The third paragraph contrasts current bank strategies with debt relief, arguing that the latter is a more effective approach to the debt problem.

1. A

As we've seen, the purpose of the passage as a whole is to state the causes of the debt crisis, and suggest what can be done about it. Choice (A) best conveys this idea. The other answer choices focus on details: (B) refers to the first paragraph, (C) to the second, and (D) and (E) to the third.

2. C

This roman numeral question poses three questions and asks which are answered in the passage. Question I is about a cause of the debt crisis, which is covered in the first sentence of the passage. The question asks about management errors by developing countries, and the passage lists "imprudent management." Since the passage answers question I, (B) and (D) can be eliminated. Question II asks if anything is currently being done about the debt crisis. This question is answered in the last paragraph, which discusses current bank strategies. So you can eliminate (A), too. Finally, question III asks how taxpayers in lending countries feel about debt relief. In the last sentence of the passage, the author says debt relief can be accomplished without burdening taxpayers, but never addresses the attitudes of the taxpayers themselves. Because the passage does *not* answer question III, you can eliminate (E). Since the passage answers questions I and II, but not III, the correct answer is (C). Keep in mind that it's usually possible to use option combinations in the answer choices to eliminate incorrect choices.

3. E

This question asks about bank responses to the debt crisis in the 1980s, the subject of the second paragraph. This paragraph says that banks curtailed their lending until they had sufficient reserves. (E) is a nice paraphrase of this information. (B) and (C) are *au contraire* choices. (A) and (D) bring up issues not dealt with in the second paragraph.

4. D

The key to most passages is not so much an overall comprehension of their content, but rather knowing where in them to look for information. In this passage, the author's opinion appears in the last few sentences, where he states that current approaches to the debt crisis are inadequate because debt service prevents long-term economic growth in developing countries. A good paraphrase of this notion appears in (D).

(A) and (C) distort information in the passage and, moreover, relate to the first paragraph rather than the third, which is the one you're interested in here. (B) and (E) contradict the passage.

5. C

Since this is an "all/EXCEPT" question, you're looking for the choice that is *not* contributing to the current debt crisis. Begin by consulting the first paragraph because it lists the causes of the debt crisis. The author mentions high interest rates, imprudent lending, and no relief from inflation as causes of the crisis. Therefore, you can eliminate (B), (D), and (E). (A), self-interested commercial banks, comes up in the third paragraph, which says that the economies of developing countries are being damaged in order to profit the banks and their shareholders. That leaves (C) as the correct answer. Indeed, not only is (C) not cited as a contributing factor to the current debt crisis, but it is contradicted by information in the passage as well.

6. A

For a "continuation" question, you need to look at where the passage leaves off and pick an answer consistent with that issue. In this passage, the author finishes by talking about debt relief. If the passage were to continue, it would take up the issue of debt relief. That makes (A) the correct answer. (B) is not logical because the last sentence is about debt relief itself; the author wouldn't suddenly take up the issue of alternatives to debt relief. (C), (D), and (E) play on issues brought up earlier in the passage.

PASSAGE 2—DESERT PLANTS

Topic and Scope: Desert plant adaptations and how they aid in these plants' survival.

Purpose and Main Idea: The author is trying to describe the physiological traits that desert plants have adapted in order to survive in arid conditions.

Paragraph Structure: The first paragraph describes some general adaptations. The second paragraph discusses adaptations based on the principle that a large surface area facilitates water and gas exchange.

7. E

The whole passage focuses on structural and behavioral adaptations that desert plants have made in order to survive. While the word "genetic" is used only once (in the last sentence of paragraph 1), it's clear that many of these modifications are genetic. Spines and thorns, which are identified in the second paragraph as modified leaves and branches, are inferably among these genetic adaptations. In the last sentence, it's further stated that they protect against predation (I) and also that they help minimize water loss (II). Option III is confirmed in the third sentence of the second paragraph; most of a desert plant's food is produced in its stem, not in its leaves, so it's pretty clear that spines and thorns (again, modified leaves and branches) have little or nothing to do with food production.

8. D

Like question 7, this is another detail question, this time focusing on the functioning of guard cells, mentioned in the sentence that concludes paragraph 1. This sentence discusses two closely related plant features: the stomata and the guard cells. You read first that daytime closing of the stomata is an adaptation that helps to minimize daytime water loss. The second half of the sentence clearly implies that it's the guard cells that control this opening and closing of the stomata. So, the guard cells force the stomata to close during the day, to minimize water loss, and then they later cause the stomata to open, when conditions for gas exchange between the plant and its environment are more favorable. The first two options are thus clearly suggested. The third option, however, is an unjustified inference. Nothing at all is stated to link the functioning of guard cells to sudden downpours.

KAPLAN

9. C

The stem is looking for the weather-related condition that would especially benefit plants with shallow root systems. Shallow root systems are mentioned up in the second sentence, and the point is that these specially adapted roots allow desert plants to take advantage of heavy, irregular flows of water. One example would be a very heavy, torrential downpour. The only choice that comes close to this is a flash flood. Flash floods result from unexpected, torrential rainfall. (A) and (B) are impossible; neither drought nor windstorms involve water. (D) won't work because a light rain doesn't fit with the idea of a large, sudden quantity of water. (E), finally, is pretty impossible, too. First, this choice doesn't suggest a *heavy*, intermittent snowfall, and second, nothing is said in the passage to suggest snow would be of special benefit to shallow rooted plants.

10. B

The second paragraph contains several examples of structures that in desert plants perform different functions than those they normally perform in plants in other environments. Spines and thorns in desert plants are modified leaves and branches, to reduce water loss. And, as a result of their lack of normal leaves, most desert plants produce their food in their green, fleshy stems. As for the wrong choices, three of them—(A), (D), and (E)—simply can't be answered. There's no information to support any of these statements. Finally, in choice (C), while the passage does indicate that a small leaf surface area is a critical factor for desert plants, nothing suggests that leaf surface area isn't critical for plants in most other environments. Since the general principle is that a large surface area facilitates gas and water exchange, one can infer that the larger leaf surface area of other plants helps in this process.

11. D

We are told in the second paragraph that most desert plants produce food in their stems, not their leaves. Therefore, (D) is the correct answer: it names something that's not mentioned in the passage. Choices (A), (B), and (C) are mentioned in the first paragraph, and (E) is mentioned in the second paragraph.

12. D

The passage mentions several different adaptations and the purpose of each. The creosote bush produces a toxin that prohibits competing root systems from intruding on its space, therefore protecting its access to water. Guard cells function to "minimize daytime water loss." The second paragraph starts by talking about adaptations that facilitate gas and water exchange. Spines and thorns are adaptations that protect against predators. There is no mention of any adaptation shielding plants from the heat, so (D) must be the answer.

PASSAGE 3—MIGRATION

Topic and Scope: The great migration; specifically, how the migration experience transformed the social thought of European intellectuals who came to America, especially Tillich.

Purpose and Main Idea: The author's purpose is to describe the changes in the social thought of European intellectuals who immigrated to America, using Tillich as an example. The main idea is simply that, as a consequence of the migration experience, European thinkers in America transformed their ideas to have more relevance to "real world" issues.

Paragraph Structure: The first paragraph introduces the topic and scope of the passage. The second paragraph describes in general terms how the social thought of European intellectuals was transformed. And the third paragraph provides a specific example of this transformation by describing the case of Tillich.

13. C

To answer this question, it's important to realize that the author's purpose is to discuss the transformation of social thought that resulted from the great migration. Tillich is merely an example of how this transformation manifested itself among European emigrés; he is not the primary focus of the passage. Therefore, (B), which places emphasis on Tillich, is out. (A) and (D) fail to mention "social thought." (D) mentions only "thought," not "social thought." Finally, (E) gets in the idea of social thought but leaves out the migration experience. (C), which includes the important elements of the author's purpose—the effects of the great migration on social thought—is correct.

14. B

Hughes is mentioned in the first paragraph as the author of a book that says something about European expatriates in the United States. He's also cited in the third paragraph in the course of analysis of Tillich's thought. In other words, Hughes is cited as a source of information, as (B) suggests.

Choices (A), (C), and (D) can't be right, because the passage doesn't tell us whether Hughes was a European or an American, or whether he had any direct contact with the emigrés. Choice (E) is a bit more tempting, since the author cites Hughes's interpretation of Tillich's ideas. But that doesn't mean that Hughes is a disciple—a follower—of Tillich. Choice (B) is the only answer that's really supported by the passage.

15. E

Before you check the options, review the information about Tillich in the last paragraph. He combined religiosity with existentialism and made religious symbols more meaningful to people. These achievements are echoed in options I and III. None of the choices includes just I and III, so you know the correct answer must be (E), which includes all three options. To confirm option II, again look back at the passage, which does say that Tillich "avoided the esoteric academic posture of many Old World scholars." Option II makes more or less the same point, so it's indeed part of the correct answer.

16. A

This is a detail question, so the correct answer is there in the text—in this case, in the second paragraph, which says that oppression forced social thinkers to reject moral isolation. (A) gets at this notion. (B) brings in "leaders," but they aren't mentioned in the passage. (C) substitutes "morality" for "moral isolation." They are not the same, and the morality of the emigrés was never in question. (D) is entirely wrong; the passage doesn't accuse the emigrés of "antisocial behavior." The most tempting wrong choice is (E). However, "rethink" in (A) is much more characteristic of the thrust of the passage than the word "justify" in (E). Don't answer detail questions on a hunch. Go back to the text and find the answer.

17. B

The passage uses the word "deprovincialization" twice to characterize the transformation of social thought. Among the choices, the closest paraphrase is (B), greater social consciousness. Notice that two choices, (A) and (C), allude to Tillich, but the question asks about social thought in general, not about him. Besides, these choices distort Tillich's approach. (D) and (E) are *au contraire* choices.

18. D

This question doesn't zero in on a particular piece of the text, so just read through the choices and look for one that "jumps out" as consistent with the purpose of the passage. (D) is consistent with what the author's trying to accomplish. "Prephrasing" his purpose would have made it easy to pick this choice.

Looking at the other choices, (A) is contradicted in the first paragraph. Also, it deals with a minor point that the author doesn't pursue in the remainder of the text. The word "abandonment" makes (B) too broad a choice. Be suspicious of choices that make sweeping generalizations. (C) focuses on American rather than European thinkers. Finally, (E) is an *au contraire* choice. If anything, the migration experience enhanced Tillich's influence.

KAPLAN

READING COMPREHENSION PRACTICE SET THREE

Time: 25 Minutes/18 Questions

Directions: Each passage in this section is followed by several questions. After reading the passage, choose the best response to each question and mark it on your answer sheet. Your replies are to be based on what is actually stated or implied in the passage, and not on your own knowledge. You may refer to the passage while answering the questions.

PASSAGE 1—SELF-EMPLOYED WOMEN

Although it is well documented that women face difficulties in reaching senior positions in business, studies indicate that business proprietorship offers one way for-
(5) ward. Stanworth and Curran suggest that members of ethnic and religious minorities have often started their own businesses as a means of advancement. One advantage of ownership is the absence of "organizational
(10) selectors"—proprietors need not meet employment criteria based on age, gender, or experience. Recent data confirm that women perceive self-employment as a means for overcoming subordination. In 1985, 4 percent
(15) of employed women in Britain were self-employed; more recent estimates are put at 6 percent. Between 1977 and 1980, the number of woman-owned enterprises in the U.S. increased by 33 percent.

(20)   Goffee and Scase classify self-employed women into four types by considering commitments to both entrepreneurial and conventional female values. Innovative entrepreneurs question conventional assumptions
(25) about the social position of women.

Innovators seek business ownership because of their inability to fulfill ambitions within more common career structures. Work is a central interest and is much more important
(30) than conventional female roles. In a related category are radicals—proprietors who are active in collective political and economic ventures which promote female issues. Unlike innovators, their businesses are not oriented
(35) mainly to profit making; rather, accumulated assets are used to further the long-term interests of women. Goffee and Scase designate a number of women as conventionals. Committed to entrepreneurship, they also
(40) remain attached to conventional female roles. Unlike many innovators, resentment about limited career prospects is rarely a motive for business start-up. Conventionals "are less likely to have been previously employed in
(45) large-scale organizations. Before starting their businesses, most were 'secondary' workers who moved in and out of the labor market depending upon employment prospects and according to domestic commitments." Goffee
(50) and Scase suggest that entrepreneurs in a fourth category, domestics, have a limited commitment to entrepreneurial ideals and are strongly attached to a traditional female role. These women "regard their business as
(55) secondary to their roles as mothers and wives. Proprietorship offers opportunities for self-fulfillment and autonomy within parameters delineated by their other obligations."

KAPLAN

1. Which of the following correctly describes one of the four types of female entrepreneurs discussed in the passage?

   (A) A conventional has a strong attachment to conventional gender roles and a weak attachment to entrepreneurial ideals.

   (B) An innovator has a limited attachment to both conventional gender roles and entrepreneurial ideals.

   (C) A radical has a limited attachment to conventional gender roles and a strong attachment to entrepreneurial ideals.

   (D) An innovator has a strong attachment to both conventional gender roles and entrepreneurial ideals.

   (E) A domestic has a limited attachment to entrepreneurial ideals and a strong attachment to conventional gender roles.

2. Which of the following summarizes a main idea of the passage?

   (A) There are few fundamental distinctions among female entrepreneurs.

   (B) Women entrepreneurs, in their motives and objectives, do not differ significantly from their male counterparts.

   (C) Entrepreneurship is increasingly seen by women as providing access to formerly unavailable economic opportunities.

   (D) The development of a single set of policy guidelines designed to facilitate female entrepreneurship is desirable.

   (E) Numbers of female entrepreneurs continue to grow despite opposition within the predominantly male business world.

3. Which of the following addresses a distinction made in the passage between innovators and radicals?

   (A) Innovators attempt to revise current definitions of women's social roles; radicals do not.

   (B) Innovators are committed to organizing cooperative business ventures; radicals are not.

   (C) Innovators view work primarily as a means of securing personal and financial success; radicals do not.

   (D) Radicals are motivated by antagonism towards previous employers; innovators are not.

   (E) Radicals direct themselves mainly towards profit-making goals; innovators do not.

4. According to the passage, which of the following is true of conventionals?

   (A) A commitment to entrepreneurship affects their attachment to a traditional female role.

   (B) Their entrepreneurial values are shaped by past job-related experiences.

   (C) Their political values are similar to those of domestics.

   (D) Their previous participation in the labor market was often irregular.

   (E) An attachment to a conventional female role inhibits their business activities.

5. It can be inferred from the passage that the author believes that the work of Goffee and Scase offers

   (A) a compelling though narrow view of self-employed women

   (B) a well-intended but unfinished analysis of female entrepreneurial behavior

   (C) an effective assault on the system men have used to circumscribe women's careers

   (D) a necessary alternative to the views of Stanworth and Curran

   (E) a meaningful contribution to current studies of female entrepreneurship

6. The information given in the passage about the work of Goffee and Scase supports each of the following generalizations about female proprietorship *EXCEPT* that it

    Ⓐ fosters links among minority groups

    Ⓑ offers opportunities for nonmonetary rewards

    Ⓒ provides a means for political advances

    Ⓓ allows access to previously unattainable economic goals

    Ⓔ curtails the importance of the conventional female role

7. Goffee and Scase's distinction between innovators and radicals would be most weakened if it were shown that relatively few women

    Ⓐ become self-employed because of anger towards former employers

    Ⓑ use business profits to combat male dominance in society

    Ⓒ start a business in order to avoid organizational selectors

    Ⓓ are able to enter and leave the labor force at will

    Ⓔ feel that sex discrimination plays a major role in their lives

PASSAGE 2—BAADE

In 1943, Baade obtained photographs of stars in the galaxy Andromeda. Using these photographs, Baade divided stars into two groups. The brightest members of Population I

(5) were hot, blue stars with surface temperatures up to 30,000 degrees Kelvin. The brightest Population II stars (called "red giants") were large, cool, and red, and fainter than Population I stars. Later observations showed that most

(10) Population I stars occur in the arms of spiral galaxies, while Population II stars are most common between the arms and in the centers of spiral galaxies, and in elliptical galaxies.

According to Baade, the two populations

(15) compose distinct stellar age groups. Since the rate at which stars consume their fuel is directly proportional to their brightness, and brightness increases with mass, large, bright stars burn their fuel more quickly than dim-

(20) mer stars. Baade concluded that the brightest Population I stars were probably less than one million years old while Population II stars were older.

Baade found support for his views in the

(25) distribution of red giants. It is believed that most of a star's hydrogen fuel is gradually converted to helium. When the helium core comprises about one tenth of a star's mass, the star expands and its surface cools. This

(30) phase lasts until the red giant consumes all of its fuel and disintegrates in either a single explosion or a series of outbursts. Most red giants occur in Population II.

The composition of red giants supports

(35) Baade's conception. It is thought that all elements evolved from hydrogen as a result of nuclear reactions in stars. When a star explodes, it throws out heavy elements. Thus, the dust and gas from which new stars are

(40) produced gradually become richer in heavier elements. Studies of red giants in both populations reveal that heavier elements are more abundant in Population I giants. Thus, Population II stars evolved from material

(45) poor in heavier elements and are older.

While Baade's basic insights have been sustained, analyses of stars in our galaxy have shown variations in concentrations of heavy elements, indicating that the stars must be of

(50) assorted ages. As a consequence, stars are now classified into five distinct populations.

8. The primary purpose of this passage is to

   (A) explain how to determine the age of a star

   (B) describe a system of star classification and some of the evidence supporting it

   (C) discuss Population II stars

   (D) compare and evaluate competing theories of stellar evolution

   (E) examine the importance of Baade's contributions to astronomy

9. According to the passage, Baade considered all of the following to be characteristics of Population I stars *EXCEPT:*

   (A) They are relatively young stars.

   (B) The brightest members are hot, blue stars.

   (C) They are found mainly between the arms of spiral galaxies.

   (D) They are brighter than Population II stars.

   (E) They have surface temperatures of up to 30,000 degrees Kelvin.

10. According to the passage, when the core in which hydrogen has been totally consumed amounts to approximately one-tenth of a star's mass, then

    (A) the star will expand and its outer layer will cool

    (B) its life as a normal star will end

    (C) the star may disintegrate in a single explosion

    (D) the star will throw out the heavy elements it has produced

    (E) its classification will change from Population I to Population II

11. Which of the following statements can be inferred from the passage as characteristic of red giants?

    I. They are all Population II stars.

    II. Each red giant is cooler than it once was.

    III. They all have a low percentage of heavy elements.

    (A) I only

    (B) II only

    (C) I and II only

    (D) I and III only

    (E) I, II, and III

12. The passage provides support for all of the following statements *EXCEPT:*

    (A) The death of a star involves either one major or several minor explosions.

    (B) The chemical compositions of red giants support the classification of stars into different age groups.

    (C) Population II stars are older than Population I stars.

    (D) Elliptical galaxies have existed for a longer period of time than spiral galaxies.

    (E) The chemical composition of a star is indicative of its age.

PASSAGE 3—CORAL REEFS

Many aspects of coral reefs remain puzzling to scientists. One mystery concerns the relationship between Scleractinia, the coral type whose colonization produces reefs, and
(5) their symbiotic partners, a unicellular algae present in the coral's endodermic tissues. It is known that both organisms play an integral part in the formation of a reef's foundation by together secreting and depositing calcium
(10) carbonate, which reacts with sea salt to form a hard limestone underlayer. Scientists also know that, because of algal photosynthesis,

the reef environment is oxygen-rich, while similarly high amounts of carbon dioxide are
(15) removed rapidly. All of this accounts for the amazing renewability of coral reefs despite the erosion caused by waves. The precise manner in which one symbiotic organism stimulates the secretion of calcium carbonate
(20) by the other, however, remains unclear.

In addition to the above unanswered question, scientists have proposed various theories to explain the transformation of "fringing reefs" (those connected above sea level to land
(25) masses) into "barrier reefs" (those separated from shorelines by lagoons) and finally into island atolls. Although Darwin's view of the transformation is considered partially correct, some scientists feel that the creation of reef
(30) formations has more to do with the rise in sea level that occurred at the end of the last Ice Age than with a gradual submergence of the volcanic islands to which fringing reefs were originally attached. However, recent drillings at
(35) one atoll have revealed a substantial underlayer of volcanic rock, which suggests that Darwin's explanation may be largely correct.

The term "coral reef" is something of a misnomer. The *Scleractinia* themselves gener-
(40) ally comprise only 10 percent of the total mass of life forms of an average reef community: Algae, along with foraminifera, annelid worms, and assorted molluscs, can account for up to 90 percent of the reef mass.
(45) Moreover, the conditions under which reef growth occurs are determined by the needs of the algae, not those of the coral. Reefs flourish only in shallow, highly saline waters above 70° F, because the algae require such an environ-
(50) ment. Non-reef-building coral, meanwhile, occur worldwide.

13. The author cites which of the following as characteristic of coral reefs?

   I.   The coexistence of a multitude of organisms
   II. Widely varying environmental conditions
   III. A tough limestone underlayer

   (A) II only
   (B) III only
   (C) I and II only
   (D) I and III only
   (E) I, II, and III

14. The author suggests that coral reefs are able to survive the process of erosion

   (A) primarily through the activities of algae
   (B) despite the high oxygen content of the reef environment
   (C) as a result of the combined relations of coral and algae
   (D) only if they have an above-surface connection to the shoreline
   (E) because of the volcanic rock at their base

15. It can be inferred from the passage that Darwin

   (A) believed that reefs became atolls through the sinking of volcanic islands
   (B) should have expanded his studies of reefs to include those found at atolls
   (C) theorized that each reef formation was formed by an entirely different process
   (D) is less persuasive on the topic of reef formation in light of recent discoveries
   (E) was more interested in algae and coral than in other organisms living at reefs

KAPLAN

16. The passage does *NOT* discuss the relationship between

    (A) algal photosynthesis and high oxygen content

    (B) Darwin's views and evidence supplied by recent research

    (C) volcanic rock and the life forms found at reefs

    (D) sea salt and calcium carbonate

    (E) wave action and the renewal of reefs

17. Which of the following questions is most completely answered by the passage?

    (A) What percentage of coral worldwide is of the reef-building type?

    (B) How do rises in sea level affect reef formation?

    (C) What are the requisite environmental conditions for coral reef formation?

    (D) How does coral stimulate the calceous secretions of symbiotic algae?

    (E) What is the principal reason for the transformation of fringing reefs into atolls?

18. It can be inferred that the author would agree with all of the following statements *EXCEPT:*

    (A) Coral cannot produce reefs without algae.

    (B) The water around a coral reef contains high levels of oxygen.

    (C) Darwin's theory about the causes of reef formation is at least partly accurate.

    (D) The term "coral reef" should be abandoned by scientists.

    (E) Coral are more resistant to cold temperatures than the algae that live in their tissues.

ANSWERS AND EXPLANATIONS

1. E
2. C
3. C
4. D
5. E
6. A
7. B
8. B
9. C
10. A
11. B
12. D
13. D
14. C
15. A
16. C
17. C
18. D

PASSAGE 1—SELF-EMPLOYED WOMEN

Topic and Scope: Different motives and values that motivate different women to start their own businesses.

Purpose and Main Idea: The author summarizes the four categories into which Goffee and Scase have divided female entrepreneurs.

Paragraph Structure: The first paragraph provides a general introduction to the topic. It says that a significant number of women have started their own businesses as a way of avoiding the discrimination to which they are often subject in male-owned businesses. The second paragraph sorts women who start their own businesses into four categories: *innovators*, who are motivated mainly by the desire for career success; *radicals*, whose motivation is primarily ideological; *conventionals*, who are committed both to their businesses and to traditional female roles; and *domestics*, for whom traditional female roles are the first priority.

1. E

This is a detail question, so the answer's in the text itself. In fact, all this question requires is that you check the choices against the definitions in the second paragraph. (A), (B), (C), and (D) are "half-right, half-wrong" choices. Each combines a correct piece of information with an incorrect piece. Only (E) gets the definition completely right.

2. C

"Prephrasing" the answer to this global question would have allowed you to move quickly and confidently through the answer choices. The first paragraph makes the point that comes up in (C).

(A) is an *au contraire* choice; the second paragraph reveals that there are many fundamental distinctions among female entrepreneurs. (B) is outside the scope of the passage, since the text never even mentions male entrepreneurs. (D) is wrong because the author describes "female entrepreneurship" without advocating any particular official actions to "facilitate" it. Finally, (E) distorts information in the first paragraph, which mentions that women have difficulty reaching senior positions in business. However, the author never claims that female entrepreneurship is opposed by the business world; certainly, this is not a main idea of the passage.

KAPLAN

3.   C

Paying close attention to terms can sometimes make it easy to relocate details. According to the second paragraph, innovators are very committed to their work and start their own businesses to fulfill their ambitions—sentiments that often clash with conventional gender roles. Radicals, though they also reject traditional female roles, start businesses not for profit but primarily to advance general female interests. The choice that gets at this distinction is (C): innovators work primarily for personal and financial success but radicals do not. (A) and (B) ascribe the motives of radicals to innovators, while (D) and (E) do the precise opposite, attributing innovator qualities to radicals.

4.   D

This is yet another detail question, so, again, the answer is right there in the text. Conventionals, according to the passage, are committed to both entrepreneurship and traditional female roles. They are not motivated by resentment about limited careers, and tend to be people who have "moved in and out of the labor market." These facts contradict (A), (B), and (E), while political values (C) are never even mentioned. However, (D), irregular participation in the labor market, is a nice paraphrase of "in and out of the labor market."

5.   E

Since the author quotes Goffee and Scase at considerable length and without criticism, it may be assumed that she thinks that they have something significant to say about women in business. That makes (E) the correct answer. (A) and (B) can be eliminated because the author never presents the work of Goffee and Scase as "narrow" or "unfinished." The other two choices are inaccurate as well. (D) implies that Goffee and Scase oppose the views expressed in the first paragraph, whereas the author presents their ideas as a logical complement. Notice how (C), like wrong answers from previous questions, exaggerates the "male versus female" issue—an issue that never rated more than a brief mention in the passage.

6.   A

The correct answer to this "all/EXCEPT" question either will not be mentioned at all in the passage or will refer to something in the wrong part of the passage. This question concerns Goffee and Scase, who are featured in the second

paragraph. Since the only mention of minorities is in the first paragraph, (A) is correct: The work of Goffee and Scase pertains to women, not minorities. The remaining four choices are all supported by the research of Goffee and Scase: "non-monetary rewards," (B), for domestics; "political advances," (C), for radicals; "access . . . to goals," (D); and "curtails the importance of the conventional female role," (E), for innovators.

7.   B

First look at the distinction at issue. You've already examined it in question 3, where it was noted that innovators want personal success while radicals want to further the interests of women in general. Thus, you're looking for an answer that denies this difference in motivation. You can eliminate (C), which plays on information in the first paragraph, and applies to many women in business. Choice (D) is also poor, because it applies to conventionals, not the two categories mentioned. (A) is mentioned in regard to innovators, but you can get rid of it because it does not address the difference between personal and political motivation. (B) and (E) address this distinction, but (B) is stronger because it directly states that few women are in business to advance a political agenda. This does deny the main difference between the two groups. (E) is fuzzier— even if most women don't feel discriminated against, they may still have distinctly different goals.

PASSAGE 2—BAADE

Topic and Scope: Baade's star observations; specifically, his system for classifying stars.

Purpose and Main Idea: The author's purpose is to describe Baade's star classification scheme and the evidence behind it. Since this is a descriptive passage, the author doesn't offer a specific main point of his own.

Paragraph Structure: The first paragraph introduces Baade's scheme by differentiating Population I and II stars. The second paragraph picks up on this contrast, distinguishing the two groups by age. The third and fourth paragraphs provide evidence in support of the notion that Population II stars are older: first, the more frequent occurrence of red giants in this population and, second, the composition of red giants themselves. The last paragraph indicates that, although Baade's basic insights are still considered valid, his two star categories have now been expanded to five.

8. B

If you put the purpose of the passage into your own words, you should have come up with something like "describe Baade's star categories and show how evidence supports them." (B) contains these ideas, though in more general terms.

Remember that the correct response to a global question must cover everything in the passage. (A) ignores the first and last paragraphs, which are not concerned with star ages. (C) focuses only on Population II stars, while the passage clearly differentiates between Population I and II stars. No theories of stellar evolution are presented, so (D) is wrong. (E) might have been tempting because it focuses on Baade, but it does so without mentioning his star categories, which are the main focus of the passage; (E) would be appropriate for a more general and biographical passage than this one.

9. C

"According to the passage" indicates a detail question, so the correct answer is to be found in the text itself. Population I stars are discussed in the first two paragraphs: They are bright (brighter than Population II stars), they are hot (up to 30,000 degrees Kelvin), the brightest among them are blue, they are young, and they occur *in* the arms of spiral galaxies. Since this is an "all/EXCEPT" question, the correct answer cannot be one of these facts. This eliminates (A), (B), (D), and (E). That leaves (C), which is indeed correct, because it is Population II stars that are found *between* the arms of spiral galaxies.

10. A

This development is discussed in the third paragraph. "When the helium core comprises about one-tenth of a star's mass, the star expands and its surface cools." (A) paraphrases this development. Notice that (B), (C), and (D) come from either too far along in the third paragraph or from the fourth paragraph. Choice (E), logical as it may appear, is never mentioned at all.

11. B

According to the passage, red giants occur primarily among Population II stars, and they are older, cooler, dimmer,

and redder than Population I stars. Their hydrogen has mostly changed to helium, and they are poorer in heavier elements than other stars. Option I is not a valid inference because of the word "all." The author says at the end of the third paragraph that "most," but not "all," red giants are in Population II. (B), therefore, must be the correct choice. Option II is supported by information in the third paragraph. Option III, on the other hand, is another absolute assertion that the passage doesn't support; the passage says that Population I red giants have "more abundant" heavy elements than Population II red giants. They are not all alike, nor do we know anything about a "low percentage."

12. D

Remember to look for the choice that is *not* supported by information in the passage. (A) appears nearly verbatim at the end of the third paragraph. (B) and (E), which get at the same point, constitute the principal focus of the fourth paragraph. (C)'s point is made several times in the passage. (D), however, looks different immediately. Elliptical galaxies are mentioned only once—at the end of the first paragraph—where it's stated that older Population II stars are found in them. But these stars are found in spiral galaxies as well, so it can't be concluded that elliptical galaxies are older than spiral galaxies. (D), therefore, is correct.

PASSAGE 3—CORAL REEFS

Topic and Scope: Coral reefs; specifically, the renewability, transformation, and composition and environment of coral reefs.

Purpose and Main Idea: The author's purpose is to discuss several aspects of coral reefs. Since this is a descriptive passage rather than an argumentative passage, the author makes no specific point.

Paragraph Structure: The first paragraph talks about the renewability of coral reefs. The second paragraph discusses their transformation, summarizing two theories on this issue. And the third paragraph describes the composition of coral reefs and the environment in which they can exist.

13. D

The third paragraph mentions that coral reefs are made up of many different creatures, so option I is part of the answer. Therefore, you can eliminate (A) and (B). Option II is contradicted by the same paragraph, which says that reefs can flourish only in a very specific environment because the algae have very specific needs. Thus, since option II isn't part of the answer, you can eliminate (C) and (E) as well. So (D), I and III only, must be correct. Checking option III just to be sure, it can be found in the first paragraph.

14. C

The answer to this question appears in the first paragraph. The paragraph's next-to-last sentence states that "All of this accounts for . . . renewability . . . despite . . . erosion." Thus, the answer must appear in the previous sentences. These sentences discuss the symbiotic relationship between coral and algae, so the correct answer is (C). (A) might have been tempting because the sentence before "All of this accounts . . ." refers to algae, but the focus of the first paragraph is on symbiosis, so the correct answer must include both coral and algae. (B) distorts the logic of the passage—oxygen contributes to renewability; "despite" is not appropriate here. (D) and (E) come from the wrong part of the passage—from later paragraphs that don't deal with the issue of erosion.

15. A

Darwin is discussed in the second paragraph of the passage. This paragraph mentions his theory of reef transformation: the theory of gradual submergence of volcanic islands. That makes (A) correct. (B), (C), and (D) are *au contraire* choices. (E) is outside the scope of the passage; the text does not address the question of what parts of the reef most interested Darwin.

16. C

The relationships in (D), (A), and (E) are discussed in the third, fourth, and fifth sentences of the first paragraph, respectively. (B) is mentioned in the second paragraph. (C), however, connects items that are not associated with each other in the passage. Volcanic rock is discussed in the second paragraph, while life at reefs is brought up in the third.

17. C

(A) is tricky because it tries to get you to look at the third paragraph and see "10 percent." This percentage, however, refers to a particular type of reef life form; no

percentage is given for reef-building coral worldwide. (B) appears promising since sea level and reefs appear in the second paragraph, but the mechanism by which sea level contributes to reef-building is never explained. (C), though, looks good; the second-to-last sentence provides considerable detail about where reefs can form. Checking the last two choices, (D) can be eliminated because the author specifies in the last sentence of the first paragraph that the answer to this question is unknown. Likewise, (E), the transformation of reefs, is never resolved. Two theories are presented and the author leans towards one of them, but never gives a definitive answer.

18. D

It might seem that the author would agree with statement (D), since the term "coral reef" is described in lines 38–39 as "something of a misnomer" (rather misleading, that is). But the fact a term is a misnomer doesn't necessarily mean that people need to stop using it. While the author calls the term a misnomer because of the large variety of life forms in a reef community, there is never any reason to believe the author wants to change it.

CRITICAL REASONING PRACTICE SET ONE

Time: 25 Minutes/16 Questions

Directions: For each question in this section, select the best of the answer choices given.

1. One problem with labor unions today is that their top staffs consist of college-trained lawyers, economists, and labor relations experts who cannot understand the concerns of real workers. One goal of union reform movements should be to build staffs out of workers who have come up from the ranks of the industry involved.

   The argument above depends primarily on which of the following assumptions?

   (A) Higher education lessens people's identification with their class background.

   (B) Union staffs should include more people with firsthand industrial supervisory experience.

   (C) People who have worked in a given industry can understand the concerns of workers in that industry.

   (D) Most labor unions today do not fairly represent workers' interests.

   (E) A goal of union reform movements should be to make unions more democratic.

2. Opening a plant in war-torn Country X is not inadvisable, despite what critics of the plan may say. Ten years ago we opened our plant in Country Y in the middle of a revolution; that plant has been generating substantial profits ever since.

   Which of the following is the author of the argument above most reasonably intending the reader to conclude?

   (A) Wars are profitable for the author's particular business.

   (B) Country X is a more politically stable nation than is Country Y.

   (C) Critics of the proposed plant in Country X are likely to be biased.

   (D) The proposed plant in Country X will generate profits in spite of its present war.

   (E) The proposed plant in Country X will be more successful than the plant in Country Y.

3. Since the deregulation of the air travel industry in the late 1970s, air fares have been relatively low and the number of passenger miles flown has been increasing. In recent months, however, air fares have risen but the number of passenger miles flown is still going up.

   Which of the following can most reasonably be inferred from the statements above?

   (A) The cost of air travel does not affect the number of passenger miles flown.

   (B) People are now flying to destinations that they formerly reached by train or by other modes of transportation.

   (C) Factors other than low air fares must be contributing to the rise in the number of passenger miles flown.

   (D) Takeovers in the deregulated air travel industry have been responsible for the rise in air fares.

   (E) Air fares can climb even higher without causing a drop in the number of passenger miles flown.

KAPLAN

4. One Zydol capsule contains twice the pain reliever found in regular aspirin. A consumer will have to take two aspirin in order to get the relief provided by one Zydol. And since a bottle of Zydol costs the same as a bottle of regular aspirin, consumers can be expected to switch to Zydol.

Which of the following, if true, would most weaken the argument that consumers will be discontinuing the use of regular aspirin and switching to Zydol?

   (A) A regular bottle of aspirin contains more than twice as many capsules as does a bottle of Zydol.

   (B) The pain reliever in Zydol is essentially the same pain reliever found in regular aspirin.

   (C) Some headache sufferers experience a brief period of dizziness shortly after taking Zydol but not after taking regular aspirin.

   (D) Neither regular aspirin nor Zydol is as effective in the relief of serious pain as are drugs available only by prescription.

   (E) A Zydol capsule is twice as large as the average aspirin.

5. At a certain college, graduate teaching assistants conduct discussion sections but have no input into grading. It has been suggested that graduate assistants be given some grading responsibility, but many undergraduates oppose that proposal. They argue that if grades are assigned by graduate assistants, regular full-time faculty will devote less time and attention to undergraduate work.

The information in the passage above answers which one of the following questions?

   (A) Are grades assigned by graduate teaching assistants inherently as fair as those given by regular faculty?

   (B) Are some undergraduates in favor of maintaining the full-time faculty's interest in their schoolwork?

   (C) May regular full-time faculty conduct discussion sections at the college?

   (D) Does graduate student contact with undergraduates' work make the grades assigned by regular faculty less valid?

   (E) Are regular faculty members in favor of giving graduate assistants some teaching responsibility?

6. Air travel is becoming increasingly more dangerous. In the last year there have been seven major collisions resulting in over 700 deaths, more deaths than in any previous year.

Which statement, if true, would most weaken the argument above?

   (A) Since the volume of air traffic has been increasing all the time, an increase in the number of deaths due to collisions does not necessarily mean greater danger.

   (B) The increase in collisions can be explained by statistical coincidence, hijackings, and unusual weather.

   (C) Mortality per passenger mile is lower for air travel than for any kind of surface transportation.

   (D) The increase in deaths due to collision in air travel has proceeded at a rate identical to that for deaths in all other major forms of transportation.

   (E) Last year the average number of passengers per flown plane was significantly lower than that of previous years.

7. According to a recent study, attending a single-sex high school aids an adolescent's physical growth. Cited as evidence is the finding that during the first two years of high school, the average boy in an all-boys school grew five inches, and the average girl in an all-girls school grew four inches.

The answer to which of the following questions is needed in order to evaluate the reasoning presented in the study?

   (A) Why was it that the first two years of high school were chosen as the focus of the study?

   (B) Did some of the boys in the study grow less than five inches while they were in high school?

   (C) How much do the average male student and the average female student in a co-educational school grow during their first two years of high school?

   (D) Did the girls in the study have as nutritious a diet as the boys during the time the study was being conducted?

   (E) What was the average height of the boys and the average height of the girls upon entering high school?

8. Although most people know that exercise is good for the body, few realize the extent to which it is valuable to the mind. The blood circulates more rapidly after physical exertion, thus allowing all of the body's organs to operate more efficiently. This increased activity enables the brain to receive more oxygen, thereby creating a higher capacity for concentration.

    The main point in the argument above is that

    (A) the greater the amount of oxygen the brain receives, the better the brain functions.

    (B) exercise is a mental, as well as physical, activity.

    (C) exercise helps the brain more than it does the rest of the body.

    (D) people can greatly improve their powers of concentration by exercising more often.

    (E) exercise serves more than one purpose.

9. Ernesto: Sales of VCRs—videocassette recorders—will decline in the next few years because the saturation level among U.S. households has virtually been reached.

    Milton: Every year a greater number of popular feature films is released on cassette—at least six per month. Clearly VCR sales will remain constant, if not rise.

    Which of the following is the best logical evaluation of Milton's response to Ernesto's argument?

    (A) He cites evidence that, if true, disproves the evidence cited by Ernesto in drawing his conclusion.

    (B) He points out a gap in the logic followed by Ernesto in drawing his conclusion.

    (C) He cites an issue ignored by Ernesto and that outweighs the issues raised by Ernesto.

    (D) He does not speak to Ernesto's point because he fails to raise the issue of whether VCR sales may be linked to sales of other leisure-related products.

    (E) He fails to respond to Ernesto's argument because he assumes that nothing will significantly retard the sale of VCRs, which was the issue that Ernesto raised.

10. Archaeologists have discovered various paintings on the walls and ceiling of a Chinese cave whose entrance was blocked by a volcanic eruption in the 25th century B.C. and only recently cleared by an earthquake. Since the paintings depict warriors using Type C bronze weapons, these archaeologists have concluded that Type C bronze weapons were already widely used in this area by 2500 B.C., far earlier than was previously believed.

    Which of the following pieces of additional evidence would most seriously weaken the archaeologists' conclusion?

    (A) Another entrance to the cave remained clear until a second volcanic eruption 1,000 years after the first.

    (B) Archaeologists have evidence that Type C bronze weapons were in wide use in areas of present-day India as early as 2500 B.C.

    (C) Alternative methods of dating place the time of the volcanic eruption somewhat earlier, at around 3000 B.C.

    (D) Most experts believe that Type C bronze weapons were not in use anywhere in present-day China until 2000 B.C.

    (E) The paintings were very faded when the archaeologists found them, making identification of the depicted weapons difficult.

KAPLAN)

11. Considering the current economy, the introduction of a new brand of cereal is unlikely to expand total sales of cereal, but rather will just cause some existing buyers of cereal to switch brands. So it makes no sense for the Coolidge Corporation to introduce another brand of cereal, since they will only hurt sales of the brands of cereal they already produce.

    Which of the following, if true, would most seriously weaken the argument above?

    (A) Total sales of cereal will increase as the total population increases.

    (B) Many new brands of cereal sell extremely well for the first year of their existence.

    (C) Coolidge Corporation currently produces fewer brands of cereal than its competitors do.

    (D) Some cereal buyers regularly switch from brand to brand, even when no new brands have been introduced.

    (E) Research indicates that the new brand will attract more buyers of competitors' cereals than buyers of other Coolidge brands.

12. A public health official reported that 60 percent of the children at summer school have never had the measles or chicken pox, and that of this 60 percent not one child has ever been observed to eat the cheese served in the school lunches. From this he concluded that children who abstain from cheese products protect themselves from most childhood disease.

    Each of the following, if true, would strengthen the official's argument EXCEPT:

    (A) Medically speaking, whatever serves to inhibit measles and chicken pox will generally inhibit the entire spectrum of childhood diseases.

    (B) The observations the official carried out were extremely accurate, and all those observed to abstain from cheese at school did, in fact, abstain.

    (C) The children's eating habits are the same at school as anywhere else, and those who abstain from cheese products at school do so in general.

    (D) Recent research has pointed to a deficiency in cheese products as one of the major causes of measles and chicken pox infections.

    (E) Most cheeses and cheese products harbor bacteria that are known to be causative agents for many childhood diseases, such as measles and chicken pox.

13. A confidential survey revealed that 75 percent of the employees of Company P are dissatisfied with their jobs. However, an investigation into working conditions at the company showed nothing uncommonly bad. Therefore, Company P's consulting firm concluded that the employees' dissatisfaction must result from an unusually high incidence of psychological problems on their part.

    Each of the following, if true, casts doubt on the consulting firm's conclusion *EXCEPT:*

    (A) In the investigation of working conditions, no account was taken of the fact that for the past year many Company P employees worked on a joint venture with Company O, at Company O's facilities.

    (B) Workers in many companies are dissatisfied although there are no apparent problems with their working conditions.

    (C) The consulting firm's conception of what constitutes uncommonly bad working conditions is not identical to that of Company P's employees.

    (D) The reasons given by Company P's employees for their dissatisfaction varied greatly from employee to employee.

    (E) A battery of tests performed on Company P's employees one month ago revealed no significant psychological stresses or problems.

14. Director: Our engineers are considering two different sites—one on the Abaco River and one on the Bornos River—for a hydroelectric plant. Although we have the technical expertise to build roughly the same plant in either place, producing roughly the same amount of electricity per hour, building the plant on the Abaco site will cost over twice as much money. With our budget currently in deficit, we should build the dam at the Bornos site.

    Which of the following, if true, best explains the difference in building costs for the two proposed dam sites?

    (A) Many farms along the lower Bornos River valley would benefit from the controlled flow of water a dam would make possible.

    (B) The Abaco site is in an inaccessible area, requiring the building of new roads and the importation of laborers.

    (C) The Bornos site is near a large city whose residents could use the resulting lake for inexpensive recreation.

    (D) The Abaco site is in an area that contains many endangered species that would be threatened by the new dam.

    (E) The Abaco River has a relatively low volume of flow, making it impossible to expand an Abaco plant to meet future electricity needs.

KAPLAN

15. In 1988, 50 people with emotional disturbances underwent hypnosis to be cured of their mood swings. A follow-up survey in 1993 revealed that 5 had fairly stable emotional conditions at the time of the survey. These 5 subjects can therefore serve as models of the types of people for whom hypnosis is likely to be successful.

    Which of the following, if true, casts the most doubt on the suitability of those five subjects as models in the sense described?

    (A) The five subjects have very different personalities and backgrounds.

    (B) Since 1988, the five subjects have experienced dramatic mood swings interspersed with periods of relative stability.

    (C) Those people who were still suffering from unstable emotional conditions at the time of the 1993 survey had shown no improvement since 1988.

    (D) Many psychologists are less concerned about a patient's mood swings than about the patient's willingness to express his or her problems and fears.

    (E) The emotional condition of most of the 45 subjects who were still unstable at the time of the 1993 survey had actually worsened since 1988.

16. The cause of the peculiar columnar growth pattern displayed by junipers growing near burning underground veins of lignite coal has never been convincingly explained. Until recently, the accepted theory posited that the abundance of carbon monoxide in the local atmosphere caused the columnar growth. However, a new theory holds that the cause is the persistent heat present near these underground fires that, while not intense enough to inflame the trees, can nonetheless change their normal growth pattern.

    The existence of which of the following would provide the strongest support for the new theory?

    (A) A columnar juniper growing in an atmosphere of intense heat and an absence of carbon monoxide

    (B) A normal juniper growing in an atmosphere of intense heat and an absence of carbon monoxide

    (C) A columnar juniper growing in an atmosphere of normal heat and a high concentration of carbon monoxide

    (D) A normal juniper growing in an atmosphere of intense heat and a high concentration of carbon monoxide

    (E) A columnar juniper growing in an atmosphere of intense heat and a high concentration of carbon monoxide

ANSWERS AND EXPLANATIONS

1. C
2. D
3. C
4. A
5. B
6. A
7. C
8. E
9. E
10. A
11. E
12. D
13. D
14. B
15. B
16. A

1. C

The Conclusion: Union reform movements should build staffs out of workers who have come up the ranks.

The Evidence: Union movements are currently suffering from a problem: Their staffs consist of college-educated professional types who don't understand the concerns of the worker.

If the author believes that hiring up-from-the-ranks workers (an idea introduced in the conclusion) will cure that problem, he must be assuming that these former workers do understand workers' real concerns.

There's no need to assume that higher education lessens people's identification with their class background, (A), since the author hasn't said that the lawyers, economists, and experts who don't understand workers come from a working-class background. Supervisory experience, (B), isn't the same as coming up through the ranks. Labor unions having problems, which the author admits, isn't the same as (D), most of them unfairly representing workers' interests. That's an overstatement. "Democratic," (E), is a new term, and one the argument doesn't need.

2. D

The Conclusion: None is stated, but as the question stem alerts us, one is implied.

The Evidence: A plant opened in Country Y during a revolution ten years ago has always generated substantial profits.

The author draws an analogy between the two plants. Since the one in Country Y has made money, so too, she implies, will the one in Country X.

The author's point is that the plant can be successful despite the war, (A), not that the plant will be successful because of the war. The author presents the two countries as similar, so she's not arguing that (B), one is more stable than the other. The author is attacking her opponents' argument, but not (C), their motives. She makes no judgment, (E), as to which plant will be more successful. Remember, comparing and contrasting things that are considered equivalent in the stimulus is a common wrong answer type for inference questions.

3. C

The Conclusion: There is none stated. One is implied, though, and we're to locate it among the answer choices.

The Evidence: Since deregulation, low air fares have correlated with increased miles flown. Recently, prices have risen, but the number of passenger miles flown is still increasing.

The passage begins with a correlation and then breaks it in the next sentence. What can you infer from this? Not very much, you may have thought, and you'd be right. The key to this question is not drawing an unwarranted sweeping conclusion from the evidence. What you can safely conclude is that the air fare doesn't, by itself, determine the amount of air travel.

That air fares don't have any effect on air travel, so (A) is too strong. We can't infer why passenger-miles flown have increased, (B); it might be at the expense of other forms of transportation, but it might not be. The author merely states that the air fares have risen recently, but never mentions a cause, (D), like "takeovers." So far, the recent rise in air fares hasn't reduced passenger miles flown, but that doesn't mean that a further increase won't, (E).

4.   A

The Conclusion: Consumers can be expected to switch to Zydol.

The Evidence: Although one has to take two aspirins to get the relief provided by one Zydol, nevertheless a bottle of Zydol costs the same as a bottle of aspirin.

The implication is that Zydol is more cost-effective than aspirin: You get a much better bargain with a bottle of Zydol. But if the aspirin bottle contains more than twice as many tablets as the Zydol bottle, then it's the aspirin bottle that gives you more pain reliever for your money.

The argument concerns which is the better bargain, not which is the better pain reliever. Thus, it doesn't matter (B) that the ingredient is the same. (C) points to some consumers who won't want Zydol. Perhaps, but one, these may be very few, and two, this doesn't attack the author's reasoning, which is based on cost. Pain sufferers who don't have a doctor's prescription are left with the same choice between Zydol and aspirin, so (D) doesn't weaken Zydol's case against aspirin. Even if you make an unwarranted leap and assume (E), that there may be fewer of the large Zydol pills per bottle, choice (A) clearly does a better job of arguing along this line.

5.   B

The Undergraduates' Conclusion: If grades are assigned by graduate assistants, regular full-time faculty will devote less time to undergraduate work.

Their Evidence: There really isn't any; just the idea that giving grading responsibilities to graduate students will somehow move regular full-time faculty away from the undergraduates' work.

The only thing to do is go through the choices to see which question we can answer. Since the undergraduates are against the proposal, it's safe to conclude that they want the full-time faculty to stay interested in their work. We have no information about the fairness of graduate assistants' grades, (A). All we know about the discussion sections, (C), is that graduate assistants now hold them; we aren't told whether or not full-time faculty may hold them. (D) asks about the validity of the faculty's grades. We know that some people have proposed that graduate assistants be given some grading responsibility, but that doesn't imply (D), that they believe the faculty's grades have been made less valid by the graduate students' "contact" with undergraduates. And we're told absolutely nothing about (E), the faculty's opinion of the proposal.

6.   A

The Conclusion: Air travel is becoming more dangerous.

The Evidence: In the last year, there have been seven collisions and over 700 deaths, the highest number of deaths ever.

We want something that suggests that the increase in fatalities doesn't prove an increase in danger. If more and more people are traveling by airplane, an increase in the number of deaths doesn't prove that air travel is becoming more dangerous. The question of how dangerous air travel is can't be answered unless we know the proportion, not the number, of passengers who get killed.

The author's contention isn't undermined by (B), the reasons for the lack of safety. Pointing out more dangerous methods of transportation, (C) doesn't deny that the danger of air travel is increasing. Likewise, the fact that other forms of transportation are also getting more dangerous, (D), doesn't dent the author's claim. Fewer passengers per place, (E), means more collisions, but we already know how many collisions there were.

7. C

The Conclusion: Attending a single-sex high school promotes growth.

The Evidence: During the first two years, the average student in an all-boys school grew five inches and the average girl in an all-girls school grew four inches.

The question stem tells you that something has been left out of the argument. The conclusion compares single-sex schools to coed schools, but the evidence only cites data from single-sex schools. Until we know how much the average student grows in co-educational schools, we have no evidence that the growth in single-sex schools is greater.

Even if we knew the answer to (A), we'd still have no evidence from the coed schools. (B) is a rather silly question; we're dealing with average growth, so we'd expect some boys to grow more than the average and some less. The reasons for the growth difference between boys and girls, (D), isn't relevant to the growth differences between coed and single-sex schools. Since the study is only interested in how much students grow during the first two years of high school, it's irrelevant how tall they are to start with, (E).

8. E

The Conclusion: Exercise is good for the mind as well as for the body.

The Evidence: Exercise increases the speed at which blood circulates, allowing the brain to receive more oxygen and thus concentrate better.

The main point is the conclusion, that exercise is good for the mind as well as the body. More generally, exercise serves more than one purpose.

(A) goes out on a limb; the author's point is the beneficial effects of exercise, not the unlimited benefits of oxygen. While exercise aids mental activity, it's not (B), a mental activity as such. Whether exercise aids the brain more or less than the rest of the body, (C), isn't discussed. This is a classic wrong answer type: the choice that compares two items the stimulus treats equally. While the author argues that exercise is beneficial to the mind, "greatly improving" concentration, (D), is an overstatement.

9. E

Ernesto's Conclusion: VCR sales will decline.

Ernesto's Evidence: The saturation level for households has been reached.

Milton's Conclusion: VCR sales won't decline.

Milton's Evidence: More and more films are released on videotape.

Milton simply ignores Ernesto's argument that the saturation point has been reached for VCRs. He concentrates on the new cassettes coming out, but the availability of new cassettes doesn't mean people need to buy or will buy more recorders. Milton ignores the relevant issue of saturation raised by Ernesto, and simply assumes that sales of VCRs will continue as before.

Milton's evidence doesn't disprove Ernesto's evidence, (A). The videos appearing each year have nothing to do with whether the saturation point in VCR ownership has been reached. "Finding a gap," (B), in an argument means demonstrating that the evidence doesn't lead to the conclusion; Milton merely brings up some irrelevant information that has nothing to do with Ernesto's reasoning. Milton does cite an issue that Ernesto ignored, (C), but the claim that this issue "outweighs" the issue of saturation is unsupported. Milton does fail to speak to Ernesto's point, (D), but not for the bizarre reason given here. Ernesto has absolutely nothing to say about "other leisure-related products" because there's no reason for Milton to raise this issue.

10. A

The Conclusion: People must already have been using Type C weapons in this area by 2500 B.C.

The Evidence: Depictions of the weapons exist on the walls of a cave that was sealed off in 2500 B.C.

We need to show that the paintings either don't depict weapons that were in use or that the paintings were made after 2500 B.C. The archaeologists are assuming that there was only one entrance to the cave. If there's another entrance to the cave that was only sealed much later, then people could have entered the cave and made the paintings long after the first entrance was sealed.

If anything, the existence of the weapons in India, (B), might be considered to strengthen the argument, since it shows Type C weapons were in existence as early as 2500 B.C. Pushing the date of the eruption back, (C), also strengthens the argument by making it likely that the paintings were done even earlier than claimed. Without some evidence to back it up, the opinion of the experts, (D), isn't worth much. That identification was difficult, (E), is not the same as its being uncertain or controversial.

KAPLAN

11. E

The Conclusion: Introducing a new cereal will only hurt the brands Coolidge already produces, so Coolidge shouldn't introduce another brand of cereal.

The Evidence: The introduction of a new brand of cereal doesn't increase the total number of cereal buyers, but only encourages those who already buy cereal to switch brands.

There's an assumption here: That the new brand will only attract those who currently buy other brands of Coolidge's cereal. If the new brand steals buyers from competitors' cereals, then it will help Coolidge by adding to its total sales.

Even if the population does increase and total cereal sales with it, (A), a new brand might still hurt the sales of Coolidge's established cereals. The new cereal may sell well, (B), but if that just means it's stealing lots of buyers from other Coolidge cereals, what good is it? The fact that Coolidge has only a few brands, (C), doesn't make it likely that a new cereal brand would steal buyers from competitors' brands rather than from other Coolidge brands. Neither does the fact that some brand switching is usual even when a new brand isn't introduced, (D).

12. D

The Conclusion: Not eating cheese protects children from childhood diseases.

The Evidence: All the children at summer school who have never had measles or chicken pox have also never eaten the cheese served in the school lunches.

The author deduces a causal relationship: Not eating cheese leads to protection from childhood diseases. I hope you saw that this has numerous holes. Four of the choices help to fill those holes; the fifth does not. That fifth choice is (D). If research shows that abstaining from cheese products is a major cause of some childhood diseases, then the health official's claim that children can protect themselves from disease by not eating cheese is flat-out wrong.

It's important that the author be able (A) to connect measles and chicken pox (in the evidence) to other childhood diseases. Also necessary is that the observations be accurate, (B), and the students' behavior at home mirror their behavior at school (C). Each of those speaks to the legitimacy of the correlation. Most important, though, is that there really be a causal connection, (E), rather than just a correlation, between cheese eating and childhood illness.

13. D

The Consulting Firm's Conclusion: The employees' dissatisfaction is all in their heads.

Its Evidence: 75 percent of the employees are dissatisfied. An investigation showed no uncommonly bad working conditions.

We need the one choice that doesn't weaken the consulting firm's conclusion; that's a good tip that the conclusion isn't solidly based. The mere fact that the complaints vary doesn't hurt the firm's conclusion that the complaints are based on psychological problems. In fact, it might even strengthen the firm's argument: Every employee has his or her own mental hang-up, so every employee comes up with his or her own irrational complaint.

If many employees had been working at a different company's facilities, (A), then it could be these facilities, not mental problems, that are responsible for the complaints. If the situation in Company P is fairly normal, (B), there's no need for the firm to hypothesize an unusual incidence of psychological problems among the workforce. If the firm's definition of uncommonly bad conditions differs from that of the workers, (C), then the firm may well have overlooked the real causes of employee dissatisfaction. And if a battery of tests, (E), showed no significant psychological problems, then the very cause cited by the firm is attacked.

14. B

The Director's Conclusion: We should build the dam at the Bornos site.

Her Evidence: Although the same plant can produce the same amount of electricity at either site, building at Abaco will cost twice as much money.

Looking at the question stem first here really helps you narrow your focus when reading the stimulus. The only thing you're interested in is why the Abaco site will cost more than twice as much as the Bornos site. The stimulus doesn't give you any hint as to how the sites are different, so you'll have to rely on the correct answer to provide a complete explanation by itself. If the Abaco site is in the middle of nowhere, and requires constructing new roads and importing laborers, then, of course, it's going to be more expensive to build there.

The benefits of the Bornos plant to farms, (A), don't explain its lower cost of construction. Neither do the benefits to nearby city residents, (C). Possible environmental damage caused by a plant built at Abaco, (D), is another reason for building at Bornos, but it's a different reason. The problem or issue of expansion, (E), like the environment, might merit consideration, but it's not a factor in determining the cost of building.

15. B

The Conclusion: These five people can serve as models for the type of person who can be helped by hypnosis.

The Evidence: A study showed that these five previously disturbed hypnosis subjects had stable emotional conditions.

The survey only found that at the time of the study the five seemed to be doing okay. Remember, these people were originally suffering from mood swings; maybe the study just caught them on a good day. If that's the case—if since 1988 these people have been experiencing dramatic mood swings and occasional periods of health—then hypnosis hasn't really helped them and they're not good models.

The author presented the people as models of different types of people who can be helped, not as a single model of a single personality type, so they needn't be similar, (A). It doesn't matter that the other 45 people who underwent hypnosis didn't get better (C); the argument is based on and concerns only the 5 who were stable. (E) fails to weaken the argument for the same reason. The concern of many psychologists, (D), is well outside the scope. We need a statement that speaks about hypnosis and these 5 subjects.

16. A

The New Theory's Conclusion: Heat (from the burning coal) causes columnar growth in junipers near burning underground coal veins.

The New Theory's Evidence: None really, except the correlation of columnar growth with these areas with underground fires.

The Old Theory's Conclusion: The abundance of carbon monoxide causes columnar growth.

The Old Theory's Evidence: None really, except the correlation of columnar growth with these areas with high carbon monoxide.

When you scan the choices, you see that each presents a case of the cause with or without the effect or the effect with or without the cause. Since the two theories

are in opposition, weakening the old theory is a way of strengthening the new one. Bearing in mind from the lesson the key issues in a causal argument, we recognize that a case of columnar growth where the cause claimed by the new theory (heat) is present, but the cause claimed by the old theory (carbon monoxide) is absent, strengthens the new theory at the expense of the old.

(B), where we get the new theory's alleged cause (intense heat), without the alleged effect (columnar junipers), is of no help at all. A columnar juniper in an atmosphere with high carbon monoxide but no extra heat, (C), strengthens the old theory. A case with both alleged causes without the expected effect, (D), weakens both theories. Likewise, columnar growth in the presence of both causes, (E), does nothing to promote one theory over the other.

**CRITICAL REASONING PRACTICE
SET TWO**

Time: 25 Minutes/16 Questions

Directions: For each question in this section,
select the best of the answer choices given.

1. Although air pollution was previously thought to
    exist almost exclusively in our nation's cities, the
    recent increase in the number of persons suffering
    from illnesses attributed to excessive air pollution
    leaves us no choice but to conclude that other,
    nonurban areas are now affected.

    Which of the following, if true, would most
    seriously weaken the conclusion of the argument
    above?

    (A) The nation's cities have seen a marked
         decrease in levels of air pollution.

    (B) The nation has experienced a sharp decrease
         in the number of people moving out of its
         cities.

    (C) Illnesses due to air pollution are among
         the least common causes of death to urban
         dwellers.

    (D) Many illnesses previously thought unrelated
         to air pollution are now considered to be
         caused by it.

    (E) As a result of the problems in urban areas,
         nonurban areas have passed strict pollution
         control measures.

2. Statistics show that although consumption of
    low-calorie, alternative sweeteners has gone up in
    each of the past five years, so has the percentage
    of the population that is obese. According to
    sugar manufacturers, this shows that the low-
    calorie, alternative sweeteners are not effective
    weight loss aids.

    Which of the following assertions, if true, would
    most weaken the sugar manufacturers' conclusion?

    (A) Many people who use low-calorie, alterna-
         tive sweeteners eat some foods that are not
         low-calorie.

    (B) Some low-calorie, alternative sweeteners can
         increase the appetite, making a person eat
         more than he or she normally would.

    (C) Many people use low-calorie, alternative
         sweeteners to accompany a well-balanced,
         low-calorie diet.

    (D) Obesity has declined among people who have
         consistently used low-calorie, alternative
         sweeteners.

    (E) The rise in the consumption of low-calorie,
         alternative sweeteners is primarily due to
         an increase in the number of users rather
         than an increase in the amount each user
         consumes.

3. It has long been commonplace in medical literature that the ingestion of drug L, in combination with the application of lotion M, causes the appearance of adverse reaction O. Recently, however, doubts have been cast on the role of lotion M in the appearance of adverse reaction O.

   Which one of the following research findings could most reasonably have created the doubts referred to above?

   (A) The appearance of adverse reaction O following the ingestion of drug L and the application of lotion M

   (B) The absence of adverse reaction O following the ingestion of drug L and the application of lotion M

   (C) The ingestion of drug L and the appearance of adverse reaction O in the absence of lotion M

   (D) The absence of adverse reaction O following the ingestion of drug L without the application of lotion M

   (E) The disappearance of adverse reaction O following the ingestion of drug L and the application of lotion M

4. The candy manufacturer's claim that employee "theft" costs the company thousands of dollars a year in potential sales is greatly overstated. Most of the candy eaten on the job and not paid for is eaten one piece at a time, by workers who would not be willing to buy an entire box of it anyway.

   Which of the following, if true, most weakens the argument above?

   (A) The workers eat only defective candies that could not be sold.

   (B) Candy eaten by employees represents lost potential sales to nonemployees.

   (C) A few workers account for most of the candy that is eaten but not paid for.

   (D) Most of the candies eaten by employees are consumed during the holiday season, when production outputs are at their highest.

   (E) The amount of candy eaten by employees is only a small fraction of the candy sold by the company.

5. U.S. officials complain that the country's trade deficit with Japan is due to the fact that Japan's markets are not open enough to imports and investment. Japanese officials reply that the United States should concentrate on improving its school systems and investing more money in scientific research and worker training.

   It can be inferred from the statements above that the Japanese officials most probably hold which of the following opinions?

   (A) The United States should open its own markets to more imports and investment.

   (B) The trade deficit between the United States and Japan is more the result of poor American industrial performance than Japan's import restrictions.

   (C) The trade deficit between the United States and Japan is a result of Japan's closed markets.

   (D) U.S. school systems foster a mistrust of Japan that prevents U.S. businesspeople from negotiating intelligently with Japan.

   (E) Better education and worker training can help shrink the trade imbalance, but should not be counted on to close the gap entirely.

6. Children who attend private high schools may initially feel that they can succeed without doing the work required, but as they grow older they realize the necessity of serious study. Each year the overwhelming majority of students disciplined for plagiarism and cheating on their exams is found in the freshman class.

The argument above would be most weakened if which of the following were true?

   Ⓐ As they move up in grade, students learn how to cheat without being caught.

   Ⓑ First-time offenders for plagiarism and cheating on exams are not disciplined.

   Ⓒ The proctors for freshman exams are the least vigilant.

   Ⓓ Acts of vandalism are most often committed by members of the sophomore class.

   Ⓔ Public school students are no less likely than private school students to believe that they can succeed in life without working hard.

7. The conflict between an artist's work and the context in which it is placed is a traditional problem in aesthetics. Recent exhibits have given it a new urgency. Too often a painter's canvases have been hung in an improper context because the gallery managers have not understood what the painter envisioned as the work's proper environment.

As an attempt to solve the problem described above, it would be most reasonable to

   Ⓐ bring artists and gallery managers into closer contact, so as to increase the artist's input into the way the exhibit is held

   Ⓑ provide brochures at the exhibit that describe the artist and how he or she intended the exhibit to look

   Ⓒ redesign galleries so that their décor contains nothing that would distract the audience from the works themselves

   Ⓓ provide a uniform environment for all the works in an exhibition so that they appear within the same context

   Ⓔ instruct gallery managers in the fine points of aesthetic theory so that they will be able to tell what, if anything, a painting means

8. To improve the physical fitness of its students, School District 4 instituted a policy whereby students would be given extra credit in physical education for extracurricular athletic activities. School officials call the program a success, since participation in after-school sports has doubled since the program was instituted.

Which of the following, if true, most seriously weakens the claim of the school officials?

   Ⓐ Most students who joined after-school sports did so only to get extra credit.

   Ⓑ Most children who are in poor physical condition cannot be persuaded to join after-school sports by such an incentive program.

   Ⓒ Few students who joined after-school sports during the extra credit program will continue to play the sport after the school year ends.

   Ⓓ Most of the new athletes are students who had never before participated in after-school sports.

   Ⓔ Fitness tests show no significant improvement in the physical condition of students after they join after-school sports.

9. It takes four weeks for a team of five professional window washers working regular full-time hours to properly clean every window of the Empire State Building. The building's owner demands that all the windows always be clean. Yet even if the five washers work consistently throughout their regular work week, they will not be able to finish cleaning all the windows before some windows will again need cleaning.

It can be correctly inferred on the basis of the statements above that which of the following must be true?

- Ⓐ If an Empire State Building window is to be kept clean, it must be cleaned by a professional window cleaner.
- Ⓑ The owner's demand for proper cleaning of all the windows will never be fulfilled.
- Ⓒ If a team of five window washers cleans all the Empire State Building's windows in less than four weeks, some of the windows will not be properly cleaned.
- Ⓓ In order to ensure that all of the Empire State Building's windows are clean, the owner must have his window washers work overtime.
- Ⓔ Some Empire State Building windows must be cleaned more frequently than once every four weeks if they are to be kept clean.

10. Cultural anthropologists who have been observing and interviewing customers in retail stores have announced a definitive theory to explain the effect that in-store product displays have on consumer purchasing behavior.

Which of the following, if true, would be least likely to represent a benefit of the theory to retailers?

- Ⓐ Retailers will be able to eliminate costly product displays that fail to increase sales.
- Ⓑ Retailers will gain insight into how consumers determine whether or not to buy a particular product.
- Ⓒ The new theory will make consumers aware of how product displays influence their purchasing decisions.
- Ⓓ The new theory will determine what types of retail display gimmicks produce a negative reaction in consumers.
- Ⓔ The new theory will explain why consumers often purchase at different stores goods that could be bought at just one store.

11. Archaeologists have recently found, in various grave sites in the Mexican state of Veracruz, small ceramic animals with attached wheels. At first, this find might seem to discredit the belief that the wheel and its uses were unknown in pre-Colombian culture. On reflection, however, it would seem that the discovery actually bears out this belief. To be familiar with these toys and yet not to apply the principle of the wheel to daily tasks such as carting, transportation, and pottery making must indicate a lack of understanding of the wheel and its potential benefits.

    Which of the following best expresses the argument made in the passage above?

    Ⓐ If the pre-Colombian people of Veracruz had understood the principle of the wheel, they would not have attached wheels to ceramic animals.

    Ⓑ If the pre-Colombian people of Veracruz had understood the principle of the wheel, they would have adapted it to everyday use.

    Ⓒ If the pre-Colombian people of Veracruz had uses for the wheel in their everyday lives, they would have adapted the idea of the wheel from the wheeled ceramic figures.

    Ⓓ The pre-Colombian people of Veracruz must have known of the wheel and its uses because they attached wheels to ceramic animals.

    Ⓔ Since the pre-Colombian people of Veracruz did not know of the wheel or its uses, the ceramic animals found in the grave sites must be the remains of later cultures.

12. Doubling the cost of public transportation to compensate for money lost by declining ridership would be disastrous. The greater expense would only further discourage commuters who are already dissatisfied with the poor condition of buses and trains. If the fares are increased, many commuters will choose to drive their cars instead, causing pollution and traffic congestion. As a result, the city will lose money and become even more noisy and smog-filled than it is now.

    Which of the following is an assumption made in advancing the argument above?

    Ⓐ Commuters who decide to drive instead of using public transportation will not share rides with one another.

    Ⓑ Commuters will not park their cars in garages and thereby spend more money than they would by using buses or trains.

    Ⓒ The condition of public transportation will not improve as a result of the fare increase.

    Ⓓ Commuters who use their own cars currently outnumber those who use buses and trains.

    Ⓔ A significant number of people who now use public transportation have cars or can easily obtain them.

13. The cost of transatlantic air fare has nearly doubled over the past five years, yet airlines are doing a booming business. Clearly, people today have more money to spend on vacations than they did five years ago.

    All of the following, if true, would weaken the argument above *EXCEPT:*

    Ⓐ Most people buying transatlantic tickets today use them for business trips, so air fare is refunded by their companies.

    Ⓑ There are fewer airlines in existence today than five years ago.

    Ⓒ People are taking shorter vacations and staying in cheaper hotels than they used to.

    Ⓓ Crossing the Atlantic by ship requires more time than most people can afford.

    Ⓔ Domestic airline flights have seen a steady increase in passengers.

KAPLAN

14. Truck driver: The gasoline tax is too high and it must be lowered. It has been raised every year for the past five years, while other sales taxes have not. If the government persists in unfairly penalizing truck drivers, our increased operating costs will either hurt consumers or put us out of business.

    State official: But your gasoline tax dollars maintain and improve the very roads you depend on. Without those additional revenues, road conditions would deteriorate, costing you and consumers much more in maintenance and repairs.

    If the statements made above are true, the best characterization of the logical relationship between the two arguments is that the state official's response

    Ⓐ points out that the truck driver's proposal will actually worsen the problem it is intended to solve

    Ⓑ is circular, assuming the truth of its conclusion in order to justify its conclusion

    Ⓒ points out that the truck driver is selfish because more people are aided by the gasoline tax than are penalized

    Ⓓ is merely an attempt to excuse the government's policies without providing any justification for those policies

    Ⓔ points to an inherent contradiction between the cause the truck driver cites and the effects the truck driver thinks will follow from the cause

15. Archaeologists recently unearthed a prehistoric statuette, portraying the figure of a woman, that had been carved from a mastodon bone. A team of researchers carefully studied the statuette, which they named the Venus of Orleans. Since it was similar in shape and design to another bone carving, the so-called Venus of Grenoble, they concluded that in all likelihood it was carved at the same time, about 70,000 years ago. Skeptics point out, however, that carbon-14 testing indicates that the recently discovered statuette is only about 50,000 years old.

    Which of the following, if true, would tend most to weaken the force of the skeptics' objection?

    Ⓐ Carbon-14 dating places the age of the Venus of Grenoble at 70,000 years.

    Ⓑ No other, similar, statuettes have been found at the site where the Venus of Orleans was unearthed.

    Ⓒ The carbon-14 dating process is unreliable for objects dating from before 60,000 B.C.

    Ⓓ The carbon-14 dating process has provided unreliable dates for many objects older than 100,000 years.

    Ⓔ Some speculation persists that the Venus of Orleans was carved out of the femur or thigh bone of a prehistoric ox.

16. The study of foreign languages is finally becoming a serious endeavor in U.S. education. The number of American college students enrolled in non-English language courses has increased by 20 percent over the past five years. Spanish, with over 500,000 students, is the most popular; its enrollment has increased by 30 percent. Meanwhile, enrollment in Japanese and Russian has nearly doubled, and now comprises 8 percent of total foreign language study. Clearly, there is now an increased interest in foreign language study. When these students join the workforce, they will enhance not only U.S. businesses' ability to compete internationally, but also our country's reputation abroad.

The answer to which of the following questions would be LEAST relevant to evaluating the above claims?

(A) Do students enrolled in foreign language classes continue their studies long enough to attain competence in those languages?

(B) By what percentage has overall enrollment in U.S. colleges and universities increased over the past five years?

(C) Does a significant number of students of foreign languages go into professions in which the ability to speak other languages is useful?

(D) Has the study of "dead" languages like Latin and Ancient Greek increased at a similar rate to that of modern languages?

(E) How does the percentage increase in foreign language enrollment over the past five years compare to previous increases in enrollment?

ANSWERS AND EXPLANATIONS

1. D
2. D
3. C
4. B
5. B
6. A
7. A
8. E
9. E
10. C
11. B
12. E
13. E
14. A
15. C
16. D

1. D

The Conclusion: Nonurban areas are now affected by air pollution.

The Evidence: An increase in the number of persons suffering from illnesses attributable to air pollution.

If more illnesses are now considered to be caused by air pollution, then it's possible for people who had been sick for what were considered other reasons to account for the increase in the number of people suffering from illnesses caused by air pollution. The general health of the population hasn't necessarily declined, just been reclassified, and so air pollution hasn't necessarily affected nonurban areas. The GMAT test makers are fond of this trick.

(A), "decreased air pollution in the cities," doesn't weaken an argument that says it's rising outside cities. (B) says fewer people are moving out of cities, and this has no clear effect. The new sufferers from air pollution would be nonurban, so the idea that not many urban dwellers die from air pollution, (C), won't weaken the argument. Antipollution measures, (E), are irrelevant. There could still be lots of pollution in nonurban areas, pollution that floated out from urban areas, for example.

2. D

The Sugar Manufacturers' Conclusion: Low-calorie sweeteners aren't effective in helping people lose weight.

The Sugar Manufacturers' Evidence: Statistics show that although the consumption of these sweeteners has gone up, so has the percentage of obese people.

The manufacturers assume that the sweeteners are in some way responsible for the public's failure to lose weight. But if the consumers of the sweeteners aren't becoming more obese, then, despite the increase in the percentage of the public that is overweight, those using alternative sweeteners actually lost weight.

Another possible cause for weight gain, (A), weakens the argument, but it doesn't go as far as (D), which says that those who use the sweeteners have actually lost weight. (B) strengthens the manufacturers' claim, saying that some low-calorie sweeteners actually increase appetite. (C) tells us nothing about how effective low-calorie sweeteners may or may not be. And the sugar manufacturers' claim doesn't depend on an increase in the amount each user consumes, (E), rather than an increase in the number of users.

3. C

The Conclusion: There are new doubts as to the role of lotion M in the appearance of reaction O.

The Evidence: This is what we're looking for: What caused the doubts?

In (C), lotion M is absent, yet O has taken place with drug L. O in the absence of M suggests that M is superfluous and casts the doubt we need.

(A) has drug L plus lotion M resulting in reaction O, just as was always thought. (B), in which O is absent despite the use of L and M, and (E), in which reaction O goes away following the use of L and M, each cast doubt on the whole commonplace, not just lotion M. (D), in which L doesn't cause O in the absence of M, would cast doubt on the role of L, and lend credence to the idea that M causes O. Watch out for *au contraire* choices on Strengthen/Weaken questions!

4. B

The Conclusion: Candy manufacturers don't really lose thousands every year in potential sales through workers eating candy.

The Evidence: Workers eat the candy one piece at a time and wouldn't buy a whole box anyway.

The argument as stated assumes that the candy would, if not eaten, only be sold to the people who are eating it—the workers. We can undermine this assumption by pointing out that the candy could easily be sold to other people.

If the workers eat only candy that couldn't be sold, (A), then the manufacturers probably aren't losing potential sales. This is an *au contraire* choice. It doesn't matter how many workers are eating the candy, (C); what's important is how much is disappearing and whether it could be sold if it weren't being eaten. The issue of when the candy is eaten, (D), is irrelevant to whether the company is losing potential sales. Even if the eaten candy is a small fraction of the candy sold, (E), it could still represent a substantial loss of potential sales money.

5. B

The Conclusion: We need to infer a conclusion from the evidence provided.

The Evidence: The Japanese respond to a claim that their closed markets are responsible for the trade deficit with the claim that the United States needs to improve schools and to spend more money on research and training.

Inferably, the Japanese think that changes the United States should make would help shrink the deficit. So they likely believe the deficit exists because the U.S. industrial performance—a function of things like education, research, and training—is poor.

The Japanese don't address U.S. markets, (A); they focus on U.S. industrial performance. It is the U.S. officials' opinion, (C), that the deficit results from Japanese protectionism. The Japanese don't say what specifically is wrong with U.S. schools, (D), just that they need improvement. Neither have they implied, (E), that something in addition to improving industrial performance is necessary.

6. A

The Conclusion: Private high school kids start out willing to let academics "slide," but they learn the value of serious study as the years go by.

The Evidence: Most kids caught and punished for cheating are freshmen.

The assumption is that upperclassmen don't cheat as much, but if they learn how to cheat without getting caught, the link between evidence and conclusion is severed.

A policy of going easy on first offenders, (B), has no impact on the logic—the statistics remain the same. (C) could somewhat weaken the argument by implying that upperclassmen don't cheat as much as freshmen because upper-class proctors are more vigilant, but we're starting to argue on behalf of the choice. It could also strengthen the argument by implying that a higher percentage of upperclassmen who cheat get caught. Vandalism (D) has nothing to do with the matter at hand. Equally irrelevant is (E)'s distinction between private and public school students' attitudes towards life.

7. A

The Conclusion: Paintings are too often hung in inappropriate contexts.

The Evidence: (actually more of an explanation) Gallery managers don't know what context would be proper.

To solve the problem, we'd want to bring the managers and artists together so that the artist can have a say in how the paintings are hung. This eliminates the gallery managers' ignorance, which is the root cause of the problem.

KAPLAN

(C) and (D) both play with the gallery's décor, but making it uniform or insignificant won't help if the artist has a particular decor in mind. (B)'s suggestion of brochures isn't good enough. Describing the appropriate environment isn't the same as providing it. And there's no reason to assume (E): that if a manager knows what the work means he'll be able to tell what context the painter had in mind.

8. E

The School Officials' Conclusion: A program intended to increase the physical fitness of students has been a great success.

The Evidence: Participation in after-school sports has doubled since the program began.

It's assumed that participation in after-school programs necessarily leads to better physical fitness. Denying this weakens the argument. Maybe the after-school sports are pool and bowling, which provide little physical conditioning.

The students' motivation, (A), is irrelevant; the end result of the program is what's important here. The school officials' claim concerns students in general, not just ones in poor condition, (B), so the program could still be a success even if the truly sickly don't join. How long students take part in after-school sports, (C), doesn't really matter. And (D)'s claim strengthens the argument by making it reasonable that the policy has encouraged the new athletes.

9. E

The Conclusion: Even if the five washers work consistently throughout the regular week, they won't finish cleaning before some windows again need cleaning.

The Evidence: It takes four weeks for the team of five washers to clean every window.

What can we conclude? If any given window can be revisited four weeks later, yet some of them already need cleaning, then some windows won't stay clean if attended to only once every four weeks. They get dirty more quickly than this.

(B), (C), and (D) are wrong because they ignore the possibility of two teams working, or of washers working overtime. There's no reason why the owner's demand couldn't be fulfilled, (B), by having 2 teams of 5 washers or by having one team work overtime. For all we know, one team working overtime could properly clean all the windows in less than 4 weeks, (C). Contrary to (D), it may be that

three teams of washers working part-time can accomplish the task. As for (A), no distinction between professional and amateur washers has been or can be made.

10. C

The Conclusion: A group of anthropologists claim to have formulated a "definitive" theory of consumer purchasing behavior.

The Evidence: There isn't any provided.

You need the choice that would be least likely to represent a benefit of the theory to retailers. This is an inference question, one where you will infer benefits of the theory. Clearly, if the theory makes consumers aware of how displays influence them, they will be less at the mercy of crafty retailers. This is a benefit to consumers, not retailers.

(A) and (D) point out that retailers will be able to use the new theory to display products to maximum advantage by cutting costs and pleasing customers. (B) names the overall benefit of the new theory, It will tell retailers why shoppers buy a particular product. And (E), if true, would help a retailer maximize the amount of shopping that customers do in his or her particular store.

11. B

The Conclusion: The pre-Colombian people of Veracruz must not have understood the principle and uses of the wheel.

The Evidence: Ceramic animals with attached wheels were found in Veracruz grave sites. Yet this culture did not use the wheel for tasks like carting, transportation, and pottery-making.

The author argues that these people didn't understand the wheel because they didn't employ it in their everyday activities. Thus, if these people had understood the uses of the wheel, they would have used it in their daily lives.

The author never hints that if they understood the wheel they wouldn't have used it on the animals, (A). Nor does the author argue that they didn't have uses for the wheel, (C); it's that they didn't understand the wheel enough to make use of it in their daily lives. As for (D), the author states the opposite, that they must not have known of the wheel's uses despite the wheels on the animals. (E) is way off topic—the author doesn't even hint that the animals came from a later culture.

12. E

The Conclusion: If the cost of public transportation is doubled, the city will lose money and become even more noisy and smog filled.

The Evidence: The added expense will deter commuters from using trains and buses—they will drive instead, resulting in pollution and congestion.

To state that the fare increase would have a major impact on the level of pollution and congestion by increasing the use of private cars, the author must assume that enough people have ready access to cars to make this impact.

People could, contrary to (A), share rides and still have a great negative impact on pollution and congestion, so long as the number of cars increases significantly. The amount of money commuters spend, (B), isn't the issue—the effect on the city is. Even if public transportation conditions did improve, (C), people would have already abandoned commuters in the system. Nor does the author have to assume that cars outnumber those in buses and trains, (D). The actual numbers aren't a part of this argument.

13. E

The Conclusion: People have more money to spend on their vacations.

The Evidence: Airlines are doing fine even though they're charging high fares to cross the Atlantic.

The idea that domestic flights are also booming doesn't sever the connection between booming business and vacation money—it shows more booming business.

The fact that most of the flights presented as evidence aren't bought by vacationers, (A), breaks the connection between booming business and vacation money. Airlines can do a booming business even if business as a whole is down, as long as, (B), there are fewer airlines. If people are skimping elsewhere, (C), then even if they're paying a lot for air fare, they needn't have more vacation money. And if in many cases people have no choice but to fly, (D), they must pay the higher fares no matter how little money they have.

14. A

The Truck Driver's Conclusion: The gas tax must be lowered.

The Truck Driver's Evidence: Increased costs will either put the truckers out of business or will hurt consumers.

The Official's Conclusion: The tax must remain.

The Official's Evidence: Highways will fall into disrepair without tax revenues, costing truckers and consumers even more.

The official wants the trucker to realize that cutting gas taxes won't help, but will likely raise costs for both industry and consumers. So she's arguing that the trucker's proposal, if carried out, will actually make matters worse.

(B)'s circular argument is more or less a restatement of the conclusion—that's not what's happening here. The official doesn't accuse the trucker of selfishness, (C); moreover, the trucker also warns of the harm done to consumers by the gas tax. The official does provide justification of the tax policy, (D); the revenue pays for road upkeep. There's no inherent contradiction between high taxes and the destruction of the trucking industry, (E); nor does the official claim there is.

15. C

The Skeptics' Conclusion: The Venus of Orleans isn't 70,000 years old.

The Skeptics' Evidence: Carbon-14 testing indicates that the statue is only about 50,000 years old.

The skeptics contend that the 70,000 year dating is false. As evidence they present carbon-14 dating results that show the statuette to be only 50,000 years old. This argument is weakened if results from carbon-14 dating are unreliable when the object pre-dates 60,000 B.C. Basically, if the archaeologists are right, the skeptics' tests are worthless. So the issue is still open and the skeptics' evidence is greatly weakened.

(D) works along similar lines, but no one believes the statuette to be over 100,000 years old. (A) deals with the other statuette and, rather than casting doubt on its date, affirms it. The skeptics' argument doesn't rely on other statuettes having been found, (B), or on the material of which the statuette is composed, (E).

16. D

The Conclusion: Foreign language study is becoming a serious endeavor in American education. When foreign language students enter the workforce, they will help businesses to compete internationally and enhance the United States's reputation abroad.

The Evidence: The number of U.S. college students in language courses has increased 20 percent over the past five years.

Neither a no nor a yes answer to the question about dead languages would have any relevance whatsoever to the author's argument.

Let's see how answers to the others would affect the argument. If students only took brief courses, (A), they probably wouldn't enhance the United States' reputation or ability to compete. If overall enrollments are way up in the past five years, (B), then a 20 percent increase in the number of language students wouldn't have as great an impact or indicate a change in students' perception of foreign language study. If the students don't use the languages, (C), it can't help their employers or the country's reputation. And if this 20 percent increase is smaller than those in previous years, (E), the idea that language study is considered more seriously now is weakened.

CRITICAL REASONING PRACTICE SET THREE

Time: 25 Minutes/16 Questions

Directions: For each question in this section, select the best of the answer choices given.

1. A tariff against computers made in Country Z is needed to protect computer manufacturers in this country. With such a tariff, domestic computer manufacturers would see increased sales of their own products. And increased sales frequently lead to reduced prices.

   If the above statements are true, which of the following conclusions can most properly be drawn from them?

   (A) A tariff is a less drastic means of applying international economic pressure than an embargo.

   (B) A drop in computer prices is likely to create more jobs in the computer industry.

   (C) Domestic manufacturers will decrease computer production if a protective tariff is not established.

   (D) The lack of a protective tariff has hampered computer production in this country.

   (E) A tariff would probably lead to a drop in prices for buyers of domestically produced computers.

2. A defense contractor is about to unveil a new plane, which has taken several years and several billions of dollars to create. Many governmental observers are uneasy about its first flight, since its designers built it straight from a computer model without first building a prototype to test the plane's design, as is the usual procedure.

   Which one of the following statements, if true, would be most likely to ease the governmental observers' concerns?

   (A) The new three-dimensional computer modeling technique used by the contractor simulates the trials typically faced by a prototype.

   (B) The Secretary of Defense has proposed delaying the deployment of this plane for one year.

   (C) This plane is susceptible to some of the same problems that caused the recent crash of another innovative plane.

   (D) Many positive features of the plane cannot yet be revealed because of national security considerations.

   (E) The computer model has already passed a battery of Department of Defense quality checks.

3. At Food World Supermarket, built in 1975, the number of successful thefts has risen dramatically in the past few months. Food World has a reliable electronic security system at all customer exit doors, and this system is always in operation. Therefore, the thefts must have been committed by people who used exits other than the regular customer exit doors.

   Which of the following is an assumption that would make the conclusion above logically correct?

   Ⓐ If a surveillance system is installed in a super-market, it is always equipped at every possible exit.

   Ⓑ If an employee so wishes, he is allowed to leave through an exit that is not monitored by surveillance equipment.

   Ⓒ If a store has a reliable security system, it is impossible to pass through the system unde-tected.

   Ⓓ If a supermarket was built before 1980, it often has exits that cannot be equipped with electronic surveillance.

   Ⓔ If a store has a reliable electronic security system but is still experiencing a rise in theft, it must be the case that the employees are stealing.

4. A complete ban on the sale of semi-automatic machine guns will not reduce the incidence of violent crime committed with these guns. People who want to commit violent crimes with these guns will still get them even if they are banned.

   The argument above would be most weakened if which of the following statements were true?

   Ⓐ Banning semi-automatic machine guns will result in an increase in the number of other dangerous weapons purchased.

   Ⓑ People who do not want to break the law will not buy guns illegally.

   Ⓒ Fully automatic machine guns, presently banned, are much more difficult to obtain than other banned weapons, such as switch-blade knives.

   Ⓓ Seeing semi-automatic machine guns legally displayed for sale tends to increase people's inclination to use those weapons to commit violent crimes.

   Ⓔ The number of accidental gun deaths is lowest in those states with the most restrictive gun control laws.

5. Magazine publishers claim that illegal photocopying of articles from their magazines costs them vast amounts of revenue every year. But most people who photocopy magazine articles are teachers using them in class. Given the economics of education, these teachers could not procure an original copy of the magazine for each student.

   Which of the following is most probably the point towards which the author of the above passage is moving?

   Ⓐ Magazine publishers should provide free copies of their magazines to schools.

   Ⓑ Preventing illegal photocopying would have no effect on magazine sales.

   Ⓒ Teachers should be prevented from photo-copying magazine articles for their students.

   Ⓓ Eliminating illegal photocopying would prevent the magazine publishers' loss of revenues.

   Ⓔ Illegal photocopying does not depress maga-zine sales as significantly as publishers believe.

6. The sanitation chief, hailing the success of her voluntary conservation program, reported that the amount of garbage produced per capita in the city decreased dramatically last year. But that statistic is deceptive. Last year the city incorporated three villages from the surrounding suburban area, increasing its population by almost 30 percent. It is this increase, rather than the conservation program, that explains the statistical drop.

Which of the following, if true, would seriously weaken the author's objection to the sanitation chief's claim?

- Ⓐ Because of differences between urban and suburban life, most suburban areas produce less garbage per capita than do urban areas.

- Ⓑ The voluntary conservation program was not implemented in the three incorporated villages until very late last year.

- Ⓒ The year before last, the three villages produced as many pounds of garbage per capita as did the city.

- Ⓓ The statistics cited by the sanitation chief do not include commercial waste or garbage collected by private carters.

- Ⓔ Due to a three-week strike, some of the garbage produced by the city during the year before last year was not counted in the statistics.

7. A spokesperson for the Reader's Book Club (RBC) recently hailed the club's free gift program as a big boost for sales. A year ago, RBC began offering a free gift to any member ordering five or more books in a single month. Since then, the number of members ordering five or more books at a time from RBC has risen by nearly 35 percent.

Which of the following, if true, would most seriously weaken the spokesperson's assessment of the program's effect on sales?

- Ⓐ The number of members ordering fewer than five books in a single month also rose in the last year.

- Ⓑ Most members ordered the same number of books over the year but concentrated their orders in specific months.

- Ⓒ The cost of providing free gifts nearly offset the increased revenue from higher sales.

- Ⓓ Most other book clubs, many of which also sponsored free gift programs, saw a drop in sales last year.

- Ⓔ The membership of the Reader's Book Club rose by more than 20 percent over the last year.

Questions 8–9 are based on the following:

The United States will soon begin spot checking all shipments of imported coffee for tainting by sandfly larvae. Any coffee found to be so tainted will be destroyed. Officials predict that the spot checks will result in the destruction of approximately 10 percent of all coffee imported into this country. Even so, the checks will miss about half of the tainted coffee sent here, since it is estimated that 20 percent of all coffee worldwide is tainted by sandfly larvae.

8. The author of the passage above is necessarily assuming which one of the following?

    Ⓐ Spot inspections will not succeed in preventing unacceptable amounts of tainted coffee from entering the country.

    Ⓑ Inspectors can detect sandfly larvae in only half of the tainted shipments they inspect.

    Ⓒ The proportion of imported coffee tainted by sandfly larvae is representative of the proportion of coffee so tainted worldwide.

    Ⓓ Spot-checking will mean that only 10 percent of all imported coffee will be inspected for tainting by sandfly larvae.

    Ⓔ The 80 percent of imported coffee shipments that are not tainted by sandfly larvae should not be inspected.

9. The information in the passage above best supports which of the following conclusions?

    Ⓐ The amount of imported coffee available for consumption in the United States may soon decrease.

    Ⓑ The United States should learn to rely more on domestically produced coffee.

    Ⓒ The United States will eventually be forced to inspect all imported coffee for tainting by sandfly larvae.

    Ⓓ Coffee producers worldwide will implement a more rigorous program of insect control.

    Ⓔ The U.S. consumer will begin paying less for imported coffee in the future.

10. The threatened prosecution of businesses flying 20 by 38 foot garrison flags, which are traditionally to be flown only on national holidays, instead of the smaller post flags, which can be flown at any time, is unconscionable. Legal technicalities of this sort should never restrict patriotic expression.

Which of the following, if true, would most weaken the argument above?

    Ⓐ Many people find the garrison flags' size to be distracting and ill-suited to neighborhood aesthetics.

    Ⓑ The businesses that are flying garrison flags are primarily using the oversized flags to attract customers.

    Ⓒ The raising and lowering of different-sized flags on the correct days of the year is a laborious and time-consuming procedure.

    Ⓓ The regulations that govern the correct display of the nation's flags are part of an old and time-honored tradition.

    Ⓔ The symbolic significance of a flag's size is not generally understood by most of the customers patronizing these businesses.

11. Rating record albums to reflect the amount of frank language and violence each one contains, in the way that motion pictures are rated, will not serve to reduce the likelihood that younger children will be exposed to that kind of music.

   Each of the following, if true, could be logically cited in support of the opinion above *EXCEPT*:

   (A) Most record albums are bought by older children who generally do not limit their younger siblings' access to their albums.

   (B) It would not be feasible to use the rating system to restrict the range of music that radio stations may play.

   (C) Movie theaters almost never fail to bar children under 18 from admittance to motion pictures of an adult nature.

   (D) Record stores could not be relied upon to monitor the age of customers seeking to purchase a particular album.

   (E) Younger children who would ordinarily not be interested in music with mature content might be drawn to it if that content were indicated by a particular rating.

12. Sam: Statistics show that hospital patients who have no health insurance generally get fewer diagnostic procedures and leave the hospital sooner than do patients who are insured. People without insurance are obviously not being cared for properly.

   Dan: On the contrary, what your statistics show is that people insist on undergoing all sorts of unnecessary procedures when they know that someone else is footing the bill.

   Which of the following best describes Dan's response to Sam?

   (A) He denies the truth of Sam's statistical evidence.

   (B) He shows that Sam's argument is based on a logical fallacy.

   (C) He provides counterevidence that contradicts that cited by Sam.

   (D) He shows that Sam's argument is biased because of an unfair preconception.

   (E) He provides an alternative explanation for the facts cited by Sam.

13. Though the number of nurses employed in the United States has risen over the past ten years, 15 percent of nursing positions in hospitals are vacant today. The situation will worsen unless hospitals improve working conditions and nursing schools attract students who have not traditionally been drawn to the profession. More scholarships and loans may make nursing education more affordable, and alternative routes to nursing may prompt adults interested in nursing to go back to studying in an undergraduate program.

   Which of the following can be logically inferred from the paragraph above?

   (A) Nursing school recruitments are now at their lowest level in a decade.

   (B) In the past ten years, the number of practicing hospital nurses has fallen.

   (C) Financial considerations are the principal reason for the current nursing shortage.

   (D) The supply of nurses has been rising, but not as fast as the demand for them.

   (E) Working conditions in hospitals have become significantly worse in the past decade.

KAPLAN

14. Cowonga lion cubs in the wild often engage in aggressive and even violent play with their siblings. This activity is apparently instigated by the parent lions. Cowonga lion cubs born in captivity, however, rarely engage in aggressive play. Zoologists have concluded that this form of play teaches the young lions the aggressive skills necessary for successful hunting in the wild, and that such play is not instigated in captivity because the development of hunting skills is unnecessary there.

The zoologists' conclusion would be most strengthened by demonstrating that

(A) Cowonga lions raised in captivity are unable to hunt successfully in the wild

(B) the skills developed from aggressive play are similar to those used for hunting in the wild

(C) the young of other types of predatory animals also engage in aggressive play

(D) parent lions that were raised in captivity do not instigate this play in their young

(E) none of the Cowonga lions raised in the wild is incapable of hunting successfully

15. Which of the following best completes the passage below?

The question of whether a child's personality is the result of genetic material inherited from the parents or the nurturing and environment provided by the parents is a perennial subject of debate. While no one would deny that environment and upbringing play some limited, superficial role, the genetic traits the child inherits provide the basic blueprint for who, and what, the child becomes. After all, if one plants tomatoes, _____.

(A) one must tend them carefully, in order to gather good vegetables

(B) one had better choose the variety and location with equal care

(C) one will eventually get tomatoes, but not necessarily good tomatoes

(D) one must expect tomatoes to grow, not cucumbers or daffodils

(E) one must be sure to tend them well, regardless of the quality of the seeds used

16. Zoologists have determined that the size of the litters produced by mating pairs of Beringer sloths is largely determined by the parent animals' diet. Sloths that feed primarily on catalpa trees tend to produce smaller numbers of offspring than do those that feed primarily on tulip trees. A new theory posits that the parent sloths choose their diet to achieve optimal population size for a given year, producing fewer offspring in dry years when food scarcity would threaten a large population.

    Which of the following, if true, would provide the strongest support for the theory that Beringer sloths choose their diets to suit the conditions of a given year?

    (A) In a forest dominated by catalpa trees, parent sloths ate far more tulip leaves than catalpa leaves in dry years.

    (B) In a forest dominated by tulip trees, parent sloths ate somewhat more tulip leaves than catalpa leaves in wet years.

    (C) The population of sloths in a particular area varied widely over several years during which precipitation remained relatively constant.

    (D) In a forest with roughly equal numbers of catalpa and tulip trees, parent sloths ate far more catalpa leaves than tulip leaves in dry years.

    (E) In a forest with roughly equal numbers of catalpa and tulip trees, parent sloths ate far more tulip leaves than catalpa leaves in dry years.

ANSWERS AND EXPLANATIONS

1. E
2. A
3. C
4. D
5. E
6. C
7. B
8. C
9. A
10. B
11. C
12. E
13. D
14. A
15. D
16. D

1. E

The Conclusion: A tariff should be imposed on Country Z's computers.

The Evidence: A tariff will increase sales of domestic computers. Increased sales often result in lower prices.

Basically, it's putting one and one together. If the tariff will increase sales and if increased sales often lower prices, then there's a good chance that the tariff will lower domestic computer prices.

Embargoes, (A), are outside the scope of the argument, which concerns the effects of a tariff, not alternatives to it. (B) mentions a possible effect of the tariff—reduced prices; unfortunately, though, there's no mention in the stimulus of this resulting in increased jobs. A tariff, we're told, will lead to increased production; that doesn't mean, though, that *no* tariff will force, (C), *reduced* production. (D) is an overstatement. The tariff will increase sales and probably production; that doesn't mean, however, that lack of a tariff has hampered production.

2. A

The Conclusion: The plane's first flight is a cause for worry.

The Evidence: The designers didn't use a prototype; they built the plane straight from a computer model.

"Easing the observers' fears" is really a matter of weakening the reasoning behind those fears. They fear the lack of a prototype and the reliance on only a computer model. If, though, the computer simulated the experience that a prototype would have gone through, the need for a prototype is diminished.

(B), postponing the first flight merely postpones the observers' fears; it doesn't allay them. And pointing out potential problems, (C), just makes matters worse. Remember: *au contraire* answers are very common on Strengthen or Weaken questions. The plane's good features, (D), aren't the issue; they haven't been tested on a prototype either. Nor is the battery of tests, (E), a comfort: they were performed on the computer model, not on a prototype.

3. C

The Conclusion: The thefts *must* (note that keyword) have been committed by people who used exits other than the regular customer exit doors.

The Evidence: The number of successful thefts has risen even though Food World has a reliable electronic security system at all customer exit doors.

In order to conclude that the thefts aren't taking place out the customer doors, the author must assume that the security system works. However, reliable doesn't necessarily mean infallible.

(A) plainly can't be assumed, since the author is concluding that the thefts took place at unequipped doors. (B) and (E) both play off the same red herring: employee theft. The issue is where the thefts are occurring, not who is committing them. The author seems to think that noncustomer exit doors are the problem, but there's no need to assume that these can't be equipped with a surveillance system.

4.   D

The Conclusion: A ban on semi-automatic machine guns will not reduce the incidence of violent crime committed with these guns.

The Evidence: People who want to commit violent crimes with these guns will still get them

There's not a whole lot of evidence here, just a couple of claims. To weaken the argument, we want to show that banning the guns will result in less criminal use of the guns. If much of the use isn't truly premeditated, but occurs to criminals when they see the guns displayed, then banning the guns (and their display) will result in less criminal use.

The author didn't argue that the ban would reduce crime, just the criminal use of these guns, so (A) attacks the wrong argument. (B) talks about law-abiding people, who aren't a part of the argument. The fact that some banned weapons are harder to get than others, (C), is irrelevant. Watch out for pointless comparisons—they are as common as wrong answers. Accidental deaths, (E), are also outside the scope.

5.   E

The Conclusion: The stem tells us that the author is moving towards a point, so we read the stimulus with an eye towards an eventual conclusion that's not on the page.

The Evidence: Most people who photocopy magazine articles are teachers using them in class. These teachers could not afford a copy of the magazine for each student.

If the publishers claim illegal copying costs them, and the author responds that most copiers can't afford to buy

the original issues, he's probably disputing the claim that copying costs publishers, (E). He's doing this by showing that the lost sales aren't really sales at all.

While he does take a "relax and calm down" attitude towards the publishers, he doesn't go so far as to tell them to give away free copies, (A). He argues that few copies represent lost sales, not that (B) none of them does. (C) and (D) can be dismissed because they run directly counter to the author's argument by presenting the illegal copying as a significant problem for publishers.

6.   C

The Conclusion: The drop in per capita garbage is not due to the chief's conservation program.

The Evidence: The city incorporated three villages, whose extra residents accounted for the per capita drop.

Well, the author plainly believes (assumes) that the suburban villagers are deflating the per capita garbage figure, so he assumes that suburbanites produce less garbage. If, though, they produce every bit as much garbage, then the drop can't be due to their incorporation into the city and the statistics.

He assumes (A), so it strengthens rather than weakens his argument. (B) makes it less likely that the conservation program is responsible for the drop, which also strengthens his argument. As long as the same type of garbage is eliminated from both years' statistics, (D), the effect of this on the different arguments is anyone's guess—a clear sign of a wrong answer. More garbage the year before last year, (E), just increases the drop; it does not, however, affect the author's attempt to explain this drop.

7.   B

The Conclusion: The free gift program increased sales.

The Evidence: The number of orders of five or more books has increased by 35 percent.

The representative argues from evidence of sales of five books or more to a conclusion about total sales. If the large sales have increased at the expense of other sales, then it's not necessarily the case that total sales have risen. People may be taking advantage of the offer without buying any more books.

If smaller orders are also up, (A), then the argument is strengthened. The argument concerns sales, not revenue, so (C) is off the point. If the argument concerned the competitiveness of RBC, then (D) might be relevant. As it stands, though, other clubs and their promotions have no effect on the representative's claims. And membership, (E), like revenues, is off the point. The representative hails the program as a success based on supposedly increased sales.

8. C

The Conclusion: The spot checks will miss half of the imported coffee tainted by sandfly larvae.

The Evidence: Only 10 percent of imported coffee will fail the spot checks, whereas 20 percent of coffee worldwide is tainted.

The evidence contains a figure for coffee worldwide; the conclusion, for coffee imported to the United States. Here we have a twist on a common GMAT theme. The argument isn't *based* on a sample; it *concludes* something about a sample (imported coffee) based on evidence about the whole (all coffee). The same key issue is at work, though: The sample must be representative. In order for the math to work, 20 percent of imported coffee (the same figure as for all coffee) must be tainted.

The author assumes that spot checks will detect some tainted coffee; there's no evidence, though, that this amount (10 percent) is unacceptable, (A). The inspectors themselves predict finding only half the tainted coffee, (B), so the author needn't assume this. Furthermore, it's not clear that they will miss half of the tainted coffee they inspect. These are spot checks; they may miss half the tainted coffee because they don't check that coffee. (D) misreads the numbers: It's not that 10 percent will be inspected, but that inspections will fail 10 percent. (E) is nonsensical. If inspectors knew which 80 percent was untainted, there would be no need for inspections.

9. A

Bearing in mind the situation described in the stimulus, we attack the choices, looking for one that seems likely. We don't look far. (A)'s claim that there may soon be less coffee is a likely outgrowth of the policy that's described. Spot checks will destroy 10 percent of imported coffee. While the amount of coffee imported may subsequently be increased, there is a good chance that, for some period of time, less coffee will be available.

The argument is descriptive, so (B)'s prescriptions about what should be done go awry. There's no support for the drastic conclusion, (C), that all coffee will have to be

checked. Nor is there support for a conclusion, (D), about the reaction of coffee producers. Coffee prices, (E), like these other issues, are also unpredictable.

10. B

The Conclusion: Businesses flying garrison flags should not be prosecuted.

The Evidence: Legal technicalities should not prevent patriotic expression.

The author's argument depends upon the patriotism of the businesses flying these large flags. If, however, the businesses are not expressing patriotism, but merely touting their wares, the argument falls apart.

Aesthetic judgments, (A), are irrelevant; the author would merely argue that these, too, shouldn't be allowed to restrict patriotic expression. If switching flags is a big hassle, (C), then the author's argument is strengthened. (D) is similar to invoking aesthetics; the author would just argue that patriotism overrides tradition. (E) is as much an argument for the author; pointing out that the significance of the flags' size (which is the basis for the threatened prosecutions) is lost on most people.

11. C

The Conclusion: Ratings won't prevent young children from hearing filthy music.

The Evidence: There is none (except the analogy to theaters); we have to supply it.

It's an "all of the following EXCEPT" question, so we figure out what we have to do and jump to the choices. We want support for the author's claim. If older children will allow younger children access, (A), then the ratings are sidestepped. Likewise, if the radio stations, (B), play the songs. (C) has the theater restrictions working. This is either a weakener or irrelevant (depending on whether the author's analogy to theaters is an illustration or support).

For the record, if record stores won't restrict the children from buying, (D), then the ratings are ineffective. And if the ratings attract young listeners, (E), they will actually be counterproductive.

12. E

Sam's Conclusion: The uninsured get poor hospital care.

Dan's Conclusion: The insured insist on unnecessary tests.

The Evidence: (for both) Hospital patients who have no

health insurance generally get fewer diagnostic procedures and leave the hospital sooner than do patients who are insured.

As the breakdown above points out, the two agree on the facts, they just disagree on what the facts mean. Each has a different explanation for the discrepancy in hospital procedures. Dan, then, accepts the evidence but provides as a conclusion an alternative explanation for it.

Choices (A), (B), and (C) all have Dan disputing the evidence, or basis for Sam's argument. It's the interpretation that he disputes. He doesn't show a bias or preconception, (D).

13. D

The Conclusion: Unless steps are taken, the nursing shortage will worsen.

The Evidence: There's a 15 percent vacancy rate, which looks likely to worsen.

More than a straightforward argument, the stimulus is an exploration of the nursing shortage and approaches to handling it. Prephrasing here might get us the idea that working conditions aren't ideal or that there aren't enough students enrolling in nursing programs. As it turns out, though, it's simpler than that. If there are more nurses than ever, yet the shortage is worsening, then demand is rising faster than the supply.

There's no evidence that enrollments are actually down, (A), and we know that the number of nurses hasn't fallen, (B). Financial considerations, (C), seem to hurt nursing school enrollments, but that's a far cry from being "the principal reason for the nursing shortage." The same reasoning eliminates (E): Working conditions have something to do with the shortage, and they need improving, but we can't infer that they have worsened significantly.

14. A

The Zoologists' Conclusion: The play teaches the young lions the aggressive skills necessary for successful hunting in the wild.

Their Evidence: Cubs in the wild often engage in aggressive play with their siblings, play that is instigated by their parents. Cubs born in captivity, however, rarely engage in aggressive play.

There's cause and effect here. The zoologists believe that the play teaches hunting skills. Where there is need of the effect (hunting skills) there is the cause (play); where

there is no need of the effect, the cause is lacking. That's a correlation, but the key issue remains: Does the play cause the hunting skills? The fact that lions raised in captivity, without the play, can't hunt tells us that without the alleged cause, there is no effect. This greatly strengthens the connection between the two.

The fact that the play and hunting are similar, (B), does little to show that the former leads to the latter; both could be effects of something more basic and instinctive. The behavior of other animals, (C), is beyond the scope of the zoologists argument. Presumably, the parents raised in captivity, (D), are raising their young in captivity, so this adds nothing new. And the fact that wild lions learn to hunt, (E), has no effect on the hypothesis; the question is how they learned to hunt.

15. D

The Conclusion: Children's personalities are primarily the result of genetics.

The Evidence: Genetics provide the basic blueprint for who a child becomes.

There's not much evidence given (it's a restatement of the conclusion). The sentence with the blank is intended to provide more: an example or illustration, where tomatoes are compared to children. Since the author believes in the primacy of genetics, we need a completion, involving tomatoes, that illustrates this. If one plants tomatoes, then one will get tomatoes (it's genetic), not some other plant.

Careful tending, (A) and (E), parallels nurture or upbringing, which the author doesn't consider very important. Equal care devoted to variety and location, (B), would illustrate that both nature and nurture are equally important. (C), getting tomatoes but not necessarily good tomatoes, is close but no cigar. (D) does a better job of illustrating that certain outcomes are genetically impossible. Moreover, the issue of quality comes from nowhere, making this an incorrect GMAT argument completion.

16. D

The New Theory's Conclusion: Parent sloths choose their diet to achieve optimal population size for a given year by producing fewer offspring in dry years when food is scarce.

The Evidence: The size of the litters is largely determined by the parent animals' diet. Sloths that feed primarily on catalpa trees tend to produce smaller numbers of offspring than do those that feed primarily on tulip trees. With stimuli

KAPLAN

like this, it's often a good idea to jot down some shorthand describing what the theory says:

dry → scarce → catalpa

wet → not scarce → tulip

We want support. Nothing leaps to mind, so we look to the choices. Each describes a scenario; we need the one that "fits" the new theory. Sloths deliberately going for tulips over catalpa in dry years, (A), is contrary to the theory. (B) is in line with the theory—tulip leaves in wet years—yet because this forest was dominated by tulip trees, it could just be that the sloths ate most what they found most. (C) tells us nothing about diet and it's not obvious what it means, so it's out. (D), however, gives us what we want. Catalpa leaves in dry years is in line with the theory, and the trees are equally available. This makes it more likely that the sloths sought out the catalpa. Tulip leaves in dry years, (E), is directly counter to the theory.

PART FOUR

Putting It All Together

Here, at last, is your chance to see what an actual GMAT verbal section feels like. The following practice verbal section contains a typical mix of medium-to-hard GMAT verbal questions. If you can answer most of these questions correctly under timed conditions, you can also expect to do well on the real GMAT.

One thing, however, that we could not simulate in this book is the computer-adaptive nature of an actual GMAT. If you want that experience (and we recommend it strongly), we have two suggestions.

First, you can get your hands on some of Kaplan's great GMAT prep materials. One option is to pick up the latest edition of *Kaplan GMAT: Premier Program*. It comes with a CD that contains four full-length, computer-adaptive GMATs, along with section-length practice quizzes.

You can also TRY OUT the Kaplan GMAT Quiz Bank! You get more than 1000 questions that you can access 24/7 from any internet browser, each with comprehensive explanations. You can even customize your quizzes based on question type, content, and difficulty level. Take quizzes in Timed Mode to test your stamina or in Tutor Mode to see explanations as you work. Best of all, you also get detailed reports to track your progress. Visit Kaptest.com/GMAT for more details on the Quiz Bank and for more on other online and classroom-based options.

Your other option is to get the *GMATprep®* software from the test maker's website, www.mba.org. It's free, and contains two full-length CATs (detailed explanations of answers are not included) and a 15-question practice section for each question type, with answers and explanations. If you don't want to download the software over the Internet, you can have a CD-ROM version of the software sent to you free. If you choose to receive the software this way you should expect up to two weeks for delivery within the United States and up to four weeks for delivery outside of the United States. You may wish to consider this timing when registering for your test.

How to Take This Practice Section

Before taking this practice test, find a quiet place where you can work uninterrupted for 75 minutes. Make sure you have a comfortable desk, a timer, a couple of pencils, and several sheets of scratch paper.

Use the answer grid on the next page to record your answers. Also, to simulate the actual GMAT experience, we ask that you do all your work on scratch paper and not write on the Verbal Section itself. Make sure as well that you answer the questions in order. As you know, there's no skipping around on the actual GMAT.

You'll find the answer key and explanations following this section.

Good luck!

PRACTICE SECTION ANSWER SHEET

1. Ⓐ Ⓑ Ⓒ Ⓓ Ⓔ   15. Ⓐ Ⓑ Ⓒ Ⓓ Ⓔ   29. Ⓐ Ⓑ Ⓒ Ⓓ Ⓔ
2. Ⓐ Ⓑ Ⓒ Ⓓ Ⓔ   16. Ⓐ Ⓑ Ⓒ Ⓓ Ⓔ   30. Ⓐ Ⓑ Ⓒ Ⓓ Ⓔ
3. Ⓐ Ⓑ Ⓒ Ⓓ Ⓔ   17. Ⓐ Ⓑ Ⓒ Ⓓ Ⓔ   31. Ⓐ Ⓑ Ⓒ Ⓓ Ⓔ
4. Ⓐ Ⓑ Ⓒ Ⓓ Ⓔ   18. Ⓐ Ⓑ Ⓒ Ⓓ Ⓔ   32. Ⓐ Ⓑ Ⓒ Ⓓ Ⓔ
5. Ⓐ Ⓑ Ⓒ Ⓓ Ⓔ   19. Ⓐ Ⓑ Ⓒ Ⓓ Ⓔ   33. Ⓐ Ⓑ Ⓒ Ⓓ Ⓔ
6. Ⓐ Ⓑ Ⓒ Ⓓ Ⓔ   20. Ⓐ Ⓑ Ⓒ Ⓓ Ⓔ   34. Ⓐ Ⓑ Ⓒ Ⓓ Ⓔ
7. Ⓐ Ⓑ Ⓒ Ⓓ Ⓔ   21. Ⓐ Ⓑ Ⓒ Ⓓ Ⓔ   35. Ⓐ Ⓑ Ⓒ Ⓓ Ⓔ
8. Ⓐ Ⓑ Ⓒ Ⓓ Ⓔ   22. Ⓐ Ⓑ Ⓒ Ⓓ Ⓔ   36. Ⓐ Ⓑ Ⓒ Ⓓ Ⓔ
9. Ⓐ Ⓑ Ⓒ Ⓓ Ⓔ   23. Ⓐ Ⓑ Ⓒ Ⓓ Ⓔ   37. Ⓐ Ⓑ Ⓒ Ⓓ Ⓔ
10. Ⓐ Ⓑ Ⓒ Ⓓ Ⓔ   24. Ⓐ Ⓑ Ⓒ Ⓓ Ⓔ   38. Ⓐ Ⓑ Ⓒ Ⓓ Ⓔ
11. Ⓐ Ⓑ Ⓒ Ⓓ Ⓔ   25. Ⓐ Ⓑ Ⓒ Ⓓ Ⓔ   39. Ⓐ Ⓑ Ⓒ Ⓓ Ⓔ
12. Ⓐ Ⓑ Ⓒ Ⓓ Ⓔ   26. Ⓐ Ⓑ Ⓒ Ⓓ Ⓔ   40. Ⓐ Ⓑ Ⓒ Ⓓ Ⓔ
13. Ⓐ Ⓑ Ⓒ Ⓓ Ⓔ   27. Ⓐ Ⓑ Ⓒ Ⓓ Ⓔ   41. Ⓐ Ⓑ Ⓒ Ⓓ Ⓔ
14. Ⓐ Ⓑ Ⓒ Ⓓ Ⓔ   28. Ⓐ Ⓑ Ⓒ Ⓓ Ⓔ

1. Fossils found recently in Pakistan provide evidence <u>supporting the theory of land mammals returning to the water that later</u> evolved into modern whales.

   (A) supporting the theory of land mammals returning to the water that later

   (B) supporting the theory that land mammals, after returning to the water,

   (C) that supports the theory of land mammals that returned to the water and that later

   (D) in support of the theory that land mammals returned to the water and that they later

   (E) of support for the theory of land mammals that returned to the water and after

2. Although modern roller coasters have loops in which they turn upside-down, <u>old-fashioned roller coasters have more and longer straight drops</u>.

   (A) old-fashioned roller coasters have more and longer straight drops

   (B) the old-fashioned roller coaster has more and longer straight drops

   (C) whereas old-fashioned roller coasters have more and longer straight drops

   (D) old-fashioned roller coasters having more and longer straight drops

   (E) old-fashioned roller coasters drop longer and straighter

3. The Governor's recent direct mail survey on the environment showed that 80 percent of those who responded, and thus allegedly the vast majority of the state's residents, support increased state spending for the environmentally safe disposal of solid waste. But we should expect that most of the people who respond to an environmental survey are in favor of spending money to protect the environment.

   Which of the following best expresses the author's point?

   (A) The survey was mailed only to those citizens who are environmentalists.

   (B) Most citizens are poor judges of how the state's revenues should be spent.

   (C) The survey failed because it neglected to ask citizens where the money for the increased spending would come from.

   (D) Those who responded to the survey are not truly representative of the state's residents.

   (E) The state does not need to spend more money to dispose of solid waste.

4. The dollar amount of federal tax revenues gained from personal income tax has increased markedly in recent years. Clearly, people are being more honest in declaring their annual earnings than they used to be.

   The argument above would be greatly weakened by each of the following *EXCEPT*:

   (A) Fewer income tax deductions are allowed now than in the past.

   (B) The nation's population has increased.

   (C) Tax revenue from of the corporate sector has decreased.

   (D) The average yearly income of the nation's residents has increased.

   (E) The rate of personal income taxation has increased.

GO ON TO THE NEXT PAGE

KAPLAN

PASSAGE 1—FORSET

Having rejected Catholicism, English society after the Protestant Reformation felt compelled to impose new order on an uncertain universe. Claiming knowledge of a divine
(5) plan that linked the celestial and natural worlds into one "great chain of being," some English thinkers depicted humans as the highest link on the portion of the chain representing the natural world. Furthermore,
(10) they conceived of human society as a vertical series of political strata. One metaphor, occurring in Shakespeare's *Coriolanus*, among other places, likened society to the human body. Queen Elizabeth I chided a recalcitrant
(15) Parliament by asserting that "the feet do not rule the head." Edward Forset echoed this assertion in 1606, when he elaborated a hierarchy in which the body was topped, literally and morally, by the head and the soul. In
(20) Forset's scheme, both soul and monarchy possessed "unity" or "indivisibility"; the soul united and reigned over the physical body, and the sovereign united and reigned over the body politic. Popular acceptance of the idea of
(25) stability as God's will gave Elizabeth and her immediate successors a potent, though short-lived, ideological restraint on rebellious thought and activity.

5. The passage suggests that many English people saw the idea of a new social order as

   Ⓐ necessary in order to fill a vacuum created by the decline of the monarchy

   Ⓑ an idiosyncratic viewpoint advocated by a few eccentric thinkers

   Ⓒ an amusing but not terribly urgent social issue

   Ⓓ a disguised attempt by the Catholic Church to restore its lost influence in English affairs

   Ⓔ unavoidable because an older order that had provided them with structure and security no longer existed

6. The passage suggests that, in the years following the Protestant Reformation, English monarchs were able to maintain their political influence primarily because

   Ⓐ popular opinion was tightly controlled by a small group of thinkers

   Ⓑ English society accepted that a hierarchical society was consistent with divine will

   Ⓒ monarchs accepted a social position basically equal to that of most other people

   Ⓓ Parliament was politically passive and offered no significant resistance

   Ⓔ English society traditionally supported a strong monarchical authority

7. Which of the following sentences would most logically follow the last sentence of this passage?

   Ⓐ Subsequently, popular acceptance of a divinely ordered social structure continues to shape English politics for an unusually lengthy period.

   Ⓑ However, because Forset's ideas were judged to be too radical, they initially failed to make a substantial impact on the balance of power in English government.

   Ⓒ Forset's arguments for a strict, hierarchically ordered society found especially enthusiastic support among many members of the English Parliament.

   Ⓓ This acceptance undoubtedly helped check growing assertiveness of those social classes that spoke through Parliament.

   Ⓔ Thus, freed of her problems with Parliament, Elizabeth was able to focus on the threat to social stability posed by the thinking of men like Forset.

GO ON TO THE NEXT PAGE ▷

KAPLAN

8. When a movie that is panned by most film critics is a popular success, it is often taken as evidence of the poor taste of general audiences. But film critics belong to a fairly homogeneous class and their preferences are often rooted in the prejudices of that class. Their opinions are no more likely to be an unerring guide to quality than those of the average moviegoer.

   The passage above best supports which of the following conclusions?

   (A) Judgments of film quality by professional film critics are usually incorrect.

   (B) Judgments of quality applied to movies are meaningless.

   (C) Film critics usually consider popular movies to be of poor quality.

   (D) Professional critics generally agree on the quality of any given movie.

   (E) When film critics and general audiences disagree about a movie's quality, the critics' opinion is not necessarily more accurate.

9. The State University debating club is always looking for money to renovate their headquarters in Stockton Hall. The latest plan is to contact alumni club members from the 1930s, 1940s, and 1950s and ask for contributions. Other such efforts have been tried in the past, however, and club headquarters are still in poor condition.

   If the author concludes that the debating club will not raise enough money to renovate their headquarters, which of the following best describes the way he supports his conclusion?

   (A) He bases a conclusion on an analogy.

   (B) He casts doubt on the reasoning ability of his opponents.

   (C) He points out a logical fallacy.

   (D) He bases a prediction on past experience.

   (E) He disparages the motives of his opponents.

10. John F. Kennedy increased the participation of the United States in the war in Vietnam, <u>which Lyndon B. Johnson did</u> when he succeeded Kennedy.

    (A) which Lyndon B. Johnson did

    (B) which Lyndon B. Johnson was to be doing

    (C) as Lyndon B. Johnson

    (D) as did Lyndon B. Johnson

    (E) as Lyndon B. Johnson did do

11. <u>The reason why Scipio Africanus wept after his defeat of Hannibal was because he knew</u> that, having attained this stunning victory, his fortunes could only turn for the worse.

    (A) The reason why Scipio Africanus wept after his defeat of Hannibal was because he knew

    (B) Scipio Africanus' weeping after his defeat of Hannibal was because he knew

    (C) Scipio Africanus wept after his defeat of Hannibal because he knew

    (D) The reason Scipio Africanus wept after his defeat of Hannibal was because he knew

    (E) Scipio Africanus wept after his defeat of Hannibal, the reason being that he knew

12. The shipbuilding industry in eighteenth-century England created a need <u>that pine and flax from Russia be made into masts and sails.</u>

    (A) that pine and flax from Russia be made into masts and sails

    (B) for pine and flax from Russia that are made into masts and sails

    (C) that there be a production of masts and sails out of pine and flax from Russia

    (D) that masts and sails are made out of pine and flax from Russia

    (E) for pine and flax from Russia to be made into masts and sails

GO ON TO THE NEXT PAGE

KAPLAN

PASSAGE 2—GROUP MANAGEMENT

Corporate managers often work in groups because of the complexity of strategic problems. A consensus-seeking group's effective-

(5) ness may be impaired, however, if the group values harmony over open evaluation of ideas. Consequently, some theorists advocate building decisional conflict into the group process. Doing so, they argue, should yield better decisions. While conflict potentially

(10) offers benefits, a group's effectiveness also depends on members' reactions to group experiences. Ideally, the group process wins the commitment of its members. The process, though, may generate so much divisiveness

(15) that implementation and future cooperation are undermined. Management groups thus face an apparent dilemma: Decisional conflict may yield better decisions at the risk of weakening managerial effectiveness. Conversely,

(20) the harmony that facilitates cooperation and implementation may come at the cost of inferior decisions.

Efforts to build conflict into group decision making have focused on two approaches,

(25) dialectical inquiry and devil's advocacy. Both work by dividing the group into two competing subgroups, relying on formal debate to prevent uncritical acceptance of the seemingly obvious, and continuing until participants

(30) agree on a decision. The approaches differ in the roles played by the subgroups. In dialectical inquiry, the subgroups present opposed sets of assumptions and recommendations, and debate until they reach agreement. In

(35) devil's advocacy, the second subgroup critiques the assumptions and recommendations of the first, but offers no alternative. The first subgroup revises its ideas and presents them for a second critique. The process con-

(40) tinues until the subgroups agree.

The varying roles of the subgroups have led to disagreement among theorists over the effectiveness of the approaches. Mason and Mitroff claim that devil's advocacy does not

(45) identify suitable alternatives, whereas dialectical inquiry's juxtaposition of opposed sets of ideas does so. Cosier, however, argues that dialectical inquiry adds potentially confusing steps to the process that would require exten-

(50) sive training, and may run counter to managers' accustomed ways of thinking; he also feels that this approach may lead to excessive compromise.

13. The author's primary purpose in the passage is to

   (A) emphasize the benefits of group decision making and reconcile two differing approaches

   (B) describe the benefits and risks of decisional conflict and alternative means of its use

   (C) defend an innovative method of group management against its critics

   (D) argue that group decision making is superior to any other decision-making approach

   (E) advocate one method of group decision making over another

14. It can be inferred from the passage that advocates of both the dialectical inquiry and devil's advocacy processes would agree with which of the following statements?

   (A) Superior decisions often reflect compromises made between opposing views.

   (B) Superior decisions stem from a consideration of opposing sets of proposals.

   (C) Managers should avoid changing their customary ways of thinking.

   (D) Formal debate can lead to a more thorough understanding of a problem.

   (E) Effective group management requires extensive training.

GO ON TO THE NEXT PAGE ⟩

KAPLAN

15. Which one of the following, if true, would counter Cosier's criticism of dialectical inquiry?

    (A) Frequent compromises among managers may lead to ill-advised actions.

    (B) Demanding that managers agree often weakens implementation of decisions.

    (C) Encouraging conflict among managers improves the quality of decisions.

    (D) Some managerial decisions must be made and implemented rapidly to be effective.

    (E) Managers willing to alter their accustomed modes of thinking often make better decisions.

16. Which of the following exemplifies the functioning of management groups, as those groups are described in the passage?

    (A) A citizens' group gathers to monitor the results of a closely contested election.

    (B) A special prosecutor's office organizes to investigate alleged misconduct on the part of government officials.

    (C) A committee of administrators forms to address the major problems of running a hospital.

    (D) A panel of experts assembles to study an issue of growing public concern.

    (E) A faculty committee forms to observe the search for a college president.

17. Manager: The success ratio for new businesses is lower than ever, with only 12 percent surviving the first two years. Furthermore, many businesses already operating are doing so at a loss, or with their lowest profit margin in decades. The blame must fall on the excessive demands of the workers. Profits drop in order to pay for new paint, radios, and artwork. We have lost sight of the fact that work is intended to be productive, not enjoyable.

Which of the following, if true, would most weaken the manager's argument?

    (A) Workers, whether they are performing productively or not, often have very difficult and highly taxing duties.

    (B) In most cases, improvements in the work environment increase productivity by increasing worker satisfaction.

    (C) The failure of many businesses in the past was due to exorbitant taxation rather than excessive demands of the workers.

    (D) The failure of a new business is not necessarily the same thing as the failure of an already existing business.

    (E) The failure of a new business is not necessarily the same thing as operating an already existing business without a profit.

18. The Republic of the Philippines encompasses more than seven thousand islands, <u>two of them with two thirds of its area.</u>

    (A) two of them with two thirds of its area

    (B) two thirds of their area being in two of them

    (C) and its area is two thirds in two islands

    (D) two of them have two thirds of its area

    (E) which have two thirds of its area in two of them

GO ON TO THE NEXT PAGE

KAPLAN

PASSAGE 3—DINOSAUR EXTINCTION

Scientists long believed that gradual changes in global climate caused the extinction of the dinosaurs. In 1979, however, a team from Berkeley discovered in Italy a layer

(5) of clay from about the time of the dinosaurs' disappearance, with an iridium level some thirty times greater than that of clays in adjacent strata. Since iridium settles fairly evenly over time and is extraterrestrial in origin, the

(10) researchers concluded that the high iridium level of this clay must have resulted from a sudden, catastrophic event. After finding similarly enriched marine rocks from the same period in Spain, Denmark, and New Zealand,

(15) the researchers calculated that some 500 billion tons of material settled on the earth in less than 150 years.

Scientists differ over the exact nature of the event. The possibility that a stellar explosion

(20) caused the deposition has been discounted, because certain radioactive isotopes are largely absent from the clay. If the material originated within the solar system, the earth must have collided with an astral body large

(25) enough to distribute the iridium-rich material around the globe. An asteroid of the required mass would have been approximately ten kilometers in diameter. A comet, being mostly ice, would have been twice as large.

(30) There is no geological evidence of the impact of such massive objects, but Grieve argues that the clay layer could have settled as fallout after an atmospheric explosion. Kyte asserts that a comet, disrupted by the earth's

(35) gravitational field, would have produced a deluge of falling debris without creating major craters. The Berkeley group suggests that an asteroid may have landed in the sea.

Whatever the type of event, the Berkeley

(40) team argues that it disrupted the planetary ecology by suspending vast clouds of matter in the stratosphere. The effects of the impact would have increased as the blockage of sunlight impeded photosynthesis, causing a mas-

(45) sive disruption at the base of the global food chain.

19. The passage is primarily concerned with

   (A) summarizing and assessing differing theories
   (B) rebutting a traditional assumption
   (C) evaluating the results of a controversial methodology
   (D) suggesting a new course of investigation
   (E) discussing the implications of a discovery

20. According to the passage, scientists used the level of "certain radioactive isotopes" (line 21) in clay from Italy in order to

   (A) assess the validity of an older theory about the extinction of the dinosaur
   (B) estimate the approximate age of adjacent clay strata
   (C) determine whether or not iridium originates extraterrestrially
   (D) estimate the amount of fallout necessary to block sunlight
   (E) eliminate a possible theory as to the origin of the clay layer

GO ON TO THE NEXT PAGE

21. Judging from the information in the passage, the argument of the Berkeley group mentioned in the last paragraph would be most strengthened by

    (A) a discovery of dinosaur fossils in strata older than the iridium-rich clay layer in Italy

    (B) a drop in the number of plant fossils in strata above those studied in Italy

    (C) a discovery of elevated levels of iridium in rocks above and below the clay strata in Spain

    (D) the development of a consensus among scientists on the probability of a comet's impact with the earth

    (E) a recalculation showing that the Italian clay layer was deposited over a period of several thousand years

22. <u>Setting a distance record, in 1984 Joe Kittinger piloted his balloon from Maine to Italy, and he became the first balloonist to cross the Atlantic solo.</u>

    (A) Setting a distance record, in 1984 Joe Kittinger piloted his balloon from Maine to Italy, and he became the first balloonist to cross the Atlantic solo

    (B) In 1984, Joe Kittinger, setting a distance record, piloted his balloon from Maine to Italy, and he became the first balloonist to cross the Atlantic solo

    (C) In 1984, Joe Kittinger piloted his balloon from Maine to Italy, setting a distance record and becoming the first balloonist to cross the Atlantic solo

    (D) Having been first to cross the Atlantic solo, and with a voyage from Maine to Italy, Joe Kittinger set a balloon distance record in 1984

    (E) Joe Kittinger, in 1984, piloted his balloon from Maine to Italy, setting a new distance record, becoming the first balloonist to cross the Atlantic solo

23. Crises in international diplomacy <u>do not always result from malice; for nations, like individuals, can find</u> themselves locked into difficult positions, unable to back down.

    (A) do not always result from malice; for nations, like individuals, can find

    (B) does not always result from malice; nations, just as individuals, finding

    (C) do not always result of malice; nations, such as individuals, can find

    (D) aren't always the results of malice; nations in the same way that individuals can find

    (E) aren't resulting always from malice; just like nations and individuals who can find

24. <u>Young female ballet dancers and gymnasts sometimes fail to maintain good eating habits caused by the desire to be as thin as possible.</u>

    (A) Young female ballet dancers and gymnasts sometimes fail to maintain good eating habits caused by the desire to be as thin as possible

    (B) Good eating habits sometimes fail to be maintained by young female ballet dancers and gymnasts caused by desiring to be as thin as possible

    (C) Because they desire to be as thin as possible, good eating habits are sometimes not maintained by young female ballet dancers and gymnasts

    (D) Because they desire to be as thin as possible, young female ballet dancers and gymnasts sometimes fail to maintain good eating habits

    (E) Young female dancers and gymnasts sometimes fail to maintain good eating habits because they desire to be as thin as possible

GO ON TO THE NEXT PAGE ⇨

KAPLAN

25. A talent agent analyzed her company's records in an attempt to determine why they were placing so few actors in roles. She attributed the company's poor performance to the fact that often the actors sent to an audition were completely inappropriate for the role.

    It can be concluded from the passage above that the agent believes that

    (A) certain actors are inappropriate for certain roles

    (B) the actors her company represents are not very good

    (C) it is difficult to predict how appropriate an actor will be for a role

    (D) her company does not send enough actors to audition for major roles

    (E) directors often cast actors who are inappropriate for the role

26. Patient: Doctor, you decreased my Olanon from seven milligrams to two but you eliminated the Doril-T entirely. You said you prescribed the Doril-T in order to prevent possible side effects of the Olanon. Since I am still taking the Olanon, shouldn't I also be taking the Doril-T?

    Doctor: Since you did not experience any side effects from the seven milligrams of Olanon, there is no reason to fear side effects from two milligrams of Olanon.

    Which of the following identifies a problem in the doctor's reasoning?

    (A) Medications cause side effects in proportion to the amount prescribed.

    (B) Without Doril-T, a mere two milligrams of Olanon may prove insufficient.

    (C) The Doril-T may have prevented side effects caused by the Olanon.

    (D) Since no side effects were experienced from seven milligrams of Olanon, the new prescription should have called for a greater, not lesser, amount.

    (E) The question as to why no Doril-T was prescribed is not addressed.

27. Analyst: This corporation is currently putting all its efforts into maximizing short-term profits. Whatever happened to our traditional philosophy of slow, steady growth and emphasis on long-term profitability? One aspect of the problem is seen in simple mathematics. Of our 57 district managers, only 7 have been with the corporation for five years or more. In addition, only 5 of our 16 vice presidents and only 2 of the 9 members of the board of directors have been with the corporation for five years.

    Which of the following conclusions does the author of this passage most probably want the reader to draw?

    (A) The corporation needs to seek leadership from outside sources if it is to remain profitable in the long run.

    (B) One of the reasons that the corporation's traditional financial goals have been ignored is that very few of its high-ranking employees have much experience with the corporation.

    (C) The only reason that the corporation's traditional financial goals have been ignored is that very few of its high-ranking employees have much experience with the corporation.

    (D) The corporation's traditional financial goals are outmoded.

    (E) Even though the corporation's traditional financial goals are being ignored, company management has made great strides by bringing in leadership from outside sources.

GO ON TO THE NEXT PAGE

KAPLAN

28. Hubert Humphrey's attempt in his campaign to dissociate <u>himself from the Johnson foreign policies was built around emphasis on Humphrey's Senate career</u>.

    (A) himself from the Johnson foreign policies was built around emphasis on Humphrey's Senate career

    (B) him from the Johnson foreign policies were built around emphasis on Humphrey's Senate career

    (C) him from the Johnson foreign policies was built around emphasis on Humphrey's Senate career

    (D) himself from the Johnson foreign policies were built around emphasis on Humphrey's Senate career

    (E) him from the Johnson foreign policies was built around emphasizing the Senate career of the candidate

29. Since conscious patients often died of shock on the operating table, <u>the invention of anesthesia was essential to the development of surgery as the invention of the propeller was to powered flight</u>.

    (A) the invention of anesthesia was essential to the development of surgery as the invention of the propeller was to powered flight

    (B) inventing anesthesia was as essential for the development of surgery as the invention of the propeller was for powered flight

    (C) the invention of anesthesia was as essential in the development of surgery much as the invention of the propeller had been for powered flight

    (D) the invention of anesthesia was as essential to the development of surgery as the invention of the propeller was to powered flight

    (E) the invention of anesthesia was essential to the development of surgery, so was the invention of the propeller essential to powered flight

30. New evidence suggests that women may react differently than men to high blood pressure, or hypertension. Women with hypertension are less likely to suffer from ensuing complications, such as heart attacks or strokes, and are less likely to die as a result. Women's higher estrogen levels may be related to this phenomenon: After menopause, when estrogen levels lower, women gradually become more and more susceptible to cardiovascular disease.

    Which of the following positions would be best supported by the statements in the passage above?

    (A) Very elderly women with high blood pressure are no less susceptible to complications than their male counterparts are.

    (B) When treating their female patients for hypertension, doctors should take into account whether or not the patient has gone through menopause.

    (C) Men with hypertension should receive immediate treatment, while women with high blood pressure may wait until their condition becomes severe.

    (D) Since women withstand high blood pressure more readily than men do, the benefits they receive from lowering it are relatively insignificant.

    (E) Women with very high blood pressure are as likely to suffer complications from their condition as are men with only slightly elevated blood pressure.

GO ON TO THE NEXT PAGE

KAPLAN

31. Unlike football, which is played on a standardized field, <u>baseball fields vary considerably in both size and shape</u>.

    - (A) baseball fields vary considerably in both size and shape
    - (B) baseball fields vary considerably, in size as well as in shape
    - (C) baseball is played on a field that varies considerably in both size and shape
    - (D) baseball is played on fields that vary considerably in both size and shape
    - (E) baseball is played on a field that varies considerably in size as well as in shape

32. <u>An important reason to be vaccinated would be that vaccination</u> prevents the spread of infectious diseases, such as cholera, typhoid, and typhus, that are prevalent in areas of the world that lack proper sanitation.

    - (A) An important reason to be vaccinated would be that vaccination
    - (B) Vaccination is important because it
    - (C) An important reason to be vaccinated is because it
    - (D) You should be vaccinated and this
    - (E) An important reason to be vaccinated is that vaccination

PASSAGE 4—DURKHEIM

A pioneering figure in modern sociology, French social theorist Emile Durkheim examined the role of societal cohesion on emotional well-being. Believing that scientific meth-
(5) ods should be applied to the study of society, Durkheim studied the level of integration of various social formations and the impact that such cohesion has on individuals within the group. He postulated that social groups with
(10) high levels of integration serve to buffer their members from frustrations and tragedies that could otherwise lead to desperation and self-destruction. Integration, in Durkheim's view, generally arises through shared activities and
(15) values.

Durkheim distinguished between *mechanical solidarity* and *organic solidarity* in classifying integrated groups. *Mechanical solidarity* dominates in groups in which individual
(20) differences are minimized and group devotion to a common aim is high. Durkheim identified *mechanical solidarity* among groups with little division of labor and high rates of cultural similarity, such as among
(25) more traditional and geographically isolated groups. *Organic solidarity*, in contrast, prevails in groups with high levels of individual differences, such as those with a highly specialized division of labor. In such groups,
(30) individual differences are a powerful source of connection, rather than of division. Because people engage in highly differentiated ways of life, they are by necessity interdependent. In such societies, there is greater
(35) freedom from some external controls, but such freedom occurs in concert with the interdependence of individuals, not in conflict with it.

GO ON TO THE NEXT PAGE ⟶

KAPLAN

Durkheim realized that societies may take
(40) many forms and consequently that group
allegiance can manifest itself in a variety
of ways. In both types of societies outlined
above, however, Durkheim stressed that
adherence to a common set of assumptions
(45) about the world was a necessary prerequisite
for maintaining group integrity and avoiding
social decay.

33. The author is primarily concerned with

  (A) supporting a specific approach to the study of
  the integration of social groups

  (B) comparing different ways that group
  dynamics maintain allegiance among group
  members

  (C) illustrating how a highly specialized division of labor can protect individuals from
  depression

  (D) helping people determine what type of
  society will best suit their emotional needs

  (E) contrasting a traditional view of a social
  phenomenon with a more recent one

34. The passage contrasts *mechanical solidarity* and
organic solidarity along which of the following
parameters?

  (A) The degree to which each relies on objective
  measures of group coherence

  (B) The manner and degree to which members
  are linked to the central group

  (C) The means by which each allows members to
  rebel against the group norm

  (D) The length of time that each has been used to
  describe the structure of societies

  (E) The effectiveness of each in serving the interests of its members

35. It can be inferred from the passage that

  (A) as societies develop, they progress from
  organic solidarity to *mechanical solidarity*

  (B) group integration enables societies to mask
  internal differences to the external world

  (C) Durkheim preferred *organic solidarity* to
  mechanical solidarity

  (D) individuals from societies with high degrees
  of *organic solidarity* would be unable to
  communicate effectively with individuals
  from societies that rest on *mechanical
  solidarity*

  (E) the presence of some type of group integration is more important for group
  perpetuation than the specific form in which
  it is manifest.

36. The passage states that *organic solidarity*
predominates in societies with relatively high levels
of intragroup dissimilarity because

  (A) it enables individual differences to be
  minimized

  (B) it causes societies to become more highly
  specialized, thus aiding industrialization

  (C) individuals who engage in highly specialized
  activities must rely on others to ensure that
  their basic needs are met

  (D) these societies are at greater risk of being
  affected by social stressors

  (E) these societies are more likely to engage in
  shared activities and values.

GO ON TO THE NEXT PAGE

KAPLAN

Questions 37–38 are based on the following.

Through their selective funding of research projects, pharmaceutical companies exert too much influence upon medical research in universities. Only research proposals promising lucrative results are given serious consideration, and funding is usually awarded to scientists at large institutions who already have vast research experience. As a result, only larger universities will be able to continue developing adequate research facilities, and graduate students will learn that their future research must conform to the expectations of the corporation. Research will continue to be conducted at the expense of human welfare.

37. Which of the following reactions of a pharmaceutical company representative would provide the strongest rebuttal to the comments above?

   Ⓐ Many of the research projects funded by pharmaceutical companies do not end up being lucrative.

   Ⓑ Much of the funding provided by pharmaceutical companies goes to fellowships that help pay for the educations of graduate students.

   Ⓒ If it were not for the funds that pharmaceutical companies provide, very little medical research could be conducted at all.

   Ⓓ The committee members fail to discuss other methods of funding research projects.

   Ⓔ Larger universities are the only ones equipped to conduct the kind of research sponsored by pharmaceutical companies.

38. The reasoning of the argument above depends upon which of the following assumptions?

   Ⓐ As universities become primarily research institutions, teaching will be neglected.

   Ⓑ Graduate students are not motivated by humane interests.

   Ⓒ Smaller universities would be better suited to serve as product development laboratories for pharmaceutical companies.

   Ⓓ Medical research should be funded by government-regulated foundations.

   Ⓔ The interests of pharmaceutical companies and human welfare are usually incompatible in research.

39. <u>Prosecutors use a reliable forensic method, graphology, in forgery cases, which may also be used by</u> employers to uncover clues to prospective employees' characters.

   Ⓐ Prosecutors use a reliable forensic method, graphology, in forgery cases, which may also be used by

   Ⓑ Prosecutors in forgery cases that have used graphology as a reliable forensic method and may also be usedd by

   Ⓒ Graphology, a reliable forensic method used by prosecutors in forgery cases, may also be used by

   Ⓓ As a reliable forensic method, prosecutors use graphology in forgery cases, which may also be used by

   Ⓔ Prosecutors which use graphology in forgery cases, a reliably forensic method may also be used by

GO ON TO THE NEXT PAGE ⇒

40. Until recently, parents whose teenaged child had signed a purchase contract <u>without their written agreement were not</u> liable for the child's debt.

   Ⓐ without their written agreement were not

   Ⓑ that they do not agree in writing have not been

   Ⓒ and they had not agreed in writing had not been

   Ⓓ without them agreeing in writing had not been

   Ⓔ without their written agreement are not

41. The state legislature has proposed a law that requires all new cars sold in the state to be equipped with airbags for both front seat passengers. The auto industry has lobbied against the proposed law, pointing out that front seat airbags would prevent only a small percentage of serious injuries, since in most accidents, serious injuries are avoidable by the use of seatbelts.

   Which of the following, if true, would most weaken the argument put forth by the auto industry?

   Ⓐ The government has a duty to protect the welfare of its citizens.

   Ⓑ The number of accidents per mile driven in the state is substantially higher than that for the rest of the nation.

   Ⓒ The cost of equipping automobiles with airbags will be passed on to the consumer in the form of higher prices.

   Ⓓ Most serious injuries occur when front seat passengers are not wearing their seatbelts.

   Ⓔ Because the law would apply only to new cars, it would take nearly a decade for the majority of the state's cars to become equipped with airbags.

IF YOU FINISH BEFORE TIME IS CALLED, YOU MAY CHECK YOUR WORK ON THIS SECTION ONLY. DO NOT TURN TO ANY OTHER SECTION IN THE TEST. STOP

KAPLAN

ANSWERS ON
THE NEXT PAGE

ANSWERS AND EXPLANATIONS

1.	B	22.	C
2.	A	23.	A
3.	D	24.	D
4.	C	25.	A
5.	E	26.	C
6.	B	27.	B
7.	D	28.	A
8.	E	29.	D
9.	D	30.	B
10.	D	31.	D
11.	C	32.	B
12.	E	33.	B
13.	B	34.	B
14.	D	35.	E
15.	E	36.	C
16.	C	37.	C
17.	B	38.	E
18.	A	39.	C
19.	E	40.	A
20.	E	41.	D
21.	B		

1.   B

In (A), "the theory of land mammals returning" is awkward; "the theory that land mammals returned" is better. (C) and (E) make the same mistake as (A) with "theory of." (E) also talks about "evidence of support for the theory" when it should say "evidence in support of the theory." So (A), (C), and (E) all use incorrect prepositions. (D) has the unnecessary words "that they." (B) makes the sentence short and to the point.

2.   A

First, since the sentence starts with "although," "whereas" in (C) is redundant. Now we can concentrate on parallelism. The plural "modern roller coasters" should not be compared with the singular "the old-fashioned roller coaster," so (B) is wrong. Choice (D) leaves the sentence with no main verb. This brings us to (A) and (E). Choice (E) may not seem too bad, but (A), "have more and longer straight drops," is clearer than (E) and more strictly parallel to the first part of the sentence.

3.   D

The Conclusion: The Governor's survey on solid waste disposal must have had skewed results.

The Evidence: Eighty percent of respondents support a rise in spending for environmentally safe disposal of solid waste.

The author assumes that most people who respond to this kind of survey will favor environmental safety—she's arguing that the respondents weren't representative of the population as a whole.

The author doesn't think that only environmentalists received the survey, (A), but that a disproportionate number of respondents are environmentalists. She isn't criticizing the judgment of "most citizens," (B). It's not that there's a problem with the survey itself, (C), but with the interpretation of the survey. And we don't know anything about the author's opinion on solid waste issues, (E).

4.   C

The Conclusion: People aren't cheating on their taxes as much as they used to.

The Evidence: The amount, in dollars, of taxes collected from personal income tax has gone up appreciably in recent years.

We're only concerned with revenue from the personal income tax, so any information about the corporate taxes is outside the realm of our interest.

All the wrong choices provide alternative explanations—explanations as to how we can have more tax dollars collected without people being more honest in reporting their incomes. Fewer deductions, (A), would probably cause people to pay more money in taxes. A population increase, (B), would produce more tax payers. If average income went up, (D), then average tax paid would go up as well. And if the tax rate rose, (E), the government would very likely collect more money.

PASSAGE 1—FORSET

Topic and Scope: A worldview prevalent in post-Reformation England.

Purpose and Main Idea: The author says that many English people after the Reformation conceived of the world as a system of hierarchies, in which the king's or queen's position as ruler is part of the natural order of things, and reflects God's plan.

Paragraph Structure: In a single paragraph, the author explains why early English Protestants hungered for order, and how the concept of order that some thinkers came up with coincided with the will of the British monarchs.

5. E

(E) is a fairly direct paraphrase of the idea stated in the passage's opening sentence, with the added (but easy) inference that the Catholic Church formerly provided structure and stability to English society. There is nothing to suggest (A), that the monarchy was declining. Quite the contrary, according to the rest of the passage: Elizabeth and other monarchs managed quite well to maintain their grip on power, temporarily anyway. The passage also implies something contrary to (B); rather than being seen as eccentric peculiar, the "divinely inspired" hierarchical view of Forset and other thinkers won wide acceptance. Contrary to (C), the need for order was felt to be "compelling," as it's put in the first sentence. As for (D), there's no evidence for this idea. The passage mentions the Catholic Church simply as having been rejected, nothing more.

6. B

This choice puts together the idea of hierarchy, as found in Forset and other thinkers, with the statement in the last sentence that people accepted stability as God's will. The implication is that Elizabeth and her successors maintained their influence and power because English society accepted the idea of a divinely prescribed social structure in which the monarch occupied the top of the social heap. Choice (A) exaggerates the role of the thinkers. Yes, they pretty much had the ear of the public, apparently, but to say they were a small group that had tight, almost conspiratorial control is too extreme. It's inconsistent with the passage's tone. (C) puts things backwards; as the sentence about Elizabeth and Parliament make clear, the monarchs claimed a position far above that of most people. That same sentence also makes clear that Parliament, while apparently not mounting effective resistance to Elizabeth, was nonetheless "recalcitrant," not passive. Finally, (E) could be true, but there is nothing to suggest it in the passage; what the passage does do is tie Elizabeth's success to the idea of divine sanction for social hierarchy, and this should lead you back to correct choice (B).

7. D

This choice is supported by two references in the passage. The first is the reference to a "recalcitrant Parliament"; the second is the veiled suggestion in the last sentence that there were restive elements in English society that had to be held down or kept in check by the monarchy, and that the English public's interim acceptance of a divine hierarchical scheme aided the monarchy in this situation. This choice completes the thought by adding the plausible idea that Parliament represented these rebellious interests. The other choices all fail, in one way or another, to follow the logic of the passage's ideas. Choice (A) contradicts the last sentence's suggestion that the monarchs' grip on power was short-lived. (B) contradicts the widespread acceptance and immediate influence of Forset's notions. (C) is inconsistent with the apparent opposition of Parliament to a political hierarchy in which the monarch was the unquestioned authority. (E), lastly, illogically pits Elizabeth against her staunch advocate, Forset. (In fact, though the passage doesn't mention it, Elizabeth was dead by the time Forset wrote his tract.)

8.   E

The Conclusion: Critics' opinions aren't any more reliable than those of the average person.

The Evidence: Critics tend to have similar points of view that are rooted in the prejudices of their class.

The author seems to believe that critics' opinions aren't necessarily more significant than those of the average Joe, so (E), a restatement of the main idea, is easy to conclude. Their opinions are no more likely to be a guide to quality, so when they disagree with the public, they're no more likely to be right.

Though the author says that critics' opinions aren't more correct than those of average moviegoers, he doesn't imply that they're usually incorrect, (A).

It's not that there are no right or wrong judgments about films, (B), but that critics don't always make the right judgments. We don't know how frequently critics dislike popular movies, (C), just that it's often assumed that they have valid reasons for doing so. And (D), that critics agree about any given movie, is too strong, since the author only says that their opinions tend to reflect certain class prejudices.

9.   D

The Conclusion: (as stated in the stem) The club won't raise enough money from their plan to ask alumni for donations.

The Evidence: Similar plans have been tried in the past, and the clubhouse is still in bad shape.

The author is predicting that the plan won't work because it didn't work in the past.

An analogy, (A), would be a comparison, but there's no comparison made here. You may have thought of the argument as an analogy from past to future, but (D) is a much better description of this. The author has no opponents that we know about, so (B) and (E) are somewhat far-fetched. The author does point out past failures of alumni fund-raising, but there's no logical connection drawn by the club members between those attempts and this one, and so no fallacy, (C).

10.   D

The second clause as it stands fails to clearly refer to the action of the first clause. It would be better to have said "which LBJ also did," but that still isn't correct. In this case,

"as did" is proper, not "which did." (A) and (B) use the unidiomatic "which." (C) lacks a second verb. In (E), "do" is redundant. (D) is correct because it repeats the verb: Kennedy increased, as did Johnson. "As did" correctly stands for the entire phrase "increased the participation of the United States in the war in Vietnam."

11.   C

You should never say "the reason . . . was because." This rules out (A) and (D). A possessive form of a noun, like "Scipio Africanus'," cannot stand for a pronoun, so (B) is wrong. "The reason being" in (E) is unnecessarily wordy.

12.   E

"Need for . . . to be" is one of those locutions that seems to pop up a lot on long and unwieldy sentence corrections. You can't say "a need that," so get rid of (A). A quick scan shows that (C) and (D) have the same problem as (A). They're just not idiomatically correct. (B) is illogical. The need isn't for pine and flax that "are made" into masts and sails. If the need had been for pine and flax in a ready-made form, then the correct way to say it would be "were made," not "are made," because we are talking about the past. The need was for pine and flax "to be made" into masts and sails, indicating what was to be done with the materials. That makes (E) the best choice. Even if you couldn't narrow it to one, knowledge of the idiom would allow you to eliminate three choices.

PASSAGE 2—GROUP MANAGEMENT

Topic and Scope: The value of group management; specifically, the benefits and risks of using decisional conflict in group management.

Purpose and Main Idea: Author agrees that building conflict into group management is good (it leads to better managerial decisions), but stresses that there are potential risks. Experts are divided over what form of decisional conflict is best (and least risky).

Paragraph Structure: Paragraph 1 acknowledges the value of group decision making and the use of decisional conflict, and identifies the risks, the "dilemma," involved in using decisional conflict: "Decisional conflict may yield better decisions at the risk of weakening managerial effectiveness.

Conversely, the harmony that facilitates cooperation and implementation may come at the cost of inferior decisions." Paragraph 2 identifies two methods of building conflict into group decisions (dialectical inquiry and devil's advocacy) and explains the similarities and differences. Paragraph 3 explains how experts disagree about which approach is better.

13. B

Choice (B) covers all the paragraphs. Paragraph 1 discusses the benefits and risks of decisional conflict, and paragraphs 2 and 3 focus on the two alternative approaches.

(A) ignores the discussion of the *risks* of decisional conflict. And the author never tries to "reconcile" the two approaches. The verb "defend" makes choice (C) suspect, the author never defends anything against critics. (D) doesn't work because the author never implies that group decision making is better than any other approach. And with (E), the author never indicates a preference for dialectical inquiry or devil's advocacy.

14. D

Paragraph 2 details similarities as well as differences between the two approaches. One similarity is that both rely on "formal debate," which clearly implies choice (D).

(A) is an irrelevant detail; the only mention of "compromise" is at the end of the passage where Cosier charges that dialectical inquiry could lead to compromises and inferior decisions. The problem with (B) is that only dialectical inquiry involves "opposing sets of proposals." (C) and (E), like (A), refer to irrelevant details in the last paragraph.

Note: Even without a line reference, the stem must steer you to paragraph 2. After a fast, *strategic* skimming of the passage, you should be equipped to recognize where the answer will be found.

15. E

You need the choice that's *inconsistent* with one of Cosier's criticisms, one of which is that dialectical inquiry "may run counter to managers' accustomed ways of thinking." (E) would cast doubt on this criticism: "Managers willing to alter their usual modes of thinking often make better decisions."

(A) doesn't work because it paraphrases—and therefore would support—one of Cosier's criticisms. With (B), Cosier implies nothing about "demanding that managers agree" about a decision. Choice (C) is a point that Cosier and everyone else connected with this passage would agree

with. (D), like (B), is an irrelevant point; Cosier says nothing about the need for some decisions to be made rapidly.

16. C

Application questions like this one ask you to recognize a choice that's consistent with information in the passage. (C) parallels the passage's *basic idea* about management groups: The opening sentence states that "corporate managers often work in groups because of the complexity of strategic problems." In a similar way, in (C), "a committee of administrators forms to address the major problems of running a hospital." The hospital is a type of corporation, and its administrators work as a group to solve its problems.

None of the other choices supplies a parallel situation: Monitoring election results, (A), investigating governmental misconduct, (B), studying an issue of public concern, (D), and observing a college presidential search, (E), are all different from running a corporation.

17. B

The Conclusion: Money spent to make the workplace more pleasant is the cause of stumbling and failing businesses.

The Evidence: New businesses almost always fail, and many established businesses show little or no profit. Workers want expensive perks like paint and radios.

The assumption here is that providing these niceties works only to the detriment or disadvantage of the businesses—that it's as simple as spending money and getting no return. We weaken the argument by denying this assumption, and showing that the perks increase productivity. In this case, the new paint, radios, and artwork might well be a wise investment.

Even if the workers work very hard, (A), it doesn't mean that they don't make excessive demands on their employers. It could be possible that in the past businesses went under for other reasons, (C), and yet still be true that they are now going under because of the perks. The author hasn't claimed that different types of businesses are the same thing, as in (D) and (E), but rather, that they're in trouble for the same reason.

18. A

The underlined part of the sentence is a modifying phrase; what's modified is "islands." Choice (D) gives us a run-on sentence. Choices (B) and (E) use pronouns in a confusing way. Choice (C) is just plain awkward.

PASSAGE 3—DINOSAUR EXTINCTION

Topic and Scope: The extinction of the dinosaur; specifically, recent findings suggest that the extinction was caused by "a sudden, catastrophic event" (paragraph 1).

Purpose and Main Idea: Author outlines new findings and theories that run counter to the old notion ("Scientists long believed . . . ," line 1) that the extinction resulted from gradual climate changes. Scientists differ about the exact type of event, but agree that a collision between earth and some kind of extraterrestrial body caused an environmental catastrophe that led to extinction.

Paragraph Structure: Paragraph 1: The opening two sentences are key; the discoveries in Italy led to a revision of the old view that the extinction resulted from gradual climate changes. The remainder of this paragraph—everything about iridium levels—is supporting detail. Skim confidently! Let the questions dictate a closer reading. Paragraph 2: The gist here is simply that "scientists differ over the exact nature of the event" (the opening line). All else should be skimmed. Paragraph 3: An objection is raised, then rebutted. Paragraph 4: The summary of what the Berkeley group believes, that the collision led to a massive disruption in the global food chain, which led to the demise of the dinosaurs.

19. E

Paragraph 1 discusses the discovery of high iridium levels in Italy and other locales, and the remaining paragraphs discuss the implications of that notable discovery. (E) expresses this in shorthand form.

(A) is too narrow. Paragraph 2 cites varying opinions, but that's the focus of one paragraph only. In (B), "rebutting" doesn't fit; it's too strong. It's true that the older belief about gradual climatic changes is outdated, but the passage's purpose isn't to "rebut." It's to describe new findings and their significance. With (C), the methodology of the Berkeley group is never described as "controversial." Nor does the passage "evaluate" the methodology. With (D), the passage never suggests "a new course of investigation."

20. E

The point is clear from the cited sentence: The lack of the isotopes indicated to scientists that the iridium levels *did not* result from a stellar explosion. (E) is a clear paraphrase of that information.

The "older theory about the extinction of the dinosaur," choice (A), is an irrelevant detail from the previous paragraph. With (B), the passage says nothing about the isotope level being useful for dating purposes. (C) misses the point. The question wasn't whether or not iridium originated extraterrestrially, but whether the specific source was an exploding star. The blockage of sunlight, (D), is another unrelated detail, from the final paragraph.

21. B

(B) jibes with information in the final paragraph. The Berkeley group believes that the main effect of the collision was the blockage of sunlight and a drop in photosynthesis. This would be reflected in a drop in plant fossils in strata younger than those studied in Italy.

Strata *older than* the iridium-rich level would not affect the argument of the Berkeley group, (A). With (C), the discovery of high iridium levels above and below the enriched clay layer would tend to raise questions about, not strengthen, the Berkeley group's findings. With (D), the Berkeley group's argument is that an event *of some kind* led to a massive ecological disruption. Whether the collision involved an asteroid or a comet is secondary. With (E), a finding that the clay layer was deposited gradually would weaken the Berkeley group's thesis.

22. C

One way to start with this sentence is to try to figure out what's most important. Joe Kittinger seems to have done two equally important things: He set a distance record and he became the first balloonist to cross the Atlantic solo. Choice (C) puts these two achievements on an equal footing by expressing them both in participial phrases ("setting" and "becoming"). So does (E), but it omits the "and," which is necessary. Choices (A), (B), and (D) fail to make it clear that it was by piloting his balloon from Maine to Italy that Kittinger accomplished these two things.

23. A

First, "crises" is the plural form of "crisis," so (B), with the singular verb "does," is wrong. Next, "do not always result from malice" in (A) and "aren't always the results of malice" in (D) are both fine, but "do not always result of malice" in (C) is unidiomatic, and "aren't resulting always from malice" in (E) is awkward. Now let's look at the second part of the sentence. Remember that the part on each side of the semicolon must be an independent clause. All of the answer choices except (A) either fail to provide a main verb for the second clause, like (B), (D), and (E), or use unidiomatic expressions, like (B) and (C).

24. D

The problem here has to do with the placement of the modifier. What is caused by the desire to be as thin as possible? Not good eating habits, though that's the impression you could get from (A), and not the ballet dancers and gymnasts, though that's the impression you could get from (B). Eliminate both of these choices. And who or what desires to be as thin as possible? Again, not good eating habits, though you could get that impression from (C) or (E), both of which use the passive voice unnecessarily and indeed confusingly. The correct answer is (D), in which pronoun reference and the placement of modifiers is perfectly clear.

25. A

The Conclusion: Actors from the agency are being sent to audition for roles that are inappropriate for them.

The Evidence: Few actors from the agency are being placed in roles.

The agent must assume that certain actors are inappropriate for certain parts. If she didn't believe this, the argument would make no sense because it wouldn't be possible for an actor to audition for an inappropriate part.

The actors' talent (B) isn't questioned by the agent; she focuses on the types of roles. That it's hard to predict an actor's appropriateness, (C), needn't be assumed—it has no effect on the argument. She could, on the contrary, think it easy to judge a role's appropriateness, and just believe that her company employs incompetents. Major roles, (D), are outside the scope, since the agent doesn't mention them. And if it were true that directors often cast the wrong actors, (E), then the idea that the agency isn't doing well because it's doing just that—sending out the wrong actors—doesn't wash.

26. C

The Doctor's Conclusion: The patient doesn't need to take Doril-T, the side-effect preventing drug.

The Doctor's Evidence: Since the patient didn't have side effects on 7 mg of Olanon, she won't have side effects on 2 mg.

What's the doctor missing here? The idea that the patient probably didn't have side effects on 7 mg because she was taking the Doril-T, the drug intended to prevent side effects. The doctor basically assumes that this drug had no effect, yet presents no evidence.

The doctor seems to believe, (A), that the smaller the amount taken, the less likelihood of side effects—so this isn't a flaw. We don't know and can't assume that the two drugs work together, (B), to produce the desired effect. Why would the doctor prescribe more Olanon, (D)? We're not doctors, so we can't argue this. And (E) is just plain false, since the doctor does describe why no Doril-T was prescribed—because the patient hasn't had side effects.

27. B

The Analyst's Conclusion: The company is moving away from its long-term growth commitment and putting all its eggs into the short-term profits basket.

Her Evidence: Few of the company's top managers have been with the company for more than five years.

What does the author want you to think about all of this? That these "newcomers" have caused the shift in emphasis, and thus, traditional values have been ignored. Otherwise, why argue for the shift in policy by pointing to the relatively short tenure of many of the top managers?

The author wouldn't advocate bringing in more newcomers, (A), since she thinks that they've caused all the trouble. We shouldn't go too far, however, by concluding that the newcomers are the only reason for the trouble, (C), especially since she refers to them as "one aspect of the problem." The author yearns for the traditional values, so she wouldn't want to convince us that they are outmoded, (D). And strong support for the company's hiring of newcomers, (E), is counter to the apparent feelings of our author.

28. A

This sentence talks about what Humphrey attempted to do to Humphrey, so we need the reflexive pronoun: "himself," not "him." We can rule out (B), (C), and (E). Now, "attempt," the noun, is singular, so it has to govern a singular verb: "was," not "were."

29. D

This sentence makes a comparison, so the correct answer will use the "as . . . as" formula. The first "as" is missing in (A). Choice (C) turns the second "as" into "much as," which spoils the construction. Choice (E) omits the "as . . . as" formula altogether, and creates a run-on sentence. You should also remember that the things being compared should be in parallel form, and this is not the case in (B).

30. B

The Conclusion: That's what we're looking for.

The Evidence: Women with high blood pressure are less likely to have heart attacks or strokes than are men with the same condition. This may be related to estrogen levels—after menopause, when estrogen is lowered, women are more likely to get cardiovascular disease.

What can we conclude? That doctors would be wise to take into account whether their female patients are pre- or post-menopausal, since estrogen levels will probably have an effect on their treatment needs. Perfectly reasonable.

We don't have any information that would allow us to conclude (A), that old women are as susceptible as old men, or that (E), women with very high blood pressure face the same risks as men with only slightly high blood pressure. In addition, we can't go so far as to claim that women can wait for treatment, (C). (D) is another distortion. Even though women are less likely to suffer complications from high blood pressure, we can't infer that they receive almost no benefit from lowering their high blood pressure.

31. D

Here's another comparison. Start by making sure that it's logical. Football can be compared with baseball, but not with baseball fields. This eliminates (A) and (B). And of course, a single field cannot vary in size and shape; it is different fields that vary. Since (D) uses the plural "fields," it is the correct answer.

32. B

Would be? No, it is; eliminate (A). "The reason . . . is because," in (C), is unidiomatic. In (D), there is no clear antecedent for "this." This brings us to (B) and (E). Choice (E) is unnecessarily long.

PASSAGE 4—DURKHEIM

Topic and Scope: Emile Durkheim's study of social cohesion in society.

Purpose and Main Idea: To describe two different ways that societies can maintain social integration among their members.

Paragraph Structure: The first paragraph introduces Durkheim and his study of social groups. The second paragraph discusses two ways societies can maintain social integration. The third paragraph offers a broader context for interpreting the evidence in the second paragraph.

33. B

The final paragraph gives you the key to answering this global question. The author is describing different ways that societies can function without choosing a side or advocating a specific position. You can rule out choice (A) immediately for its strong stand. Choice (C) distorts a detail beyond its acceptable scope. While the passage does discuss how social cohesion can function in societies with high degrees of labor specialization, this is not the author's main goal. Choice (D) takes a prescriptive stance, and the author never tells us how to live our lives. Finally, choice (E) makes a comparison that is not there. Both of the mechanisms for maintaining social solidarity were developed by Durkheim at the same time and are part of the same worldview, namely, his. The comparison between a traditional and a recent view is inapplicable here.

34. B

What is the crucial difference between *mechanical solidarity* and *organic solidarity*? The level of homogeneity in the group in which each functions. Neither one relies on any measure, objective or otherwise, of group coherence. Rather, they describe the way societies function naturally, ruling out choice (A). Choice (C) introduces the notion of rebellion, a concept that is not mentioned in the passage and, hence, cannot be correct. Choice (D) is wrong because the two types of solidarity were developed at the same time by Durkheim; we do not have a traditional view and a more recent view of the same phenomenon, but rather two different ways that societies can function within the same worldview. Choice (E) brings into question the effectiveness of each, and the last paragraph makes it clear that either one can serve its members needs equally well.

35. E

In this inference question, you will need to think about the author's opinion as you approach the answer choices. Choice (A) is wrong because the author never discusses the two forms of *solidarity* as being related to each other, nor does she discuss the transformation of societies over time. Choice (B) is outside the scope, as the relationship of individual societies to the world-at-large is not an issue that concerns the author. Choice (C) makes a subjective statement about Durkheim that is never suggested by the passage. Choice (D) makes a comparison between the two types of social groups that is not supported by the passage. Choice (E), however, is basically stated verbatim in the final paragraph of the passage. The particular type of integration that exists within a given society is less important than that it is present in some form.

36. C

Look to the second paragraph, where *organic solidarity* is discussed, and you will see Durkheim's reasoning for why it exists in societies with high levels of heterogeneity. *Organic solidarity* prevails in societies with fewer similarities among members, because when a society is highly specialized, its members rely on each other out of necessity, as a way to ensure that everyone's needs are met. Reading through the answers, choice (C) should jump out at you as conveying this sentiment.

Choice (A) is *au contraire.* In societies in which *organic solidarity* dominates, individual differences are relatively high. Choice (B) implies a causal relationship between *organic solidarity* and the way a society is organized, but *organic solidarity* is simply a term to describe the way a society *is* functioning; it is not an active agent of anything. Choice (D) uses information that was never mentioned in the passage—namely, that some societies are more likely to be affected by social stressors. Finally, choice (E) misappropriates information from the section on societies in which *mechanical solidarity* dominates. Societies that operate by *organic solidarity*, by contrast, tend not to be comprised of members who lead highly similar lives.

37. C

The Conclusion: Pharmaceutical companies have too much influence on university medical research.

The Evidence: Most of the time, only projects that promise profitable results are considered, and only scientists with lots of experience at large universities get funding.

The Dire Prediction: (or ultimate conclusion) Research will continue to be conducted at the expense of human welfare.

The author believes that research would be better off without the meddling of pharmaceutical manufacturers. If, without these companies' funding, though, very little research would get done, then we're better off with their funding, even if it is selective.

The companies, according to the author, are concerned with a project's *potential* profitability, so some actual failures, (A), don't weaken the argument. The author isn't critical because the companies don't help fund students, (B); the issue is which students they fund, and for what research. (D) just turns around and says, "You don't like it? Then what would be better?" A poor attempt at rebuttal, and not a GMAT weakener. The idea that only large universities can support the research, (E), misses the author's point: Only research of the type large universities can carry on is getting funded, and other types of research should be funded but aren't.

38. E

We need an assumption, and if we compare evidence and conclusion (including the author's dire prediction), we find an element for which there's no evidence: the idea of "human welfare." The author must be assuming that the interests of these companies and human welfare are usually at odds in order to conclude that research conducted in the interests of the companies won't be compatible with human welfare.

The quality of university teaching, (A), has nothing to do with this argument. The author doesn't argue that grad students aren't interested in humane pursuits, (B), but rather that they must conform to the companies' expectations. That smaller universities are better for research from the companies' perspective, (C), is way off—the companies, we're told, are only funding the larger universities. And government-regulated foundations, (D), are outside the scope. The author may well believe that some other type of funding is needed, but this particular remedy is not required by the argument.

39. C

(A) and (D) make it seem as if it's forgery cases "which may be used by employers to uncover clues to prospective employees' characters." But the employers are really using graphology to do this. (C) clarifies the sentence. (B) is incomplete and nonsensical. (E) makes it sound as if forgery cases are a forensic method.

40. A

The nonunderlined verb "had signed" lets you know you're talking about the past. So (E)'s definitely out. The child didn't sign a "contract that they do not agree," so (B) can't be right. In (C) and (D), the phrases "and they had not agreed in writing," and "without them agreeing in writing," are unclear. They make it sound as if the parents need to agree with each other. In (A), "without their agreement" makes it clear that the parents are agreeing to the contract.

41. D

The Auto Industry's Conclusion: Putting airbags in cars won't make much difference in preventing injuries.

Its Evidence: In most accidents, injuries are avoidable through the use of seatbelts.

In moving from evidence to conclusion, the auto industry is assuming that seatbelts *do*, not just *can*, prevent most serious injuries. We break the link by showing that lots of injuries occur when people don't wear belts. So airbags will, in fact, prevent injuries because although the belts *would* work, they *aren't used*.

The industry could agree with (A)'s general principle that the government has to protect people without thereby weakening its argument. Evidence about this particular state, (B), is irrelevant to an argument about the protective power of airbags in general. The high cost of airbags, (C), would be more evidence for the auto industry's argument: Assuming they won't prevent many injuries, why charge consumers for them? And (E)'s idea that it will take a long time for most cars to get airbags has no effect: This tells us that whether the bags are a good idea or not, it'll take a while to get it into practice.

PART FIVE

Analytical Writing Assessment

Chapter 6: **Before You Write**

For the GMAT Analytical Writing Assessment, you'll be required to write two essays on two different kinds of topics, one called "Analysis of an Issue," and the other called "Analysis of an Argument." Either of these may appear first on an actual GMAT. You'll be given 30 minutes to write an essay in response to each, and you'll type your essay using a simple word processing program. The general tasks required of you are similar for both essay types. You must analyze a topic, take an informed position, and explain that position in writing.

THE TWO KINDS OF TOPICS

Both essay topics have two basic parts: the stimulus and question stem. The stimulus (the first paragraph in each topic) contains the information you must analyze, and the question stem (the second paragraph) tells you what tasks to perform. But the two kinds of topics look slightly different from each other, and they specify different tasks. Let's take a closer look at our sample topics.

Analysis of an Issue

The stimulus and question stem of an Analysis of an Issue topic will look something like the example below:

> Many assert that individuals allowed to work flexible schedules at home will be both more productive and happier than colleagues working under more traditional arrangements. But others assert that the close supervision of an office workplace is necessary to ensure productivity and quality control and to maintain morale.

> Which argument do you find more compelling; the case for flexible work conditions or the opposing viewpoint? Explain your position using relevant reasons or examples drawn from your own experience, observations, or reading.

The Stimulus

As you can see from the example above, the stimulus consists of a few sentences discussing a broad issue about which reasonable people could disagree. In this sample stimulus, two points of view on the issue will be discussed. However, sometimes only one point of view is presented. In either case, you won't need prior knowledge of any specific subject matter in order to analyze the issue.

The first sentence or two will introduce the general issue itself and express a point of view. If two viewpoints are expressed, a Keyword (here it's the word *but*) will sometimes signal the introduction of the contrasting point of view. The transition will not always be quite as explicit, however. The last part of the stimulus will then discuss the contrary view of the issue. If a single viewpoint is discussed, the last part will elaborate on it a little more fully.

The Question Stem

The stem will ask you what viewpoint you find most convincing, and instruct you to explain your position, using reasons or examples to back up your assertions. Although the specific wording of the instructions may vary, the basic tasks required of you will be essentially the same.

Exactly what does this stem ask you to do?

> Which argument do you find more compelling, the case for flexible work conditions or the opposing viewpoint?

Translation: There are two, conflicting viewpoints here; take one side or the other.

> Explain your position using relevant reasons or examples drawn from your own experience, observations, or reading.

Translation: Argue your position, using specific examples. Support your points with evidence.

Analysis of an Argument

The stimulus and question stem of an Analysis of an Argument topic will look something like the example below:

> The problem of poorly trained teachers that has plagued the state public school system is bound to become much less serious in the future. The state has initiated comprehensive guidelines that oblige state teachers to complete a number of required credits in education and educational psychology at the graduate level before being certified.

> Explain how logically persuasive you find this argument. In discussing your viewpoint, analyze the argument's line of reasoning and its use of evidence. Also explain what, if anything, would make the argument more valid and convincing or help you to better evaluate its conclusion.

The Stimulus

The first part of an Analysis of an Argument topic expresses a point of view, an argument, in much the same way as in Critical Reasoning. In an Analysis of an Argument stimulus, the writer tries to persuade you of something—her conclusion—by citing some evidence. When you read the "argument" in the stimulus, be on the lookout for assumptions—things that the writer takes for granted as she makes the conceptual leap from evidence to conclusion.

The Question Stem

Question stems will ask you to decide how persuasive you find the argument. Most likely you'll be asked to explain how convincing an argument is, and discuss what might improve the argument. (It's also possible that the GMAT folks may ask you to explain why an argument is not convincing and then poke holes in it.) For this task, you'll need to first analyze the argument and evaluate its use of evidence; second, explain how a different approach or more information would make the argument better.

Let's take a closer look at the question stem to see what these questions ask you to do:

Explain how logically persuasive you find this argument . . . analyze the argument's line of reasoning and use of evidence.

Translation: Critique the argument. Discuss whether you think it's convincing or not and explain why.

. . . explain what, if anything, would make the argument more valid and convincing or help you to better evaluate its conclusion.

Translation: Spot weak links in the argument and offer constructive modifications that would strengthen them.

Now let's look at how the Kaplan Method works for each topic.

THE KAPLAN METHOD FOR ANALYTICAL WRITING

Step 1: Digest the issue/argument (2 minutes)

Step 2: Select the points you will make (5 minutes)

Step 3: Organize (1 minute)

Step 4: Write/type your essay (20 minutes)

Step 5: Proofread your work (2 minutes)

The timing guidelines are approximate. Don't worry about being precise in how you use your time. The important thing is to make sure you have time to finish.

THE KAPLAN METHOD: ANALYSIS OF AN ISSUE

Here's how we can apply the Kaplan Method to the Analysis of an Issue topic we saw before.

Step 1: Digest the Issue

Many assert that individuals allowed to work flexible schedules at home will be both more productive and happier than colleagues working under more traditional arrangements. Others assert that the close supervision of an office workplace is necessary to ensure productivity and quality control and to maintain morale.

Which argument do you find more compelling, the case for flexible work conditions or the opposing viewpoint? Explain your position using relevant reasons or examples drawn from your own experience, observations, or reading.

First, identify the issue and the different points of view. *Note:* If only *one* point of view is expressed, evaluate it and consider possible alternative viewpoints.

What's the basic issue? Try to frame it as a question.

Should people be allowed to work at home with flexible schedules?

What do those in *favor* say?

Those working at home are happier and more productive.

What do those *opposed* say?

Close supervision of workers is needed to maintain productivity, quality control, and morale.

Are there any phrases that may need some interpretation?

flexible schedules (just how flexible?)
close supervision (just how close?)
more production
quality control
maintain morale

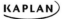

Step 2: Select the Points You Will Make

You're given *two* points of view here. So first, compare them; weigh them against each other:

Arguments in Favor:

- Productivity
- Happier workers

Arguments Opposed:

- Closer supervision
- Better quality control
- Maintain morale

Be objective. Hold off on taking a side or interpreting implications. Start by just *summarizing* information that's specified in the stimulus.

Then decide which side you'll advocate.

There's no "right" answer; you can take *either* side. (If only one point of view is expressed, focus on whether you agree or disagree with that point of view.)

In Favor of Flexibility: I'll argue that flexible schedules make sense

- Flexibility means better use of time = productivity
- Flexibility would save the company money
- Flexibility would make me/workers happier

Against Flexibility: I'll argue that flexibility is a bad idea

- Closer supervision = more productivity
- Closer supervision = easier to regulate quality
- It's easier to redress worker grievances in office setting

Map out your side of the argument; try to spot the main points of conflicting viewpoints, too. (If only one viewpoint is presented, imagine possible alternatives.)

Reasons to Favor:

- People respond well to additional responsibility and trust
- Better use of worker's time (no commuting time)
- Smaller business expenses (e.g., electricity, telephones)
- Commuting time (and costs) cut

Reasons to Oppose:

- Hidden supervisory and management costs of coordinating out-of-house work
- Harder to react to sudden emergencies and rush jobs
- Communication and technological difficulties
- Harder to communicate to workforce as a whole

List the **assumptions**:

In Favor:	Opposed:
• Worker productivity/morale is not improved by being around colleagues	• Worker productivity/morale is better when around colleagues
• Workers don't require the closer supervision offered by traditional office setup	• Feel more comfortable with traditional office setup
	• Delegating too much authority is risky

Step 3: Organize

Try renumbering points and using this as your outline.

Argument in Favor of Flexible Scheduling:

Flexible scheduling will:

1. Increase productivity
2. Make workers happy
3. Save money/cut expenses

because:

1. Most people respond well to additional responsibility and trust
2. There is better use of worker's time (no commuting time)
3. There are smaller business expenses (e.g., electricity, telephones)

Assumptions:

1. Worker productivity/morale is not improved by being around colleagues
2. Workers don't require the closer supervision offered by traditional office setup

Often, the best way to validate the assumptions contained in your argument is to address and counter the arguments of other viewpoints.

Workers don't need closer supervision because:

• Quality control won't be a problem for the company because:
• Close supervision isn't needed to "maintain morale" because:

Communication and technological difficulties are not an issue because:

• Most people respond well to additional responsibility and trust (cite an example)

Step 4: Write/Type Your Essay

What's your thesis sentence?

For:

> Allowing individuals to work at home with a flexible schedule makes good business sense for two basic reasons. This arrangement could both cut a company's operating expenses and create a more productive, more highly motivated workforce.

Opposed:

> The idea of allowing people to work at home without a clearly fixed schedule is a bad idea from a management perspective for a number of reasons. First . . . .

Step 5: Proofread Your Work

THE KAPLAN METHOD: ANALYSIS OF AN ARGUMENT

Now let's apply the Kaplan Method to the Analysis of an Argument topic we saw earlier.

Step 1: Digest the argument

> The problem of poorly trained teachers that has plagued the state public school system is bound to become much less serious in the future. The state has initiated comprehensive guidelines that oblige state teachers to complete a number of required credits in education and educational psychology at the graduate level before being certified.

> Explain how logically persuasive you find this argument. In discussing your viewpoint, analyze the argument's line of reasoning and its use of evidence. Also, explain what, if anything, would make the argument more valid and convincing or help you to better evaluate its conclusion.

Spot the topic and scope of the argument.

> Topic: *The problem of poorly trained teachers*
> Scope: *A given solution, centering on mandatory classes*

What's the conclusion?

> The problem of poorly trained teachers that has plagued the state public school system is bound to become a good deal less serious in the future.

What's the evidence?

> The state has initiated comprehensive guidelines that oblige state teachers to complete a number of required credits in education and educational psychology at the graduate level before being certified.

Most arguments will be structured in one of two ways:

<u>conclusion</u> *because* <u>evidence</u>

or

<u>evidence</u> *therefore* <u>conclusion</u>

Sum this argument up in your own words:

The problem of badly trained teachers will become less serious because
(conclusion)

of the better training they'll be getting.
(evidence)

How does the argument use its evidence?

It uses evidence of better training regulations to conclude that future improvement is likely.

Step 2: Select the Points You Will Make

Are there any assumptions—gaps between evidence and conclusion?

Yes.
- *Coursework in education will improve teachers' classroom performance*
- *Present (bad) teachers haven't already met this standard (of classroom training)*
- *Poor teachers now teaching will not still be teaching in the future or will be trained to*

Under what circumstances are these assumptions valid?

- *The required credits have to be something new. Otherwise, they can't have much effect.*
- *Since the argument predicts future improvement, the actual improvement might not occur until all current teachers are out of the system.*

Is there anything relevant that's not discussed?

Yes. How to get rid of or improve poor teachers now teaching.

What would make the argument stronger or more valid?

In this case, we need some new evidence supporting the assumptions:

- *Evidence verifying that this training will make better teachers*
- *Evidence making it clear that present bad teachers haven't already had this training*
- *Evidence suggesting why all or many bad teachers won't still be teaching in the future (or why they'll be better trained)*

Step 3: Organize

What's your outline?

1. The argument says that:

   The problem of badly trained teachers will become less serious because of the better training they'll get.

2. The argument assumes that:
   - Coursework in education will improve teachers' classroom performance
   - Present (bad) teachers haven't already met this standard (of classroom training)
   - Poor teachers now teaching either will not still be teaching in the future or will have been trained to

3. It could be improved by:
   - Evidence verifying that this training will make better teachers
   - Evidence making it clear that present bad teachers haven't already had this training
   - Evidence suggesting why all or many bad teachers won't still be teaching in the future

Step 4: Write/Type Your Essay

What is your opening sentence?

The writer concludes that the present problem of poorly trained teachers will become less severe in the future because of required coursework in education and psychology.

Step 5: Proofread Your Work

Now you've seen how to build essays for both Analysis of an Issue and Analysis of an Argument questions. Next we'll see how the method works on two other sample questions.

ANALYSIS OF AN ISSUE, TAKE 2

In response to what they view as the inordinate attention and funding given to university athletics and the detrimental effect this has on learning, some people suggest that universities should drop their intercollegiate sports programs altogether. They reject claims that participation in sports builds character and discipline, as well as the idea that sports help develop the "whole person" in ways that academics or other extracurricular activities cannot.

Do you think that intercollegiate university sports programs should be abolished? Explain your position using relevant reasons or examples drawn from your own experience, observations, or reading.

Notice that the question stem is worded differently here, but the basic idea is essentially the same: You must take a side on the issue and make your best case, using evidence in the argument and any examples you can devise.

Step 1: Digest the Issue

What's the basic issue? Try to frame it as a question.

> Should universities drop their intercollegiate sports programs?

Those in favor of abolishing sports programs would say:

> Intercollegiate sports get too much money and attention; this detracts from education.

Those opposed to abolishing them would say:

> "Education" also involves developing the whole person; sports programs serve this purpose.

Notice how another viewpoint is clearly implied in this stimulus, even though only one side is explicitly stated.

Phrases that may need interpretation?

> inordinate attention (how much is "too much"?)
>
> detriment of learning
>
> whole person
>
> character and discipline

Step 2: Select the Points You Will Make

Be objective: What are the differing viewpoints here?

Since only one viewpoint is specified here, use your imagination a bit:

Arguments for Those in Favor (of abolishing):

- Sports programs cost too much
- They get too much attention

Arguments for Those Opposed (to abolishing):

- They educate the whole person
- Sports build character and discipline

Take a side; which one do you prefer?

> I'll argue for abolishing sports.

Remember, you can still defend either point of view; pick the one for which you can make a stronger argument.

Now add reasons of your own.

Abolish Sports Programs:	Keep Them:
• Read about abuses in the news (e.g., recruiting violations)	• Most programs are clean (e.g. ?)
• Money spent on sports could go to better ends (e.g., scholarships)	• Sports raise money through ticket sales and alumni interest (they give $$$)
• Students go to college to learn, not play games and waste time	• Education also takes place outside the classroom
• Sports doesn't "teach" anything valuable	• Sports help build the "whole person" by teaching cooperation, etc.

List the **assumptions**:

Abolish Sports Programs:	Keep Them:
• Students should go to college to study and learn	• There's more to life than books
• Education should mean "hitting the books"	• There are many ways to learn—not all in the classroom
• "Jocks" are not good role models	• Who wants to be a "nerd"?

Step 3: Organize

Now, renumber these points and use them as a working outline.

Sports programs should be abolished because:

1. They're not part of education
   - Sports don't "teach" anything valuable
   - Students go to college to learn, not play games and waste time
   - Students should go to college to study and learn; "education" should mean "hitting the books"

2. They're a waste of money
   - Money spent on sports could go to better ends (e.g., scholarships)
   - Read about abuses in the news (e.g. ?)

If time permits, counter the arguments of the other side.

(Sports help build the "whole person")

   - "Jocks" are not good role models

Step 4: Write/Type Your Essay

What's your thesis sentence?

For (abolishing sports):

Getting rid of intercollegiate sports programs would allow universities to spend money on more important things and would allow students to concentrate on learning—the primary reason people go to college.

Opposed (to abolishing sports):

I think universities should keep their sports programs because these programs serve a number of valuable purposes. First, . . .

Use your notes from Steps 1–3 as a "working outline."

Step 5: Proofread Your Work

ANALYSIS OF AN ARGUMENT, TAKE 2

Newly developed CD-ROM technology will ensure that librarians are able to make any text they choose to store available to the public quickly. Hundreds of volumes can be recorded on small, durable disks—all of which can be kept within a relatively small room—and read using a computer monitor.

Explain how logically persuasive you find this argument. In discussing your viewpoint, analyze the argument's line of reasoning and its use of evidence. Also explain what, if anything, would make the argument more valid and convincing or help you better to evaluate its conclusion.

Step 1: Digest the Argument

Spot the topic and scope of the argument.

Topic: *CD-ROM technology*
Scope: *Its value as a library resource*

What's the conclusion?

Newly developed CD-ROM technology will ensure that librarians are able to make any text they choose to store quickly available to the public.

What's the evidence?

Hundreds of volumes can be recorded on small, durable disks—all of which can be kept within a relatively small room—and read using a computer monitor.

How's this argument structured?

conclusion	*because*	evidence
	or	
evidence	*therefore*	conclusion

(Here it's:

conclusion	*because*	evidence)

Sum it up in your own words:

Libraries will become more efficient (conclusion) because of CD-ROM technology, with its huge storage capacity (evidence).

How does the argument use its evidence?

It uses evidence about a technological innovation to predict the future.

Step 2: Select the Points You Will Make

Are there any assumptions—gaps between evidence and conclusion?

Yes.

- Books will be copied onto CD-ROM disks
- Libraries will be able to afford this technology
- Librarians will want to buy CD-ROM versions of books along with all needed technology (computers, etc.)
- Librarians and the public will know how to operate the CD hardware so texts are readily available and actually read
- The public will be willing to let CD-ROM disks replace or supplement paper

Under what circumstances are these assumptions valid?

- If cost is affordable
- If librarians' and library patrons' attitudes allow use of CD-ROM

How extreme is the conclusion, given the evidence?

It's too sweeping; "will ensure that" predicts the future with absolute certainty.

Is there anything relevant that's not discussed?

- Cost issues
- Attitudes of librarians and the public towards this technology

What would make the argument stronger or more valid?

- Evidence that libraries can afford the technology
- Evidence that books are/will be copied onto the CD format
- Evidence that librarians will purchase CDs and related hardware
- Evidence that librarians are/will be trained to use CDs and related hardware
- Qualifying the conclusion so it's less extreme

Step 3: Organize

1. The argument says that:
   Libraries will become more efficient because of CD-ROM technology, with its huge storage capacity.

2. The argument assumes that:

   Cost:

   - Books will be copied onto CD-ROM disks
   - Libraries will be able to afford this technology

   Attitude:

   - Librarians will want to buy CD-ROM versions of books along with all needed technology (computers, etc.)
   - Librarians and the public will know how to operate the CD hardware so texts are readily available and actually read
   - The public will be willing to let CD-ROM disks replace or supplement paper

3. It could be improved by:
   - Evidence that books are/will be copied onto the CD format
   - Evidence that libraries can afford the technology
   - Evidence that librarians will purchase CDs and related hardware
   - Evidence that librarians are/will be trained to use CDs and related hardware

4. It could also be strengthened by:
   - Changing the word "ensure" to "facilitate" or "make it possible," thereby changing a prediction of certainly to a probability. (Nobody can predict the future with absolute certainty.)

Step 4: Write/Type Your Essay

What's your opening sentence?

The argument asserts that the public will surely be able to read any text it wants because of the development of CD-ROM disks with enough memory to store hundreds of volumes on a single text.

Step 5: Proofread Your Work

Chapter 7: **Sample Essays**

One way to learn how to write better essays is to read essays written by other people and try to evaluate them yourself. In this chapter, you'll see three sample GMAT Analytical Writing Assessment (AWA) essays. Read each essay, use the checklist to rate the author's performance, and then compare your evaluation to ours.

GMAT ESSAY SCORING

GMAT essays are scored holistically, and the essays in this chapter and in the next chapter have been graded in a similar way. Holistic scoring uses a single letter or a number—on the GMAT it's a number— to provide an overall evaluation of an essay as a whole. A holistic score emphasizes the interrelation of different thinking and writing qualities in an essay—such as content, organization, or syntax—and tries to denote the unified effect of all these elements.

Your two GMAT essays will be scored on a scale of 0–6, with 0 the lowest grade and 6 the highest. The average of these two scores will be your overall score for the Writing Sample. The grading chart on the next page will give you an idea of how GMAT grading works for essays on the AWA.

Analysis of an Issue and Analysis of an Argument topics each require a different type of response, so they have slightly different sets of grading criteria. But both kinds of topics require similar essay qualities. The following table, based on information from the Graduate Management Admission Council (GMAC), will give you a general idea of the guidelines a GMAT grader will have in mind when reading your essays.

6: Outstanding Essay

- Insightfully presents and convincingly supports an opinion on the issue or a critique of the argument
- Ideas are very clear, well organized, and logically connected
- Shows superior control of language: grammar, stylistic variety, and accepted conventions of writing; minor flaws may occur

5: Strong Essay

- Presents and strongly supports an opinion on the issue or a critique of the argument
- Ideas are generally clear and well organized; connections are logical
- Shows solid control of language: grammar, stylistic variety, and accepted conventions of writing; minor flaws may occur

4: Adequate Essay

- Presents and adequately supports an opinion on the issue or a critique of the argument
- Ideas are fairly clear and adequately organized; logical connections are satisfactory
- Shows satisfactory control of language: grammar, stylistic variety, and accepted conventions of writing; some flaws may occur

3: Limited Essay

- Succeeds only partially in presenting and supporting an opinion on the issue or a critique of the argument
- Ideas may be unclear and poorly organized
- Shows less than satisfactory control of language; contains significant mistakes in grammar, usage, and sentence structure

2: Seriously Flawed Essay

- Shows little success in presenting and supporting an opinion on the issue or a critique of the argument
- Ideas lack organization
- Meaning is impeded by many serious mistakes in grammar, usage, and sentence structure

1: Fundamentally Deficient Essay

- Fails to present a coherent opinion on the issue or a critique of the argument
- Ideas are seriously disorganized
- Lacks meaning due to widespread severe mistakes in grammar, usage, and sentence structure

0: Unscorable Essay

- Essay completely ignores topic

A WORD ABOUT THE E-RATER

As you've probably heard by now, each AWA essay you write will be graded twice, once by a human grader (usually a person in academia who can use the extra cash), and once by the "E-rater," a computer program designed by ETS to cut test-administration costs. The average of these two scores becomes your overall essay score, and your two essay scores are then averaged for your final AWA score. If the E-rater's score and the human grader's score differ by more than one point, another human grader will be brought in to settle the difference. Here's how a typical AWA score might be derived:

> **"Analysis of an Issue" essay:** Human grader's score: 4, E-rater's score: 5, Overall score: 4.5
>
> **"Analysis of an Argument" essay:** Human grader's score: 4, E-rater's score: 4, Overall score: 4.
>
> Final AWA score: 4.25 (rounded up to 4.3).

ETS takes great pride in the E-rater, and its subsidiary, ETS Technologies, is now trying to sell the program on a subscription basis to colleges as an automated essay-grading program. ETS's pride and faith in the E-rater is based on the high agreement between the scores given by E-rater and those given by human graders (about 91 percent, the same as that among different human graders). But let's face some facts. A computer program cannot follow the thread of an argument. It cannot even follow the grammar of an essay very well, as anyone who's ever used a grammar-check program can tell you. So how do the E-rater's grades manage to correlate so well with those of human graders? And what does this mean to you and the way you should approach writing your essays?

For starters, you may find it insulting to have your essays graded by a computer, but you shouldn't sweat it too much. The E-rater is programmed to recognize the syntactical and grammatical variety that marks high-scoring essays, and the structural words (the "Keywords" discussed in chapter 3) that are found in well-organized essays. For instance, a good Argument essay invariably contains Contrast words such as *however* or *on the other hand*. Keywords that indicate sequential arrangement or parallelisms, such as *not only . . . but also* and *furthermore*, tend to be found in the very best essays as well, as do Keywords that signal Emphasis, Conclusion, Illustration, and Evidence. Make sure to pepper your essays with appropriate Keywords, and the E-rater will reward you accordingly.

In order to achieve the "syntactical variety" that the E-rater recognizes and rewards, you should come up with good synonyms for the phrases in your essay topic, as well as related phrases. For instance, if your Issue essay asks you to discuss the "responsibilities of business leaders towards the communities in which they reside," try to come up with and include good synonyms and related phrases for the terms of this debate—for example *responsibility:* obligation, duty, accountability; *business leader:* entrepreneur, captain of industry, chief executive; *community:* locality, neighborhood; *related phrases:* citizenship, benefactor, sponsorship, philanthropy. And, finally, if you're trying to maintain grammatical variety, just make sure to mix long sentences with short sentences, and to give yourself enough time to proofread your essays for grammatical errors.

Also note that while scores range from 0–6, about 90 percent of all scores fall between 2 and 5. By giving sufficient attention to the superficial attributes that the E-rater seeks in distinguishing good essays from bad ones, you should be able to ensure for an above-average score on the AWA section. Now let's look at some sample essays and see how we might grade them using ETS's scoring formula.

SAMPLE ESSAY 1

Insurance policies guaranteeing the policyholder's income if he or she becomes permanently disabled will surely provide the insurance industry with a popular and profitable product. The cost to a worker who is at average risk is very little, and the benefits paid to the disabled far outweigh this cost.

Explain how logically persuasive you find this argument. In discussing your viewpoint, analyze the argument's line of reasoning and its use of evidence. Also explain what, if anything, would make the argument more valid and convincing or help you to better evaluate its conclusion.

I do not think that the argument about the insurance policies are very "logically convincing." Basically, it makes the same mistakes as so many of our newspapers and television personalities. Namely, just because alot of people like something doesn't mean that it's any good if you really look at it.

The argument says that the policy is a good investment for workers. Specifically, the benefits paid to the disabled far outway the cost, which is very little, or so we're told, but there's no facts to back this up. I don't think that what's a "very little" to a rich man who lives in a mansion and gets hit on the head with a slab of cement is necessarily a "very little" to a working class individual who is in an accident. Even if their injuries are equivalent.

Instead of such "concrete" facts, the argument gives us everyone's opinion, as if everyone were a person or this meant anything. If everyone feels like voting for Adolf Hitler, does that make him a good man? No in my opinion, although it doesn't mean he's necessarily a bad man for that reason. The fact that these insurance policies are going to be popular is no argument either. Just because they're popular doesn't make them cheap or benificial.

I would find the argument more convincing if it mentioned more specific cases of people who made a lot of money by being crippled. I would be feeling better about evaluating the conclusion that such people really exist and that they exist because of these policies. It doesn't matter to me that a lot of people like these policies or think that they are profitible. What matters isn't what people think but what's true.

SAMPLE ESSAY 1—KAPLAN'S EVALUATION

	Poor	Adequate	Outstanding
Analysis of the Argument			
Identifies/Analyzes Argument's Main Features	✔		
Identifies Real or Potential Weaknesses	✔		
Recommends Improvements or New Evidence	✔		
Organization	✔		
Use of Language and Sentence Structure: Correct? Interesting?	✔		
Grammar and Syntax	✔		

Comments:

The essay completely neglects to critique the argument's internal logic. Instead of identifying and analyzing the argument's principal flaw (the inconsistency between conclusion and evidence), the essay's author faults the argument for failing to provide specific examples. Consequently, the essay also fails to note how the argument's structure could be strengthened and what sort of evidence would be needed to assess its validity. Moreover, the essay's organization doesn't help structure its points. Three paragraphs would have done the trick here. The first could have clearly identified the conclusion and evidence, the second could have evaluated the connection between them, and the third could have offered recommendations. Sentence construction and grammar both need work, too.

Holistic Score: 2

SAMPLE ESSAY 2

Insurance policies guaranteeing the policyholder's income if he or she becomes permanently disabled will surely provide the insurance industry with a popular and profitable product. The cost to a worker who is at average risk is very little, and the benefits paid to the disabled far outweigh this cost.

Explain how logically persuasive you find this argument. In discussing your viewpoint analyze the argument's line of reasoning and its use of evidence. Also explain what, if anything, would make the argument more valid and convincing or help you to better evaluate its conclusion.

The writer believes that insurance policies guaranteeing a policyholder's income if he or she becomes disabled could be a profitable and popular product for insurance companies. But insurance companies that introduce such a product are taking an unacceptable risk, for several reasons.

First, any company offering a guaranteed lifetime income may find its available assets permanently and unacceptably drained by large payments to the disabled. The writer doesn't make clear exactly what level of income insurance companies should guarantee. But let's assume they had to provide a lifetime's regular salary for every disabled policyholder. This could represent an unacceptably large outlay for the company, perhaps in the hundreds of millions of dollars.

Second, companies could never be sure what an "average" level of risk for an "average" person is. Of course, insurance companies base their business on estimates of the likelihood of all sorts of mishaps, such as car accidents or theft. But it's not possible to make a reasonable estimate of all the factors that could lead to disability. What of epidemics, such as the current AIDS epidemic that has caused havoc with so many insurance companies, not to mention with people's lives? Before HIV was discovered, it simply wasn't possible for companies to foresee that so many of their customers would get ill.

It is not the role of insurance companies to provide lifelong assistance to disabled people. This role belongs to government, which can muster the vast resources needed to properly care for the ill.

SAMPLE ESSAY 2—KAPLAN'S EVALUATION

	Poor	Adequate	Outstanding
Analysis of the Argument			
Identifies/Analyzes Argument's Main Features	✔		
Identifies Real or Potential Weaknesses	✔		
Recommends Improvements or New Evidence	✔		
Organization			✔
Use of Language and Sentence Structure: Correct? Interesting?			✔
Grammar and Syntax			✔

Comments:

This essay is quite well written but it neglects the tasks specified in the instructions. The essay's sentence structure and grammar are sound, and its organization is clear. However, it goes off on a tangent. Instead of analyzing the internal logic of the argument (i.e., discussing the extent to which the evidence supports the conclusion), the essay takes issue with only the conclusion and argues a contrary point of view. Thus, it also fails to suggest what sort of information would be needed to evaluate and/or strengthen the connection between conclusion and evidence.

Holistic Grade: 4

SAMPLE ESSAY 3

> Some people protest the destruction of famous old buildings, saying that we are losing priceless cultural and historical landmarks. But they forget these buildings weren't intended to be museums but to serve practical purposes. In replacing them, we're doing exactly what the builders of the originals did. In time, the new buildings themselves may be considered landmarks.
>
> Which argument do you find more compelling, the case for preserving old buildings or the opposing viewpoint? Explain your position using relevant reasons or examples taken from your own experience, observations, or reading.

I support the preservation of famous old buildings. I believe it is important to save these landmarks to keep a sense of culture and history. Moreover, historic buildings need not be treated as 'museums,' since there is no reason why they cannot continue to be used. There are countless examples in many cities of historic buildings that are still standing but are now used for something other than their original purpose. In Austin, Texas, restaurants are housed in nineteenth-century settlers' homes. In Charlottesville, Virginia, the original colonial section of the city has been transformed into a shopping area with restaurants and boutiques. And in New York City's Greenwich Village, an old courthouse now houses a branch of the public library. These buildings thus continue to serve citizens' practical needs while also reminding them of their past.

Would it be better to supplant these old buildings with modern, chrome-and-glass skyscrapers simply because replacing them is 'what the builders of the originals did'? If we need room for more skyscrapers, why not demolish numerous buildings that are not considered landmarks? And should any of the new structures eventually become landmarks, we will thus have preserved both traditional and modern examples of our architectural history. In short, there is no reason why historic preservation cannot be compatible with practicality.

SAMPLE ESSAY 3—KAPLAN'S EVALUATION

	Poor	Adequate	Outstanding
Analysis of the Issue			
Identifies Issue			✔
Develops a Convincing Position			✔
Uses Evidence and Examples to Support Argument			✔
Organization			✔
Use of Language and Sentence Structure: Correct? Interesting?			✔
Grammar and Syntax			✔

Comments:

An outstanding essay; this is well constructed and well written. Although brief, the essay fulfills all the tasks specified in the question. The writer takes a clear position and supports it with reasons and several good examples. By pointing out how buildings can be both historical landmarks and serve a practical purpose, the essay also addresses—and rebuts—a key point in the opposing viewpoint. Organization, sentence structure, and grammar are also sound.

Holistic Score: 6

Note: If you are interested in further practice with sample AWA topics, we highly recommend that you visit the GMAC website and print out the complete list of published AWA topics that could appear on your GMAT. This list is available at www.mba.com

| PART SIX |

Appendixes

Appendix 1: **Grammar Reference Guide**

SENTENCE STRUCTURE

Understanding the basic rules of sentence structure enables you to spot the classic GMAT errors quickly. The fundamental principles described here will play a role in nearly every Sentence Correction item you see, whether in the original version or among some of the answer choices. Especially if English is not your native language, be sure to know this basic material.

Run-on Sentences

When a sentence consists of more than one clause (a group of words that contains a subject and a verb), those clauses must be joined properly. It is never acceptable to hook two clauses together with a comma, as the "sentence" below does. That's called a **run-on sentence**.

Wrong:	Nietzsche moved to Basel in 1869, he planned to teach classical philology.

There are a number of acceptable ways to fix a run-on.

Correct:	Nietzsche moved to Basel in 1869; he planned to teach classical philology.
Also Correct:	Nietzsche planned to teach classical philology; therefore, he moved to Basel in 1869.
Also Correct:	Nietzsche moved to Basel in 1869, and he planned to teach classical philology. (The word *and*, like *or*, *for*, *but*, *nor*, and *yet*, is what's called a *coordinating conjunction*.)
Also Correct:	Because Nietzsche planned to teach classical philology, he moved to Basel in 1869. (The word *because*, like *although*, *if*, *though*, etc., is what's called a *subordinating conjunction*.)
Also Correct:	Nietzsche, who planned to teach classical philology, moved to Basel in 1869. (The word *who*, like *which*, *where*, *whom*, *that*, and *whose*, is what's called a *relative pronoun*.)

KAPLAN

Sentence Fragments

Every sentence must contain at least one complete independent clause. If there is no independent clause at all, or if what's supposed to be the independent clause is incomplete, you've got a **sentence fragment**.

Wrong: While most people, who have worked hard for many years, have not managed to save any money, although they are trying to be more frugal now.

This sentence fragment consists of nothing but subordinate clauses. One of the subordinate clauses must be made into an independent clause.

Correct: Most people, who have worked hard for many years, have not managed to save any money, although they are trying to be more frugal now.

Also Correct: While most people, who have worked hard for many years, have not managed to save any money, they are trying to be more frugal now.

SUBJECT-VERB AGREEMENT

Remember, in English, a subject and its verb must **agree** in number and person. **Number** refers to whether a subject (or a verb) is singular or plural. **Person** refers to first person (*I*, *we*), second person (*you*), and third person (*he, she, it, one, they*).

Intervening Phrases

When the subject of a sentence is followed by a phrase (a group of words that does not have a subject and verb) or relative clause, the words are not part of the subject. They simply add information about that subject.

Learn to recognize groups of words that can come between the subject and verb!

1. **Relative clauses**, which contain important information about the subject of another clause, are very often placed in between a subject and verb. (The previous sentence contains a relative clause.)

Wrong: John Clare, *who during the mid-nineteenth century wrote many fine poems on rural themes*, were confined for decades to an insane asylum.

The subject is *John Clare*, which is singular, but the verb is *were*, which is plural. The fact that the relative clause ends with a plural noun (*themes*) is supposed to distract you from the fact that the subject and verb don't agree.

Correct: John Clare, who during the mid-nineteenth century wrote many fine poems on rural themes, *was* confined for decades to an insane asylum.

2. **Appositives** often come between a subject and a verb. Appositives are nouns, pronouns, or noun phrases that are placed next to nouns to describe them further.

Wrong:	John Smith, *the man who led British expeditions to several American sites*, have left several written accounts of dramatic events there.
Correct:	John Smith, the man who led British expeditions to several American sites, *has* left several written accounts of dramatic events there.

Relative clauses and appositives are sometimes set off from the rest of the sentence by commas. When this is the case, it's a dead giveaway that those words are not part of the subject. That makes checking for subject–verb agreement much easier; just ignore the words set off by commas and concentrate on the subject and the verb.

3. The **prepositional phrase** is an all-time favorite.

Wrong:	Wild animals *in jungles all over the world* is endangered.
Correct:	Wild animals in jungles all over the world *are* endangered.

Prepositional phrases, and some relative clauses and appositives, are not set off by commas. It's harder to recognize intervening phrases and clauses when they're not set off by commas, but if you remember to check each sentence carefully for such things, you'll be able to pick them out anyway.

Compound Subjects

When two nouns or groups of nouns are joined by *and*, they're called a **compound subject** and are therefore plural.

Correct:	*Ontario and Quebec* contain about two thirds of the population of Canada.

There are some connecting phrases that may look as though they should make a group of words into a compound subject—but they don't result in a compound subject.

Wrong:	George Bernard Shaw, as well as Mahatma Gandhi and River Phoenix, were vegetarians.

And is the only connecting word that results in a compound and plural subject. The following words and phrases do not create compound subjects:

along with	*as well as*
together with	*besides*
in addition to	

Correct:	*George Bernard Shaw*, as well as Mahatma Gandhi and River Phoenix, *was* a vegetarian.
Wrong:	Neither Thomas Jefferson nor Alexander Hamilton were supportive of Aaron Burr's political ambitions.

KAPLAN

When words in the subject position are connected by *either . . . or* or *neither . . . nor*, the verb agrees with the last word in the pair. If the last word is singular, the verb must be singular. If the last word is plural, the verb must be plural.

Correct:	Neither Thomas Jefferson nor *Alexander Hamilton was* supportive of Aaron Burr's political ambitions.
Correct:	Neither Thomas Jefferson nor *the Federalists were* supportive of Aaron Burr's political ambitions.

Both . . . and is the only pair that always results in a plural subject.

Correct:	*Both* Thomas Jefferson *and* Alexander Hamilton *were* unsupportive of Aaron Burr's political ambitions.

Unusual Sentence Patterns

When you're checking for subject-verb disagreement, remember that the subject doesn't always appear before the verb.

Wrong:	Dominating the New York skyline is the Empire State Building and the Chrysler Building.

The subject of this sentence is a compound subject, *the Empire State Building and the Chrysler Building*. The verb should be plural.

Correct:	Dominating the New York skyline *are* the Empire State Building and the Chrysler Building.

Subjects That Are Not Nouns or Pronouns

An entire clause can serve as the subject of a sentence. When used as subject, a clause always takes a singular verb:

Whether the economy will improve in the near future *is* a matter of great concern.

Infinitives and gerunds can be used as subjects. Remember that they're singular subjects:

To err is human.
Rollerblading is dangerous.

See the section on verbs for more on infinitives and gerunds.

MODIFICATION

Adjectives and adverbs aren't the only sentence elements whose job it is to modify. Phrases and even relative clauses can act as modifiers in a sentence. The following sentence contains several types of modifiers:

> Waiting to regain enough strength to eat, a cheetah, which expends most of its energy in the chase, must rest beside its prey.

Waiting to regain enough strength to eat is a phrase that describes the cheetah, as does the relative clause *which expends most of its energy in the chase*. The phrase *beside its prey* modifies the verb *rest*.

English depends heavily on word order to establish modifying relationships. In other words, most modifiers attach themselves to the first things they can get their hands on in the sentence, even if it's the wrong thing.

Introductory Modifiers

Wrong: Sifting the sand of a river bed, gold was discovered by prospectors in California in 1848.

A modifying phrase that begins a sentence refers to the noun or pronoun immediately following the phrase. But if we apply that rule here, the sentence says that the *gold was sifting sand*. See the problem? The author apparently meant to say that the prospectors were sifting sand. There are several ways to correct the sentence so that it expresses the intended meaning.

Correct: Sifting the sand in a river bed, prospectors discovered gold in California in 1848.

Also Correct: Prospectors, sifting the sand in a river bed, discovered gold in California in 1848.

Also Correct: Gold was discovered by prospectors, who were sifting the sand in a river bed, in California in 1848.

In all three cases the phrase or clause directly precedes or follows the noun it describes.

Dangling Modifiers

A modifying phrase or clause should clearly refer to a particular word in the sentence. A modifying phrase or clause that does not sensibly refer to any word in the sentence is called a **dangling modifier.** The most common sort of dangler is an introductory modifying phrase that's followed by a word it can't logically refer to.

Wrong: Desiring to free his readers from superstition, the theories of Epicurus are expounded in Lucretius's poem *De rerum natura*.

The problem with this sentence is that the phrase that begins the sentence seems to modify the noun following it: *theories*. In fact, there is really nowhere the modifier can be put to make it work properly, and no noun to which it can reasonably refer (*Lucretius's*, the possessive, is functioning as an adjective

KAPLAN

modifying *poem*). Get rid of dangling constructions by clarifying the modification relationship or by making the dangler into a subordinate clause.

Correct: Desiring to free his readers from superstition, Lucretius expounded the theories of Epicurus in his poem *De rerum natura*.

Now the phrase *desiring to free his readers from superstition* clearly refers to the proper noun *Lucretius*.

Other Modifiers

In correcting some of those misplaced introductory modifiers, we move the modifier to a position inside the sentence rather than at the beginning. This is perfectly acceptable, but just remember that modifying phrases inside a sentence can also be misplaced.

Wrong: That night they sat discussing when the cow might calve in the kitchen.

The problem here is the phrase *in the kitchen*, which seems to refer to where the cow might have her calf. What the author probably meant to say is the following correct sentence:

Correct: That night they sat in the kitchen discussing when the cow might calve.

This sentence is correct because the phrase comes directly after the word it modifies: the verb *sat*.

Wrong: As a young man, the French novelist Gustave Flaubert traveled in Egypt, which was a fascinating experience.

It's not that *Egypt* itself was a fascinating experience, but that traveling there was fascinating.

Correct: Traveling in Egypt as a young man was a fascinating experience for the French novelist Gustave Flaubert.

PRONOUNS

When doing Sentence Correction questions, always try to locate the antecedent of a pronoun (that is, the word to which the pronoun refers). Most of the pronoun problems you'll encounter on the test result from a problem in the relationship of the pronoun and its antecedent.

Pronoun Reference

In GMAT English, a pronoun must refer clearly to one and only one antecedent.

1. Watch out for sentences in which pronouns refer to indefinite antecedents, paying particular attention to the pronoun *they*. (Avoid references to some vague *they*.)

Wrong:	They serve meals on many of the buses that run from Santiago to Antofagasta. (Who are *they*?)
Better:	Meals are served on many of the buses that run from Santiago to Antofagasta.

Note: It's quite all right to use *it* like this:

It seldom rains in Death Valley.

2. Sometimes a sentence is structured so that a pronoun can refer to more than one thing, and as a result the reader doesn't know what the author intended.

Wrong:	Pennsylvania Governor William Keith encouraged the young Benjamin Franklin to open his own printing shop because he perceived that the quality of printing in Philadelphia was poor. (*Which* man perceived that the quality of printing in Philadelphia was poor?)

Pronouns are assumed to refer to the nearest reasonable antecedent. Nonetheless, it is best to avoid structural ambiguity of the sort that occurs in this sentence.

Better:	Because *he* perceived that the quality of printing in Philadelphia was poor, Pennsylvania Governor *William Keith* encouraged the young Benjamin Franklin to open his own printing shop. (*Keith* perceived that the quality of printing was poor.)
Better:	Because the young *Benjamin Franklin* perceived that the quality of printing in Philadelphia was poor, Pennsylvania Governor William Keith encouraged *him* to open *his* own printing shop. (In this version, *Franklin* is the one who perceived that the printing was poor.)

3. Sometimes it's easy to see what the author meant to use for the antecedent, but when you examine the sentence more closely that antecedent is nowhere to be found. Correct the problem either by replacing the pronoun with a noun or by providing a clear antecedent.

Poor:	The proslavery writer A. C. C. Thompson questioned Frederick Douglass's authorship of *The Narrative*, claiming that he was too uneducated to have written such an eloquent book.

What's the antecedent of *he*? It should be the noun *Frederick Douglass*, but the sentence contains only the possessive form *Douglass's*. As a rule, avoid using a possessive form as the antecedent of a personal pronoun.

Better:	The proslavery writer A. C. C. Thompson questioned whether Frederick Douglass actually wrote *The Narrative*, claiming that *he* was too uneducated to have written such an eloquent book.

Oddball Problems

Here are two oddball pronoun reference problems to watch out for:

DO SO

Wrong:	It is common for a native New Yorker who has never driven a car to move to another part of the country and have to learn to do it.
Better:	It is common for a native New Yorker who has never driven a car to move to another part of the country and have to learn to *do so*.

ONE AND YOU

When we give advice to others or make general statements, we often use the pronouns *one* and *you*. "You should brush your teeth every day." "One never knows what to do in a situation like that."

It is never acceptable to mix *one* and *you*, or *one* and *yours*, or *you* and *one's* in a sentence together.

Wrong:	One shouldn't eat a high-fat diet and avoid exercise, and then be surprised when you gain weight.
Correct:	*One* shouldn't eat a high-fat diet and avoid exercise, and then be surprised when *one* gains weight.
Also Correct:	*You* shouldn't eat a high-fat diet and avoid exercise, and then be surprised when *you* gain weight.

Also, never use *one* or *one's* to refer to any antecedent except *one*.

Wrong:	A person should leave a light on in an empty house if one wants to give the impression that someone is at home.
Correct:	A *person* should leave a light on in an empty house if *he or she* wants to give the impression that someone is at home.
Also Correct:	*One* should leave a light on in an empty house if *one* wants to give the impression that someone is at home.
Also Correct:	*One* should leave a light on in an empty house if *he or she* wants to give the impression that someone is at home.

Pronoun Agreement

Always use singular pronouns to refer to singular entities and plural pronouns to refer to plural entities. First, identify the antecedent of a given pronoun, and don't allow yourself to be distracted by a phrase that comes between the two. The GMAT will frequently try to confuse you by inserting a phrase containing plural nouns between a pronoun and its singular antecedent, or vice versa.

Wrong:	A cactus will flower in spite of the fact that they receive little water.
Correct:	A *cactus* will flower in spite of the fact that *it* receives little water.

Wrong:	The number of people with college degrees is many times what they were last summer.
Correct:	The *number* of people with college degrees is many times what *it* was last summer.

Note: The number is always singular. (The number of cookies he ate *was* impressive.) *A number* is always plural. (A number of turkeys *were* gathered outside the shed.)

Pronoun Case

One type of pronoun problem you can't catch by looking at the relationship between a pronoun and its antecedent is wrong case.

	Subjective Case	**Objective Case**
First Person:	*I, we*	*me, us*
Second Person:	*you*	*you*
Third Person:	*he, she, it, they, one*	*him, her, it, them, one*
Relative Pronouns:	*who, that, which*	*whom, that, which*

When to Use Subjective Case Pronouns

1. Use the subjective case for the subject of a sentence:
   She is falling asleep.

2. Use the subjective case after forms of *to be*:
   It is *I*.

3. Use the subjective case in comparisons between the subjects of understood verbs:
   Gary is taller than *I* (am).

When to Use Objective Case Pronouns

1. Use the objective case for the object of a verb:
   I called *him*.

2. Use the objective case for the object of a preposition:
   I laughed at *her*.

3. Use the objective case after infinitives and gerunds:
   Asking *him* to go was a big mistake.

4. Use the objective case in comparisons between objects of understood verbs:
   She calls you more than (she calls) *me*.

There probably won't be many times when you are in doubt as to which case of a pronoun is correct. However, the following hints may prove helpful:

When two or more nouns or pronouns are functioning the same way in a sentence, determine the correct case of any pronoun by considering it separately:

Beatrice and (*I* or *me*) are going home early.

Without *Beatrice*, should the sentence read: *Me am going home early* or *I am going home early*? *I am going*, of course, so *Beatrice and I are going home early.*

A common mistake in the use of RELATIVE PRONOUNS is using *who* (subject case) when *whom* (object case) is needed, or vice versa. If you tend to confuse the two, try the following system.

Scholars have disagreed over (*who* or *whom*) is most likely to have written *A Yorkshire Tragedy*, but some early sources attribute it to Shakespeare.

1. Isolate the relative pronoun in its own clause: *whom is most likely to have written* A Yorkshire Tragedy.

2. Ask yourself the question: Who or whom wrote *A Yorkshire Tragedy*?

3. Answer with an ordinary personal pronoun: *He* did. (If you are a native speaker of English, your ear undoubtedly tells you that *him did* is wrong.)

4. Since *he* is in the subjective case, we need the subjective case relative pronoun: *who*. Therefore this sentence should read:

Scholars have disagreed over *who* is most likely to have written *A Yorkshire Tragedy*, but some early sources attribute it to Shakespeare.

VERBS

Here are some important terms and concepts to review before you read this section:

Verb: A word that expresses an action or a state of being.

Verbal: A word that is formed from a verb but is not functioning as a verb. There are three kinds of verbals: *participles*, *gerunds*, and *infinitives*.

It is important to realize that a verbal is not a verb, because a sentence must contain a verb, and a verbal won't do. A group of words containing a verbal but lacking a verb is not a sentence.

Participle: Usually ends in *-ing* or *-ed*. It is used as an adjective in a sentence:

Let *sleeping* dogs lie.
It is difficult to calm a *frightened* child.
Peering into his microscope, Robert Koch saw the tuberculosis bacilli.

Gerund: Always ends in *-ing*. It is used in a sentence as a noun:

Skiing can be dangerous.
Raising a family is a serious task.
I was surprised at his *acting* like such a coward.

Note from the third sentence that a noun or pronoun that comes before a gerund is in the possessive form: *his*, not *him*.

Infinitive: The basic form of a verb, generally preceded by *to*. It is usually used as a noun, but may be used as an adjective or an adverb.

> Winston Churchill liked *to paint*. (Infinitive used as a noun.)
> The will *to conquer* is crucial. (Infinitive used as an adjective—modifies the *will.*)
> Students in imperial China studied the Confucian classics *to excel* on civil service exams. (Infinitive used as an adverb—modifies *studied.*)

Verb Tense

On the GMAT you'll find items that are wrong because a verb is in the wrong tense. To spot this kind of problem, you need to be familiar with both the way each tense is used individually and the ways the tenses are used together.

Present Tense

Use the present tense to describe a state or action occurring in the present time:

> Congress *is* debating about health policy this session.

Use the present tense to describe habitual action:

> Many Americans *jog* every day.

Use the present tense to describe "general truths"—things that are always true:

> The earth *is* round and *rotates* on its axis.

Past Tense

Use the simple past tense to describe an event or state that took place at a specific time in the past, and is now over and done with:

> Hundreds of people *died* when the Titanic sank.
> Few people *bought* new cars last year.

There are two other ways to express past action:

> Bread *used to* cost a few cents per loaf.
> George Bush *did promise* not to raise taxes.

Future Tense

Use the future tense for intended actions or actions expected in the future:

> The twenty-second century *will begin* in the year 2101.

We often express future actions with the expression *to be going to:*

> I *am going to move* to another apartment as soon as possible.

The simple present tense is also used to speak of future events. This is called the **anticipatory future.** We often use the anticipatory future with verbs of motion, such as *come, go, arrive, depart,* and *leave*:

> The senator *is leaving* for Europe tomorrow.

We also use the anticipatory future in two-clause sentences when one verb is in the regular future tense:

> The disputants will announce the new truce as soon as they *agree* on its terms.

Present Perfect Tense

Use the present perfect tense for actions and states that started in the past and continue up to and into the present time:

> Hawaii *has been* a state since 1959.

Use the present perfect for actions and states that happen a number of times in the past and may happen again in the future:

> Italy *has had* many changes in government since World War II.

Use the present perfect for something that happened at an unspecified time in the past. Notice the difference in meaning between the two sample sentences below:

Present Perfect: Susan Sontag *has written* a critical essay about Leni Riefenstahl. (We have no idea when—we just know she wrote it.)

Simple Past: Susan Sontag *wrote* a critical essay about Leni Riefenstahl in 1974. (We use the simple past because we're specifying when Sontag wrote the essay.)

Past Perfect Tense

The past perfect tense is used to represent past actions or states that were completed before other past actions or states. The more recent past event is expressed in the simple past, and the earlier past event is expressed in the past perfect:

> After he came to America, Vladimir Nabokov translated novels that *he had* written in Russian while he was living in Europe.

Note the difference in meaning between these two sentences:

> The Civil War *had ended* when Lincoln was shot. = *The war was over by the time of Lincoln's death.*
> The Civil War *ended* when Lincoln was shot. = *The war ended when Lincoln died.*

Future Perfect Tense

Use the future perfect tense for a future state or event that will take place before another future event:

> By the time the next election is held, the candidates *will have debated* at least once. (Note that the present tense form [anticipatory future] is used in the first clause.)

Sequence of Tenses

When a sentence has two or more verbs in it, you should always check to see whether the tenses of those verbs correctly indicate the order in which things happened. As a general rule, if two things happened at the same time, the verbs should be in the same tense.

Wrong: Just as the sun rose, the rooster crows.

Rose is past tense and *crows* is present tense, but the words just as indicate that both things happened at the same time. The verbs should be in the same tense.

Correct: Just as the sun *rose*, the rooster *crowed*.

Also Correct: Just as the sun *rises*, the rooster *crows*.

When we're talking about the past or the future, we often want to indicate that one thing happened or will happen before another. That's where the past perfect and the future perfect come in.

Use the past perfect for the earlier of two past events, and the simple past for the later event.

Wrong: Mozart finished about two thirds of the Requiem when he died.

Putting both verbs of the sentence in the simple past tense makes it sound as if Mozart wrote two thirds of the Requiem after dying. If we put the first verb into the past perfect, though, the sentence makes much more sense.

Correct: Mozart *had finished* about two thirds of the Requiem when he *died*.

Note: Occasionally, the GMAT won't use the past perfect for the earlier event. They'll use a word like *before* or *after* to make the sequence of events clear. You should always look for the past perfect, but if it's not there, you can settle for the simple past with a time word such as *before* or *after*.

Use the future perfect for the earlier of two future events.

Wrong: By the time I write to Leo he will probably move.

The point the author is trying to get across is not that Leo will move when he gets the letter, but that by the time the letter arrives he'll be living somewhere else.

Correct: By the time I write to Leo, he *will* probably *have moved*.

When you use a participial phrase in a sentence, the action or the situation that phrase describes is assumed to take place at the same time as the action or state described by the verb of the sentence.

Wrong: *Being* a French colony, Senegal is a Francophone nation.

This implies that Senegal is still a French colony. We can make the information in the participial phrase refer to an earlier time than does the verb by changing the regular participle to what's called a **perfect participle**. The way to do it is to use *having + the past participle*.

Correct: *Having been a French colony*, Senegal is a Francophone nation.

KAPLAN

You can do the same thing with infinitives by replacing the regular infinitive with *to have + the past participle:*

> I'm glad *to meet* you. (I'm glad to be in the process of meeting you right now.)
>
> I'm glad *to have* met you. (I'm glad now that I met you earlier today, last week, or whenever.)

Subjunctive Mood

On the GMAT you may come across an item that tests your knowledge of the subjunctive. Subjunctive verb forms are used in two ways.

The subjunctive form *were* is used in statements that express a wish or situations that are contrary to fact:

> I wish I *were* a rich man. (But I'm not.)
> If I *were* you, I wouldn't do that. (But I'm not you.)

The **subjunctive of requirement** is used after verbs such as *ask, demand, insist,* and *suggest*—or after expressions of requirement, suggestion, or demand. A subjunctive verb of requirement is in the base form of the verb: the infinitive without *to:*

> Airlines insist that each passenger *pass* through a metal detector.
> It's extremely important that silicon chips *be made* in a dust-free environment.

Conditional Sentences

Conditional sentences are if-then statements:

> *If* you go, *then* I'll go, too.

We use conditional sentences when we want to speculate about the results of a particular situation. There are three types of conditional sentences.

Statements of Fact: There is a real possibility that the situation described in the *if* clause really happened, or is happening, or will happen:

> If Vladimir Putin resigns, there will be unrest in Russia.
> If John Milton met Galileo, they probably discussed astronomy.

Contrary to Fact: The situation in the *if* clause never happened, so what is said in the *then* clause is pure speculation:

> Blaise Pascal wrote that if Cleopatra's nose had been shorter, the face of the world would have changed.
> Alexander the Great said, "If I were not Alexander, I would want to be Diogenes."

Future Speculation: Some conditional sentences speculate about the future, but with the idea that the situation in the *if* clause is extremely unlikely to happen:

> If Shakespeare's manuscripts were to be discovered, the texts of some of his plays would be less uncertain.

PARALLELISM

Remember, when you express a number of ideas of equal importance and function in the same sentence, you should always be careful to make them all the same grammatical form (that is, all nouns, all adjectives, all gerunds, all clauses, or whatever). That's called **parallel structure** or **parallelism.**

Coordinate Ideas

Coordinate ideas occur in pairs or in series, and they are linked by conjunctions such as *and*, *but*, *or*, and *nor*, or, in certain instances, by linking verbs such as *is*.

Wrong:	To earn credits, an American college student can take up folk dancing, ballet, or study belly dancing.
Correct:	To earn credits, an American college student can take up *folk dancing*, *ballet*, or *belly dancing*.

Note that once you begin repeating a word in a series like the following, you must follow through:

Wrong:	A wage earner might invest her money in stocks, in bonds, or real estate.
Correct:	A wage earner might invest her money *in* stocks, *in* bonds, or *in* real estate.
Also Correct:	A wage earner might invest her money *in* stocks, bonds, or real estate.

This principle applies equally to prepositions (*in*, *on*, *by*, *with*, etc.), articles (*the*, *a*, *an*), helping verbs (*had*, *has*, *would*, etc.), and possessive pronouns (*his*, *her*, etc.). You must either repeat the preposition, helping verb, or whatever, in front of each element in the series, or include it only in front of the first item in the series.

Correlative Constructions

There is a group of words in English that are called **correlative conjunctions.** They are used to relate two ideas in some way. Here's a list of them:

both . . . and

either . . . or

neither . . . nor

not only . . . but (also)

You should always be careful to place correlative conjunctions immediately before the terms they're coordinating.

Wrong:	Isaac Newton not only studied physics but also theology.

The problem here is that the author intends to coordinate the two nouns *physics* and *theology*, but makes the mistake of putting the verb of the sentence (*studied*) after the first element of the construction (*not only*), and in so doing destroys the parallelism. Note that the solution to an error like this is usually to move one of the conjunctions.

Correct: Isaac Newton studied not only *physics* but also *theology*.

Compared or Contrasted Ideas

Frequently, two or more ideas are compared or contrasted within the same sentence. Compared or contrasted ideas should be presented in the same grammatical form.

Certain phrases should clue you in that the sentence contains ideas that should be presented in parallel form. These phrases include *as . . . as* and *more (or less)* x *than* y.

Wrong: Skiing is as strenuous as to run.
Correct: *Skiing* is as strenuous as *running*.
Wrong: Skiing is less dangerous than to rappel down a cliff.
Correct: *To ski* is less dangerous than *to rappel* down a cliff.

To Be

In certain cases, sentences with forms of *to be* must be expressed in parallel form.

Wrong: To drive while intoxicated is risking grave injury and criminal charges.

When an infinitive is the subject of *to be*, don't use a gerund after the verb, and vice versa. Pair infinitives with infinitives and gerunds with gerunds.

Correct: *To drive* while intoxicated is *to risk* grave injury and criminal charges.

Note that we wouldn't change both words to gerunds in this sentence because it wouldn't sound idiomatic.

COMPARISONS

On the GMAT, you will see a number of sentences that make comparisons. A sentence that makes a comparison must do two things: It must be clear about what is being compared, and it must compare things that logically can be compared. A sentence that makes an unclear or illogical comparison is grammatically unacceptable. When you see a comparative expression such as *like, as, more than, unlike, less than, similar to,* or *different from,* it should remind you to ask yourself two questions about the comparison in the sentence: Is it clear? Is it logical?

Unclear Comparisons

Sometimes it isn't clear what the author is trying to compare.

Wrong: Byron admired Dryden more than Wordsworth.

There are two ways to interpret this sentence: that Dryden meant more to Byron than Wordsworth did, or that Byron thought more highly of Dryden than Wordsworth did. Whichever meaning you choose, the problem can be cleared up by adding more words to the sentence.

Correct:	Byron admired Dryden more than *he did* Wordsworth.
Also Correct:	Byron admired Dryden more than *Wordsworth did*.

Illogical Comparisons

Sometimes what the author meant to say is clear enough, but what the author meant to say is not what he or she ended up saying.

Wrong:	The peaches here are riper than any other fruitstand.

This sentence is comparing *peaches* to *fruitstands*, even though that's clearly not the intention of the author. We can correct it so that we're comparing peaches to peaches by inserting the phrase *those at*.

Correct:	The peaches here are riper than *those at* any other fruitstand.

Now the pronoun *those* is standing in for *peaches*, so the sentence is accurately comparing things that can be reasonably compared: the peaches here and some other peaches.

Incomplete comparisons like this one are normally corrected by inserting a phrase like *those of, those in, those at, that of, that in,* and *that at*.

Incomplete comparisons can also be corrected by use of the possessive.

Wrong:	Many critics considered Enrico Caruso's voice better than any other tenor. (This is comparing a voice to a person.)
Correct:	Many critics considered Enrico Caruso's voice better than *any other tenor's*. (Note that this is a shortened version of: *Many critics considered Enrico Caruso's voice better than any other tenor's voice*.)

The second sort of incomplete comparison occurs when one thing is being compared to a group it is a part of. This error is corrected by inserting either the word *other* or the word *else*.

Wrong:	Astaire danced better than any man in the world.

This is wrong because he couldn't have danced better than himself.

Correct:	Astaire danced better than any *other* man in the world.

Comparative Forms

The comparative form is used when comparing only two members of a class, and the superlative for three or more.

Loretta's grass grows *more vigorously* than Jim's.
Loretta's grass grows the *most vigorously* of any in the neighborhood.

Of Buchanan and Lincoln, the *latter* was *taller*.
Of McKinley, Roosevelt, and Taft, the *last* was *heaviest*.

Idiom

Sometimes the right way to say something isn't a matter of grammar but is a matter of **idiom:** an accepted, set phrase or usage that's right for no other reason than that's just the way we say it.

Most of what we call "idioms" are pairs of words that are used together to convey a particular meaning, and many "idiom errors" result from substituting an unacceptable word—usually a preposition—for a word that is always part of the idiom.

Wrong: Brigitte Bardot has joined an organization that is concerned in preventing cruelty to animals.

The adjective *concerned* is followed by either *about* or *with*, either of which would be idiomatic here. But the expression *concerned in* simply isn't idiomatic—we just don't say it that way.

Correct: Brigitte Bardot has joined an organization that is *concerned with* preventing cruelty to animals.

Also Correct: Brigitte Bardot has joined an organization that is *concerned about* preventing cruelty to animals.

There are so many possible idiom errors of this kind that we can't list them all. The most frequently tested errors, however, are contained in appendix 3 of this book on Common GMAT Idioms.

ELLIPSIS

An **ellipsis** is the omission from a sentence of words that are clearly understood. Ellipsis is perfectly acceptable as long as it's done properly—in fact, we do it all the time. Not many people would make a statement like:

I've seen more movies this year than you have seen movies this year.

Instead, we would automatically shorten the statement to the much more concise and natural sounding:

I've seen more movies this year than you have.

In the following sentence, ellipsis is properly used:

The Spectator was written by Addison and Steele.

This is a shorter way of saying:

The Spectator was written by Addison and by Steele.

It's all right to leave the second *by* out of the sentence because the same preposition appears before *Addison* and before *Steele*, so you need to use it only once.

Now watch what happens when ellipsis is improperly used.

Wrong: Ezra Pound was interested but not very knowledgeable about economics.

This is wrong because the preposition that's needed after the word *interested* (*in*) is not the same as the preposition that follows the word *knowledgeable* (*about*).

Correct: Ezra Pound was *interested in* but not very *knowledgeable about* economics.
Wrong: London always has and always will be the capital of the United Kingdom.

This is wrong because the verb form that's needed after *has* is not the same as the one that's needed after *will*, so both must be included.

Correct: London *always has been* and *always will be* the capital of the United Kingdom.

Negatives

You will probably run across at least one item that tests your ability to recognize the difference between idiomatic and unidiomatic ways to express negative ideas. You already know that a double negative is a no-no in standard written English. You wouldn't have any trouble realizing that a sentence such as "I don't want no help" is unacceptable. But the incorrect negatives you will probably see on the exam won't be quite that obvious.

The obviously negative words are *neither, nobody, nor, nowhere, never, none, not, no one,* and *nothing.* But don't forget that *barely, rarely, without, hardly, seldom,* and *scarcely* are also grammatically negative.

In Sentence Correction, you'll find problems with these words where sentences connect two or three negative ideas. Read through the following example sentences carefully:

There were *neither* threats *nor* bombing campaigns.
There were *no* threats *or* bombing campaigns.
There were *no* threats *and no* bombing campaigns.
There were *no* threats, *nor* were there bombing campaigns.

These are the most common idiomatic ways to join two negative ideas. If you can remember these patterns, you can probably eliminate many wrong answers, because they in some way violate these idiomatic patterns.

Wrong: When Walt Whitman's family moved to Brooklyn, there were no bridges nor
                    tunnels across the East River.

The phrase *no bridges nor tunnels* is just not idiomatic—it contains a double negative. The sentence can be rewritten to correct the problem in several ways.

Correct:	There were *no bridges or tunnels* across the East River.
Also Correct:	There were *neither bridges nor tunnels* across the East River.
Also Correct:	There were *no bridges and no tunnels* across the East River.

Another situation in which negatives can cause problems is in a series. Words like *no*, *not*, and *without* must follow the same rules as prepositions, articles, helping verbs, and the like.

Wrong:	After the floods in the Midwest, many farmers were left without homes, businesses, and huge bills to replace all they had lost.

When a preposition, such as *without* in this sentence, is used in front of only the first member of a series, it's taken to refer to all three members of the series. Here, that causes the sentence to say that the farmers were left without homes, without businesses, and without huge bills to replace what they had lost, which makes no sense. There are several ways to rewrite the sentence so that it makes sense.

Correct:	After the floods in the Midwest, many farmers were left *without* homes, *without* businesses, and *with* huge bills to replace all they had lost.
Also Correct:	After the floods in the Midwest, many farmers were left *with no* homes, *with no* businesses, and *with* huge bills to replace all they had lost.
Also Correct:	After the floods in the Midwest, many farmers were left *with no* homes, *no* businesses, and huge bills to replace all they had lost.

Appendix 2: **Guide to Usage and Style**

In part five, we discussed how to analyze a GMAT essay topic, organize your thoughts, and outline an essay. Once you have an overall idea of what you want to say in your essay, you can start thinking about how to say it. This appendix emphasizes the skills you need for the second stage of the writing process: producing clearly developed and well-organized essays. The best strategy is to study this section and tackle the exercises in short, manageable blocks, interspersed with the study of other subjects in preparation for the GMAT.

Perhaps the single most important thing to bear in mind when writing essays is this: *Keep it simple*. This applies to word choice, sentence structure, and argument. Obsession about how to spell a word correctly can throw off your flow of thought. The more complicated (and wordy) your sentences, the more likely they will contain errors. The more convoluted your argument, the more likely you will get bogged down in convoluted sentence structure. Yet recall that simple does *not* mean simplistic. A clear, straightforward approach can be sophisticated.

Many students mistakenly believe that their essays will be "downgraded" by such mechanical errors as misplaced commas, poor choice of words, misspellings, faulty grammar, and so on. Occasional problems of this type will not significantly affect your GMAT essay score. The test readers understand that you are writing first-draft essays. They will *not* be looking to take points off for such errors, unless the writer makes them repeatedly. If an essay is littered with misspellings, incorrect usage, and the like, then a more serious communication problem is indicated.

Bottom line: Don't worry excessively about writing mechanics, but do try to train yourself out of poor habits and do proofread your essays for obvious errors. Your objective in taking the GMAT is admission to business school. To achieve that objective, give the business schools what they want. They do not expect eloquence in a 30-minute assignment, but they do want to see effective writing.

KAPLAN

To write an effective essay, there are three things you need to do:

1. **Be concise.**
2. **Be forceful.**
3. **Be correct.**

An effective essay is concise; It wastes no words. An effective essay is forceful; It makes its point. And an effective essay is correct; It conforms to the generally accepted rules of grammar and form.

The following pages break down the three broad objectives of concision, forcefulness, and correctness into 16 specific principles. Don't panic! Many of them will already be familiar to you. And, besides, you will have many chances to practice in the exercises we provide.

Principles 1 through 4 aim primarily at the first objective: concise writing; principles 5 through 10 aim primarily at the second objective: forceful writing; and principles 11 through 16 aim primarily at the third objective: grammatically correct writing. For a thorough understanding of the third of these objectives, though, you should consult appendix 1, the Grammar Reference Guide; in this appendix, we concentrate on principles that are rarely tested in Sentence Correction, but become important when you do your writing. Each principle is illustrated by exercises. (Answers to these exercises are at the end of this section.)

The principles of concise and forceful writing are generally not as rigid as the principles of grammatically correct writing. Concision and forcefulness are matters of art and personal style as well as common sense and tradition. But if you are going to disregard a principle, we hope you will do so out of educated choice. On the GMAT Analytical Writing Assessment, sticking closely to the principles of standard English writing should produce a concise, forceful, and correct essay.

BE CONCISE

The first four principles of good writing relate to the goal of expressing your points clearly in as few words as possible. Each principle represents a specific way to tighten up your writing.

Principle 1: Avoid Wordiness

Do not use several words when one will do. Wordy phrases are like junk food: They add only fat, not muscle. Many people make the mistake of writing phrases such as *at the present time* or *at this point in time* instead of the simpler *now*, or *take into consideration* instead of simply *consider*, in an attempt to make their prose seem more scholarly or more formal. It does not work. Instead, their prose ends up seeming inflated and pretentious. Don't waste your words or your time.

Wordy: I am of the opinion that the aforementioned managers should be advised that they will be evaluated with regard to the utilization of responsive organizational software for the purpose of devising a responsive network of customers.

Concise: We should tell the managers that we will evaluate their use of flexible computerized databases to develop a customer network.

Exercise 1: Wordy Phrases

Improve the following sentences by omitting or replacing wordy phrases.

1. In view of the fact that John has prepared with much care for this presentation, it would be a good idea to award him with the project.

   _____

2. The airline has a problem with always having arrivals that come at least an hour late, despite the fact that the leaders of the airline promise that promptness is a goal which has a high priority for all the employees involved.

   _____

3. In spite of the fact that she only has a little bit of experience in photography right now, she will probably do well in the future because she has a great deal of motivation to succeed in her chosen profession.

   _____

4. Accuracy is a subject that has great importance to English teachers and company presidents alike.

   _____

5. The reason why humans kill each other is that they experience fear of those whom they do not understand.

   _____

Principle 2: Don't Be Redundant

Redundancy means that the writer needlessly repeats an idea. It's redundant to speak of "a beginner lacking experience." The word *beginner* implies lack of experience by itself. You can eliminate redundant words or phrases without changing the meaning of the sentence. Watch out for words that add nothing to the sense of the sentence.

Here are some common redundancies:

Redundant	Concise
refer back	*refer*
few in number	*few*
small-sized	*small*
grouped together	*grouped*
end result	*result*

Redundancy often results from carelessness, but you can easily eliminate redundant elements when proofreading.

Exercise 2: Redundancy

Repair the following sentences by crossing out redundant elements.

1. All these problems have combined together to create a serious crisis.
2. A staff that large in size needs an effective supervisor who can get the job done.
3. He knows how to follow directions and he knows how to do what he is told.
4. The recently observed trend of spending on credit has created a middle class that is poorer and more impoverished than ever before.
5. Those who can follow directions are few in number.

Principle 3: Avoid Needless Qualification

Since the object of your essay is to convince your reader, you will want to adopt a reasonable tone. There will likely be no single, clear-cut "answer" to the essay topic, so don't overstate your case. Occasional use of such qualifiers as *fairly*, *rather*, *somewhat*, and *relatively*, and of such expressions as *seems to be*, *a little*, and *a certain amount of* will let the reader know you are reasonable, but overusing such modifiers weakens your argument. Excessive qualification makes you sound hesitant. Like wordy phrases, qualifiers can add bulk without adding substance.

Wordy: This rather serious breach of etiquette may possibly shake the very foundations of the corporate world.

Concise: This serious breach of etiquette may shake the foundations of the corporate world.

Just as bad is the overuse of the word *very*. Some writers use this intensifying adverb before almost every adjective in an attempt to be more forceful. If you need to add emphasis, look for a stronger adjective (or verb).

Weak: Novak is a very good pianist.

Strong: Novak is a virtuoso pianist.

                 or

     Novak plays beautifully.

And don't try to qualify words that are already absolute.

Wrong	Correct
more unique	*unique*
the very worst	*the worst*
completely full	*full*

Exercise 3: Excessive Qualification

Practice achieving concision by eliminating needless qualification in the sentences below.

1. She is a fairly excellent teacher.
2. Ferrara seems to be sort of a slow worker.
3. You yourself are the very best person to decide what you should do for a living.
4. Needless to say, children should be taught to cooperate at home and in school.
5. The travel agent does not recommend the trip to Tripoli, since it is possible that one may be hurt.

Principle 4: Do Not Write Sentences Just to Fill Up Space

This principle suggests several things:

- Don't write a sentence that gets you nowhere.
- Don't ask a question only to answer it.
- Don't merely copy the essay's directions.
- Don't write a whole sentence only to announce that you're changing the subject.

If you have something to say, say it without preamble. If you need to smooth over a change of subject, do so with a transitional word or phrase, rather than with a meaningless sentence. If your proofreading reveals unintentional wasted sentences, neatly cross them out.

Wordy:	Which idea of the author's is more in line with what I believe? This is a very interesting . . . .
Concise:	The author's beliefs are similar to mine.

The author of the wordy example above is just wasting words and time. Get to the point quickly and stay there. Simplicity and clarity win points.

Exercise 4: Unnecessary Sentences

Rewrite each of these multiple-sentence statements as one concise sentence.

1. What's the purpose of getting rid of the chemical pollutants in water? People cannot safely consume water that contains chemical pollutants.

   _____

2. I do not believe those who argue that some of Shakespeare's plays were written by others. There is no evidence that other people had a hand in writing Shakespeare's plays.

   _____

3. Which point of view is closest to my own? This is a good question. I agree with those who say that the United States should send soldiers to areas of conflict.

   _____

4. Frank Lloyd Wright was a famous architect. He was renowned for his ability to design buildings that blend into their surroundings.

_____

5. A lot of people find math a difficult subject to master. They have trouble with math because it requires very precise thinking skills.

_____

BE FORCEFUL

The next group of principles aim at the goal of producing forceful writing. If you follow these principles, your writing will be much more convincing to the reader.

Principle 5: Avoid Needless Self-Reference

Avoid such unnecessary phrases as "I believe," "I feel," and "in my opinion." There is no need to remind your reader that what you are writing is your opinion.

Weak:	I am of the opinion that air pollution is a more serious problem than the government has led us to believe.
Forceful:	Air pollution is a more serious problem than the government has led us to believe.

Self-reference is another form of qualifying what you say—a very obvious form. One or two self-references in an essay might be appropriate, just as the use of qualifiers like _probably_ and _perhaps_ can be effective if you practice using them _sparingly_. Practice is the only sure way to improve your writing.

Exercise 5: Needless Self-Reference

Eliminate needless self-references in these sentences.

1. I do not think this argument can be generalized to most business owners.

_____

2. My own experience shows me that food is the best social lubricant.

_____

3. Although I am no expert, I do not think privacy should be valued more than social concerns.

_____

4. My guess is that most people want to do good work, but many are bored or frustrated with their jobs.

_____

5. I must emphasize that I am not saying the author does not have a point.

_____

Principle 6: Use the Active Voice

Using the passive voice is a way to avoid accountability. Put verbs in the active voice whenever possible. In the active voice, the subject performs the action (e.g., we write essays). In the passive voice, the subject is the receiver of the action and the performer of the action is often only implied (e.g., essays are written).

You should avoid the passive voice *EXCEPT* in the following cases:

- When you do not know who performed the action: *The letter was opened before I received it.* (For example, see the last sentence of the above paragraph.)
- When you prefer not to refer directly to the person who performs the action: *An error has been made in computing this data.*

Passive: The estimate of this year's tax revenues was prepared by the General Accounting Office.

Active: The General Accounting Office prepared the estimate of this year's tax revenues.

Exercise 6: Undesirable Passives

Replace passive voice with active wherever possible.

1. The politician's standing in the polls has been hurt by recent allegations of corruption.

   _____

2. The bill was passed in time, but it was not signed by the president until the time for action had passed.

   _____

3. Advice is usually requested by those who need it least; it is not sought out by the truly lost and ignorant.

   _____

4. The minutes of the City Council meeting should be taken by the city clerk.

   _____

5. The report was compiled by a number of field anthropologists and marriage experts.

   _____

Principle 7: Avoid Weak Openings

Try not to begin a sentence with *there is*, *there are*, or *it is*. These roundabout expressions usually indicate that you are trying to distance yourself from the position you are taking.

Exercise 7: Weak Openings

Rewrite these sentences to eliminate weak openings.

1. It would be unwise for businesses to ignore the illiteracy problem.

   _____

2. It would be of no use to fight a drug war without waging a battle against demand for illicit substances.

   _____

3. There are many strong points in the candidate's favor; intelligence, unfortunately, is not among them.

   _____

4. It has been decided that we, as a society, can tolerate homelessness.

   _____

5. There seems to be little doubt that Americans like watching television better than conversing.

   _____

Principle 8: Avoid Needlessly Vague Language

Don't just ramble on when you're writing your GMAT essays. Choose specific, descriptive words. Vague language weakens your writing because it forces the reader to guess what you mean instead of concentrating fully on your ideas and style. The essay topics you're given aren't going to be obscure. You will be able to come up with specific examples and concrete information about the topics. Your argument will be more forceful if you stick to this information.

Weak:	Brown is highly educated.
Forceful:	Brown has a master's degree in business administration.
Weak:	She is a great communicator.
Forceful:	She speaks persuasively.

Notice that sometimes, to be more specific and concrete, you will have to use more words than you might with vague language. This principle is not in conflict with the general objective of concision. Being concise may mean eliminating unnecessary words. Avoiding vagueness may mean adding necessary words.

Exercise 8: Needlessly Vague Language

Rewrite these sentences to replace vague language with specific, concrete language.

1. Water is transformed into steam when the former is heated up to 100° C.

   _____

2. The diplomat was required to execute an agreement that stipulated that he would live in whatever country the federal government thought necessary.

   _____

3. The principal told John that he should not even think about coming back to school until he changed his ways.

_____

4. The police detective had to seek the permission of the lawyer to question the suspect.

_____

5. Thousands of species of animals were destroyed when the last ice age occurred.

_____

Principle 9: Avoid Clichés

Clichés are overused expressions, expressions that may once have seemed colorful and powerful but are now dull and worn out. Time pressure and anxiety may make you lose focus; that's when clichés may slip into your writing. A reliance on clichés will suggest you are a lazy thinker. Keep them out of your essay.

Weak: Performance in a crisis is the acid test for a leader.

Forceful: Performance in a crisis is the best indicator of a leader's abilities.

Putting a cliché in quotation marks in order to indicate your distance from the cliché does not strengthen the sentence. If anything, it just makes weak writing more noticeable. Notice whether you use clichés. If you do, ask yourself if you could substitute more specific language for the cliché.

Exercise 9: Clichés

Make the following sentences more forceful by replacing clichés.

1. Beyond the shadow of a doubt Jefferson was a great leader.

_____

2. Trying to find the employee responsible for this embarrassing information leak is like trying to find a needle in a haystack.

_____

3. The military is putting all its eggs in one basket by relying so heavily on nuclear missiles for the nation's defense.

_____

4. Older doctors should be required to update their techniques, but you can't teach an old dog new tricks.

_____

5. A ballpark estimate of the number of fans in the stadium would be 120,000.

_____

Principle 10: Avoid Jargon

Jargon includes two categories of words that you should avoid. First is the specialized vocabulary of a group, such as that used by doctors, lawyers, or baseball coaches. Second is the overly inflated and complex language that burdens many students' essays. You will not impress anyone with big words that do not fit the tone or context of your essay, especially if you misuse them.

If you are not certain of a word's meaning or appropriateness, leave it out. An appropriate word, even a simple one, will add impact to your argument. As you come across words you are unsure of, ask yourself, "Would a reader in a different field be able to understand exactly what I mean from the words I've chosen?" "Is there any way I can say the same thing more simply?"

Weak:	The international banks are cognizant of the new law's significance.
Forceful:	The international banks are aware of the new law's significance.
Wrong:	The new law would negatively impact each of the nations involved.
Correct:	The new law would hurt each of the nations involved. (*Impact* is also used to mean *affect* or *benefit*.)

The following are commonly used jargon words:

prioritize	*parameter*
optimize	*time frame*
utilize	*input/output*
finalize	*maximize*
designate	*facilitate*
bottom line	

Exercise 10: Jargon

Replace the jargon in the following sentences with more appropriate language.

1. We anticipate utilizing hundreds of paper clips in the foreseeable future.

   _____

2. Education-wise, our schoolchildren have been neglected.

   _____

3. Foreign diplomats should always interface with local leaders.

   _____

4. There is considerable evidentiary support for the assertion that Vienna sausages are good for you.

   _____

5. In the case of the recent railway disaster, it is clear that governmental regulatory agencies obfuscated in the preparation of materials for release to the public through both the electronic and print media.

   _____

BE CORRECT

Correctness is perhaps the most difficult objective for writers to achieve. The complex rules of standard English usage can leave you feeling unsure of your writing and more than a bit confused. But remember, the most important lesson you can take from this section is how to organize your thoughts into a strong, well-supported argument. Style and grammar are important but secondary concerns. Your readers will *not* mark you down for occasional errors common to first-draft writing. So just think of this section, together with the Grammar Reference Guide, as helping you to improve the details of good writing. If it begins to overwhelm you, stop and take a break. You need time to absorb this information.

Do the exercises and then compare your answers to ours. Make sure you understand what the error was in each sentence. Use what you learn in this section to help you proofread your practice essays; later, return to your practice essays and edit them. Better yet, ask a friend to edit them, paying special attention to correctness.

Principle 11: Avoid Slang and Colloquialisms

Conversational speech is filled with slang and colloquial expressions. However, you should avoid slang on the GMAT Analytical Writing Assessment. Slang terms and colloquialisms can be confusing to the reader, since these expressions are not universally understood. Even worse, such informal writing may give readers the impression that you are poorly educated or arrogant.

Inappropriate:	He is really into gardening.
Correct:	He enjoys gardening.
Inappropriate:	She plays a wicked game of tennis.
Correct:	She excels in tennis.
Inappropriate:	Myra has got to go to Memphis for a week.
Correct:	Myra must go to Memphis for a week.
Inappropriate:	Joan has been doing science for eight years now.
Correct:	Joan has been a scientist for eight years now.

With a little thought, you will find the right word. Using informal language is risky. Play it safe by sticking to standard usage.

Exercise 11: Slang and Colloquialisms

Replace the informal elements of the following sentences with more appropriate terms.

1. Cynthia Larson sure knows her stuff.

_____

2. Normal human beings can't cope with repeated humiliation.

_____

3. If you want a good cheesecake, you must make a top-notch crust.

_____

4. International organizations should try and cooperate on global issues like hunger.

_____

5. The environmentalists aren't in it for the prestige; they really care about protecting the yellow-throated hornswoggler.

_____

Principle 12: Use Commas Correctly

When using the comma, follow these rules:

A. Use commas to separate items in a series. If more than two items are listed in a series, they should be separated by commas; the final comma—the one that precedes the word _and_—is optional. Never use a comma _AFTER_ the word _and_.

Correct:	My recipe for buttermilk biscuits contains flour, baking soda, salt, shortening, and buttermilk.
Correct:	My recipe for chocolate cake contains flour, baking soda, sugar, eggs, milk and chocolate.

B. Do not place commas before the first element of a series or after the last element.

Wrong:	My investment adviser recommended that I construct a portfolio of, stocks, bonds, commodities futures, and precious metals.
Wrong:	The elephants, tigers, and dancing bears, were the highlights of the circus.

C. Use commas to separate two or more adjectives before a noun; do not use a comma after the last adjective in the series.

Wrong:	I can't believe you sat through that long, dull, uninspired, movie three times.
Correct:	I can't believe you sat through that long, dull, uninspired movie three times.

D. Use commas to set off parenthetical clauses and phrases. (A parenthetical expression is one that is not necessary to the main idea of the sentence.)

Correct:	Gordon, who is a writer by profession, bakes an excellent cheesecake.

The main idea is that Gordon bakes an excellent cheesecake. The intervening clause merely serves to identify Gordon; thus it should be set off with commas.

Correct:	The newspaper that has the most insipid editorials is the _Daily Times_.
Correct:	The newspaper, which has the most insipid editorials of any I have read, won numerous awards last week.

In the first of these examples, the clause beginning with *that* defines which paper the author is discussing. In the second example, the main point is that the newspaper won numerous awards, and the intervening clause beginning with *which* identifies the paper.

E. Use commas after introductory participial or prepositional phrases.

Correct:	Having watered his petunias every day during the drought, Harold was very disappointed when his garden was destroyed by insects.
Correct:	After the banquet, Harold and Martha went dancing.

F. Use commas to separate independent clauses (clauses that could stand alone as complete sentences) connected by coordinate conjunctions such as *and*, *but*, *not*, *yet*, and the like.

Correct:	Susan's old car has been belching blue smoke from the tailpipe for two weeks, but it has not broken down yet.

Note: Make sure the comma separates two *independent* clauses, joined by a conjunction. It is incorrect to use a comma to separate the two parts of a compound verb.

Wrong:	Barbara went to the grocery store, and bought two quarts of milk.

Exercise 12: Commas

Correct the punctuation errors in the following sentences.

1. It takes a friendly energetic person to be a successful salesman.
2. I was shocked to discover that a large, modern, glass-sheathed, office building had replaced my old school.
3. The country club, a cluster of ivy-covered whitewashed buildings was the site of the president's first speech.
4. Pushing through the panicked crowd the security guards frantically searched for the suspect.
5. Despite careful analysis of the advantages and disadvantages of each proposal Harry found it hard to reach a decision.

Principle 13: Use Semicolons Correctly

When using a semicolon, follow these rules:

A. Use a semicolon *instead of* a coordinate conjunction such as *and*, *or*, or *but* to link two closely related independent clauses.

Wrong:	Whooping cranes are an endangered species; and they are unlikely to survive if we continue to pollute.
Correct:	Whooping cranes are an endangered species; there are only fifty whooping cranes in New Jersey today.
Correct:	Whooping cranes are an endangered species, and they are unlikely to survive if we continue to pollute.

B. Use a semicolon between independent clauses connected by words like *therefore*, *nevertheless*, and *moreover*.

Correct:	Farm prices have been falling rapidly for two years; nevertheless, the traditional American farm is not in danger of disappearing.

Exercise 13: Semicolons

Correct the punctuation errors in the following sentences.

1. Morgan has five years' experience in karate; but Thompson has even more.

_____

2. Very few students wanted to take the class in physics, only the professor's kindness kept it from being canceled.

_____

3. You should always be prepared when you go on a camping trip, however you must avoid carrying unnecessary weight.

_____

Principle 14: Use Colons Correctly

When using a colon, follow these rules:

A. In formal writing the colon is used only as a means of signaling that what follows is a list, definition, explanation, or concise summary of what has gone before. The colon usually follows an independent clause, and it will frequently be accompanied by a reinforcing expression like *the following*, *as follows*, or *namely*, or by an explicit demonstrative like *this*.

Correct:	Your instructions are as follows: read the passage carefully, answer the questions on the last page, and turn over your answer sheet.
Correct:	This is what I found in the refrigerator: a moldy lime, half a bottle of stale soda, and a jar of peanut butter.
Correct:	The biggest problem with America today is apathy: the corrosive element that will destroy our democracy.

B. Be careful not to put a colon between a verb and its direct object.

Wrong:	I want: a slice of pizza and a small green salad.
Correct:	This is what I want: a slice of pizza and a small green salad. (The colon serves to announce that a list is forthcoming.)
Correct:	I don't want much for lunch: just a slice of pizza and a small green salad. (Here what follows the colon defines what "don't want much" means.)

C. Context will occasionally make clear that a second independent clause is closely linked to its predecessor, even without an explicit expression like those used above. Here, too, a colon is appropriate, although a period will always be correct also.

Correct:	We were aghast: the "charming country inn" that had been advertised in such glowing terms proved to be a leaking cabin full of mosquitoes.
Correct:	We were aghast. The "charming country inn" that had been advertised in such glowing terms proved to be a leaking cabin full of mosquitoes.

Exercise 14: Colons

Edit these sentences so they use colons correctly.

1. I am sick and tired of: your whining, your complaining, your nagging, your teasing, and, most of all, your barbed comments.

   _____

2. The chef has created a masterpiece, the pasta is delicate yet firm, the mustard greens are fresh, and the medallions of veal are melting in my mouth.

   _____

3. In order to write a good essay, you must: practice, get plenty of sleep, and eat a good breakfast.

   _____

Principle 15: Use Hyphens and Dashes Correctly

When using a hyphen or a dash, follow these rules:

A. Use the hyphen with the compound numbers twenty-one through ninety-nine, and with fractions used as adjectives.

Correct:	Sixty-five students constituted a majority.
Correct:	A two-thirds vote was necessary to carry the measure.
Wrong:	Only two-thirds of the students passed the final exam.

B. Use the hyphen with the prefixes *ex*, *all*, and *self* and with the suffix *elect*.

Correct:	The constitution protects against self-incrimination.
Correct:	The president-elect was invited to chair the meeting.

C. Use the hyphen with a compound adjective when it comes before the word it modifies, but not when it comes after the word it modifies.

Correct:	The no-holds-barred argument continued into the night.
Correct:	The argument continued with no holds barred.

D. Use the hyphen with any prefix used before a proper noun or adjective.

Correct: They believed that his activities were un-American.

E. Use a hyphen to separate component parts of a word in order to avoid confusion with other words or to avoid the use of a double vowel.

Correct: The sculptor was able to re-form the clay after the dog knocked over the bust.
Correct: They had to be re-introduced, since it had been so long since they last met.

F. Use the dash to indicate an abrupt change of thought. In general, however, formal writing is best when you think out what you want to say in advance and avoid abrupt changes of thought.

Correct: To get a high score—and who doesn't want to get a high score?—you need to devote yourself to prolonged and concentrated study.

Exercise 15: Hyphens and Dashes

Edit these sentences so they use hyphens and dashes correctly.

1. The child was able to count from one to ninety nine.
2. The adults only movie was banned from commercial TV.
3. It was the first time she had seen a movie that was for adults-only.
4. A two thirds majority would be needed to pass the budget reforms.
5. The house, and it was the most dilapidated house that I had ever seen was a bargain because the land was so valuable.

Principle 16: Use the Apostrophe Correctly

When using an apostrophe, follow these rules:

A. Use the apostrophe with contracted forms of verbs to indicate that one or more letters have been eliminated in writing. But try to avoid contractions altogether on the GMAT. (See also Principle 11: Avoid Slang and Colloquialisms.)

Full Forms:

you are	*it is*	*you have*	*the boy is*
Harry has	*we would*	*was not*	

Contracted:

you're	*it's*	*you've*	*the boy's*
Harry's	*we'd*	*wasn't*	

One of the most common errors involving use of the apostrophe is using it in the contraction *you're* or *it's* to indicate the possessive form of *you* or *it*. When you write *you're*, ask yourself whether you mean *you are*. If not, the correct word is *your*. Similarly, are you sure you mean *it is*? If not, use the possessive form *its*. You spell *his* or *hers* without an apostrophe, so you should spell *its* without an apostrophe.

Incorrect:	You're chest of drawers is ugly.
Incorrect:	The dog hurt it's paw.
Correct:	Your chest of drawers is ugly.
Correct:	The dog hurt its paw.

B. Use the apostrophe to indicate the possessive form of a noun.

Not Possessive:

the boy   *Harry*   *the children*   *the boys*

Possessive Form:

the boy's   *Harry's*   *the children's*   *the boys'*

Correct:	Ms. Fox's office is on the first floor. (One person possesses the office.)
Correct:	The Foxes' apartment has a wonderful view. (There are several people named Fox living in the same apartment. First you must form the plural, then add the apostrophe to indicate possession.)

C. The apostrophe is used to indicate possession only with nouns; in the case of pronouns, there are separate possessives for each person and number.

my, mine   *our, ours*
your, yours   *your, yours*
his, his   *their, theirs*
her, hers
its its

The exception is the neutral "one," which forms its possessive by adding an apostrophe and an *s*.

Exercise 16: Apostrophes

Edit these sentences so they use apostrophes correctly.

1. The presidents limousine had a flat tire.
2. You're tickets for the show will be at the box office.
3. The opportunity to change ones lifestyle does not come often.
4. The desks' surface was immaculate, but it's drawers were messy.
5. The cat on the bed is hers'.

Answers to Exercises

Answers to Exercise 1: Wordy Phrases

1. Since John has prepared for this presentation so carefully, we should award him the project.
2. Flights are always at least an hour late on this airline, though its leaders promise that promptness is a high priority for all its employees.
3. Although she is inexperienced in photography, she will probably succeed because she is motivated.
4. Accuracy is important to English teachers and company presidents alike.
5. Humans kill each other because they fear those whom they do not understand.

Answers to Exercise 2: Redundancy

1. All these problems have combined to create a crisis.
2. A staff that large needs an effective supervisor.
3. He knows how to follow directions.
4. The recent trend of spending on credit has created a poorer middle class.
5. Few people can follow directions.

Answers to Exercise 3: Excessive Qualification

1. She is a good teacher.
2. Ferrara is a slow worker.
3. You are the best person to decide what you should do for a living.
4. Children should be taught to cooperate at home and in school. (If there's no need to say it, don't!)
5. The travel agent said not to go to Tripoli, since one may be hurt. (Saying *it is possible that one may be hurt* is an example of redundant qualification, since both *possible* and *may* indicate uncertainty.)

Answers to Exercise 4: Unnecessary Sentences

1. People cannot safely consume water that contains chemical pollutants.
2. No present evidence suggests that Shakespeare's plays were written by others.
3. The United States should send soldiers to areas of conflict.
4. The architect Frank Lloyd Wright was famous for his ability to design buildings that blend into their surroundings.
5. A lot of people find math a difficult subject because it requires very precise thinking skills.

Answers to Exercise 5: Needless Self-Reference

1. This argument cannot be generalized to most business owners.
2. Food is the best social lubricant.
3. Privacy should not be valued more than social concerns.
4. Most people want to do good work, but many are bored or frustrated with their jobs.
5. The author has a point.

Answers to Exercise 6: Undesirable Passives

1. Recent allegations of corruption have hurt the politician's standing in the polls.
2. Congress passed the bill in time, but the president did not sign it until the time for action had passed.
3. Those who need advice least usually request it; the truly lost and ignorant do not seek it.
4. The city clerk should take the minutes of the City Council meeting.
5. A number of field anthropologists and marriage experts compiled the report.

Answers to Exercise 7: Weak Openings

1. Businesses ignore the illiteracy problem at their own peril.
2. The government cannot fight a drug war effectively without waging a battle against demand for illicit substances.
3. The candidate has many strong points; intelligence, unfortunately, is not among them.
4. We, as a society, have decided to tolerate homelessness.
5. Americans must like watching television better than conversing.

Answers to Exercise 8: Needlessly Vague Language

1. When water is heated to 100° C, it turns into steam.
2. The diplomat had to agree to live wherever the government sent him.
3. The principal told John not to return to school until he was ready to behave.
4. The police detective had to ask the lawyer for permission to question the suspect.
5. The last ice age destroyed thousands of animal species.

Answers to Exercise 9: Clichés

1. Jefferson was a great leader.
2. Trying to find the employee responsible for this embarrassing information leak may be impossible.
3. The military should diversify its defense rather than rely so heavily on nuclear missiles.
4. Older doctors should be required to update their techniques, but many seem resistant to changes in technology.
5. I estimate that 120,000 fans were in the stadium. (Even when a cliché is used in its original context, it sounds old.)

Answers to Exercise 10: Jargon

1. We expect to use hundreds of paper clips in the next two months.
2. Our schoolchildren's education has been neglected.
3. Foreign diplomats should always talk to local leaders.
4. Recent studies suggest that Vienna sausages are good for you.
5. Government regulatory agencies lied in their press releases about the recent railway accident.

Answers to Exercise 11: Slang and Colloquialisms

1. Cynthia Larson is an expert.
2. Normal human beings cannot tolerate repeated humiliation.
3. If you want a good cheesecake, you must make a superb crust.
4. International organizations should try to cooperate on global issues like hunger.
5. The environmentalists are not involved in the project for prestige; they truly care about protecting the yellow-throated hornswoggler.

Answers for Exercise 12: Commas

1. It takes a friendly, energetic person to be a successful salesman.
2. I was shocked to discover that a large, modern, glass-sheathed office building had replaced my old school.
3. The country club, a cluster of ivy-covered whitewashed buildings, was the site of the president's first speech.
4. Pushing through the panicked crowd, the security guards frantically searched for the suspect.
5. Despite careful analysis of the advantages and disadvantages of each proposal, Harry found it hard to reach a decision.

Answers for Exercise 13: Semicolons

1. Morgan has five years' experience in karate; Thompson has even more.
2. Very few students wanted to take the class in physics; only the professor's kindness kept it from being canceled.
3. You should always be prepared when you go on a camping trip; however, you must avoid carrying unnecessary weight.

Answers to Exercise 14: Colons

1. I am sick and tired of your whining, your complaining, your nagging, your teasing, and, most of all, your barbed comments.
2. The chef has created a masterpiece: the pasta is delicate yet firm, the mustard greens are fresh, and the medallions of veal are melting in my mouth.
3. In order to write a good essay, you must do the following: practice, get plenty of sleep, and eat a good breakfast.

Answers to Exercise 15: Hyphens and Dashes

1. The child was able to count from one to ninety-nine.
2. The adults-only movie was banned from commercial TV.
3. It was the first time she had seen a movie that was for adults only.
4. A two-thirds majority would be needed to pass the budget reforms.
5. The house—and it was the most dilapidated house that I had ever seen—was a bargain because the land was so valuable.

Answers to Exercise 16: Apostrophes

1. The president's limousine had a flat tire.
2. Your tickets for the show will be at the box office.
3. The opportunity to change one's lifestyle does not come often.
4. The desk's surface was immaculate, but its drawers were messy.
5. The cat on the bed is hers.

Appendix 3: **Common GMAT Idioms**

Note: All of the following have been known to appear on more than one GMAT. Entries with double ellipses (such as **between . . . and . . .**) indicate that the idiom also sets up a parallelism (between A and B).

able to (ability to)

No one has been *able to* prove that the person who wrote Shakespeare's plays was named Shakespeare.

among versus between

Use *between* when referring to two items or groups, *among* when referring to three or more.

Don't make me choose *between* Tweedledum and Tweedledee.

Among all five candidates, he's by far the best qualified.

amount versus number

Use *amount* when referring to an uncountable quantity, like soup or love, and *number* when referring to countable things, like jelly beans or people.

The *amount* of work you put into your studies will affect the *number* of points you will add to your GMAT score.

as versus like

Use *like* to compare nouns; use *as* to compare actions—in other words, use *as* when what follows is a clause.

Like fine wine, fruitcake tastes better after it has aged.

Dogs don't scratch up furniture, *as* cats often do.

as . . . as

She actually is *as* naïve *as* she appears.

associate with

Many people *associate* the smell of vinegar *with* coloring Easter Eggs.

at least as . . . as

The Eiffel Tower is *at least as* tall *as* the Statue of Liberty.

attribute to

I *attribute* his success *to* having good friends in high places.

believe to be

The expert *believes* the painting *to be* a fraud.

between . . . and . . .

You must decide *between* wealth *and* fame.

both versus **each**

Use *both* when pointing out similarities; use *each* when pointing out differences. Note that *each* is always singular.

Although *both* cooks enjoy making goulash, *each* has a different take on this classic dish.

both . . . and . . .

He is *both* an artist *and* a rogue.

compare to versus **compare with**

On the GMAT, *compare with* is the generally preferred form. Use *compare to* to point out an abstract or figurative likeness, and *compare with* to consider likenesses and differences in general.

Shall I *compare* thee *to* a summer's day?
Compared with a summer's day, it's cold outside.

connection between

I saw little *connection between* her words and her deeds.

consequence of

One *consequence of* the Supreme Court decision was increased public distrust in the judicial system.

consider

I *consider* you a very good friend.

Note: Although *consider to be* is also correct, it will never be correct on the GMAT.

continue to

Do not *continue to* deny the obvious.

contrast with

I like to *contrast* my plaid pants *with* a lovely paisley jacket.

credit with

James Joyce is often *credited with* the invention of the literary form called stream of consciousness.

debate over

This idiom only applies when *debate* is used as a noun.

They held a lively *debate over* whom to throw off the island.

decide to

She *decided to* go to the party after all.

define as

My dictionary *defines* a clause *as* group of words containing a subject and a verb.

different from

John Major's policies were not very *different from* those of Margaret Thatcher.

difficult to

It's *difficult to* disagree with such a persuasive argument.

dispute over

This idiom applies only when *dispute* is used as a noun.

The *dispute over* how to read the punchcards was never properly resolved.

distinguish between . . . and . . .

Some colorblind people cannot *distinguish between* red *and* green.

distinguish . . . from . . .

Other colorblind people find it difficult to *distinguish* blue *from* purple.

double versus **twice** (**triple** versus **three times**, etc.)

On the GMAT, *double* (*triple*, *quadruple*, etc.) is only used as a verb; when making a comparison, the preferred form is *twice* (*three times*, etc.).

He promised to *double* the company's profits in less than a year.
I ate *twice* as much as you did.

each (See **both** versus **each** above.)

each other versus **one another**

In GMAT English, *each other* is used to refer to two things, and *one another* is used for three or more.

Those two theories contradict *each other*.
Those three theories contradict *one another*.

KAPLAN)

either . . . or . . .

Today I will *either* look for a job *or* watch the Boston marathon on TV.

-er than

Winston Churchill was a bett*er* dancer *than* Neville Chamberlain ever was.

extent to which

You should appreciate the *extent to which* the same idioms repeatedly appear on the GMAT.

estimate to be

The oldest cave paintings known to exist are *estimated to be* over 50,000 years old.

fewer versus less

Use *fewer* to describe countable things, like jelly beans or people, and *less* to describe an uncountable quantity, like soup or love. (See **amount** versus **number** above.)

I ate *fewer* hotdogs and *less* potato salad than I did at last year's picnic.

forbid to

I was *forbidden to* discuss politics at the dinner table.

from . . . to . . .

From the Redwood forest *to* the Gulf Stream waters, this land was made for you and me.

just as . . . so too . . .

Just as sand flows through an hourglass, *so too* flow the days of our lives.

if versus whether

If you're ever given a choice on the GMAT, choose *whether*. The actual rule states that whenever you're discussing a choice between alternatives, you should use *whether* (as in *whether or not* to do something) rather than *if*. On the GMAT *if* is reserved for conditional "if-then" statements.

Let me know *if* I behave inappropriately in front of the royal family. (Translation: I may or may not behave inappropriately, but if I do, I should be informed).

Tell me *whether* I behaved inappropriately in front of the royal family. (Translation: Either I behaved inappropriately or I didn't; tell me the truth.)

in danger of

Conservationists fear that the West Indian manatee is *in danger of* becoming extinct.

less (See **fewer** versus **less** above.)

like versus such as

If you're ever given a choice on the GMAT, choose *such as*. The GMAT writers prefer *such as* to *like* when what follows are examples; to these writers *like* means "similar to."

I prefer salty snacks *such as* potato chips to sweet snacks *such as* candy bars.

I've never met anyone *like* him before.

likely to

You're *likely to* do well on the GMAT verbal section.

link to

Exposure to classical music has been *linked to* improved performance on mathematical aptitude tests.

model after

Louisiana's legal system is *modeled after* the Napoleonic Code.

more than

I was *more* prepared this time *than* I was the last time I took the test.

native

Use *native to*, meaning "indigenous to," when discussing plants, animals, and the like. Use *a native of* when discussing people and where they were born.

The sugar maple is *native to* Canada.

Leslie Nielsen is *a native of* Canada.

neither . . . nor . . .

Note that when a sentence has a *neither . . . nor . . .* subject, whatever follows *nor* determines whether the verb is singular or plural. (The same thing is true of *either . . . or . . .* subjects.)

Neither the players *nor* the coach was surprised by the team's victory.

not . . . but [rather, merely] . . .

It's *not* a bother *but rather* an honor to serve you.

not only . . . but also . . .

I am *not only* charming *but also* modest to a fault.

not so . . . as

It's *not so* bad *as* it seems.

not so much . . . as . . .

The company's recent success is due *not so much* to better management *as* to an improved economy.

number (See **amount** versus **number** above.)

Also note that on the GMAT *the number of* will always be singular, while *a number of* will always be plural.

The number of stars in our galaxy *is* huge.

A number of guests *are* waiting in the foyer.

one another (See **each other** versus **one another** above.)

opposition to

There has been far less *opposition* in the United States than in Europe *to* the use of genetically modified foods.

perceive as

I didn't mean for my comments to be *perceived as* criticism.

prohibit from

People are *prohibited from* entering the park after 10 P.M.

range from . . . to . . .

Scores on the GMAT *range from* 200 *to* 800.

regard as

I *regard* him *as* little more than a common criminal.

require to

The laws in many states *require* couples *to* have their blood tested before getting married.

resistance to

Stress can lower one's *resistance to* cold and flu viruses.

same as

I got the *same* score *as* he did.

seem to

He *seemed to* be at a loss for words.

so . . . as to be . . .

My new computer game is *so* entertaining *as to be* genuinely addictive.

so . . . that

In fact, it's *so* addictive *that* I spend several hours every day playing it.

such as (See **like** versus **such as** above.)

superior to

Superman's powers are clearly *superior to* those of Batman.

target at

I sometimes suspect that beer ads are *targeted at* morons.

the -er . . . the -er . . .

The bigg*er* they come, *the* hard*er* they fall, or so I have heard.

try to

Try to write a short story based on your travel experiences.

twice (See **double** versus **twice** above.)

use as

Lacking cooking implements, we *used* one of the car's hubcaps *as* a makeshift pan.

view as

Many *view* the former publishing magnate *as* a con artist extraordinaire.

whether (See **if** versus **whether** above.)

worry about

There's no need to *worry about* idioms on the GMAT; just study the ones you don't recognize.

Idioms Quiz

1. Richard Gere portrays not only an officer (and also, and as well, but also) a gentleman in this film.

2. I respect Jerry Hallowell, a.k.a., Ginger Spice, both as an entertainer (and also, and as, but also as) a humanitarian.

3. I must have either Twinkies™ (or else, or, and) Dingdongs™ for lunch.

4. You must decide (between, among) the hot and sour soup (or, and) the egg drop soup.

5. (Between, Among) the three starting pitchers, Martinez is generally (considered, considered to be, considered as) the (more, most) reliable.

6. There were (less, fewer) immigrants entering the country last year than the previous year.

7. The (number, amount) of students in my class (has, have) gone up.

8. I regard the movies of Mamie Van Doren (as, to be, as being) superior (when compared to, over, to) those of Jayne Mansfield.

9. Poor Zeppo is often perceived (as, to be, as being) the least talented of the Marx Brothers.

10. According to exit polls, a majority of those who voted for the winning candidate viewed him (as, to be, as being) the lesser of two evils.

11. Adam Sandler's movies are not very different (than, from) those of Paulie Shore.

12. It was so quiet (you, that you, as a result you) could hear a pin drop.

13. Barbra Streisand and Neil Diamond (each, both) went to the same high school.

14. Dean Martin and Jerry Lewis (both had their, each had his) own take on why the two split up.

15. Some pundits like to associate the 1960s (with, and) the decline of Western civilization.

16. We held a spirited debate (over, about, concerning) the place of *Married with Children* within the pantheon of classic situational comedies.

17. I can assure you that it was not a dispute (over, about, concerning) trivial issues.

18. Charles was forbidden (to enter, from entering) the Temple of Doom.

19. He was also prohibited (to visit, from visiting) the Garden of Earthly Delights.

20. I hereby define a "baker's dozen" (to be, as, as being) thirteen.

21. Yogi Bear was clearly more intelligent (compared to, as, than) your average bear.

22. Studying grammar is about as pleasant (when compared to, as, than) going to the dentist.

23. I attribute my stunning success (as due to, because of, to) good looks and native intelligence.

24. I attribute my good looks not so much to exquisite grooming (as, but, but rather) to an inner radiance.

25. Most people credit Philo Taylor Farnsworth (as, for, with) having invented the television back in the 1920s while he was still a teenager.

26. Swing dances from the 1940s (like, such as) the Jitterbug and the Hucklebuck have recently become popular again.

27. (Similar to, Like, As with) many female supermodels, Fabio (is also, is) known by his first name alone.

28. I did not try the clam dip, (as, like) my roommate who got sick did.

29. I've finally decided (on going, to go) camping over the holidays but I still haven't figured out (whether, if) I need to buy a tent.

30. Resistance (against, to) assimilation by the Borg is futile.

Answers

1. Richard Gere portrays *not only* an officer *but also* a gentleman in this film.

2. I respect Jerry Hallowell, a.k.a., Ginger Spice, both as an entertainer *and as* a humanitarian.

3. I must have either Twinkies™ *or* Dingdongs™ for lunch.

4. You must decide *between* the hot and sour soup *and* the egg drop soup.

5. *Among* the three starting pitchers, Martinez is generally *considered* the *most* reliable.

6. There were *fewer* immigrants entering the country last year than the previous year.

7. The *number* of students in my class *has* gone up.

8. I regard the movies of Mamie Van Doren *as* superior *to* those of Jayne Mansfield.

9. Poor Zeppo is often *perceived as* the least talented of the Marx Brothers.

10. According to exit polls, a majority of those who voted for the winning candidate viewed him *as* the lesser of two evils.

11. Adam Sandler's movies are not very different *from* those of Paulie Shore.

12. It was so quiet *that you* could hear a pin drop.

13. Barbra Streisand and Neil Diamond *both* went to the same high school.

14. Dean Martin and Jerry Lewis *each had his* own take on why the two split up.

15. Some pundits like to associate the 1960s *with* the decline of Western civilization.

16. We held a spirited debate *over* the place of *Married with Children* within the pantheon of classic situational comedies.

17. I can assure you that it was not a dispute *over* trivial issues.

18. Charles was forbidden *to enter* the Temple of Doom.

19. He was also prohibited *from visiting* the Garden of Earthly Delights.

20. I hereby define a "baker's dozen" *as* thirteen.

21. Yogi Bear was clearly more intelligent *than* your average bear.

22. Studying grammar is about *as* pleasant as going to the dentist.

23. I attribute my stunning success *to* good looks and native intelligence.

24. I attribute my good looks not so much to exquisite grooming *as* to an inner radiance.

25. Most people credit Philo Taylor Farnsworth *with* having invented the television back in the 1920s while he was still a teenager.

26. Swing dances from the 1940s *such as* the Jitterbug and the Hucklebuck have recently become popular again.

27. *Like* many female supermodels, Fabio *is* known by his first name alone.

28. I did not try the clam dip, *as* my roommate who got sick did.

29. I've finally decided *to go* camping over the holidays but I still haven't figured out *whether* I need to buy a tent.

30. Resistance *to* assimilation by the Borg is futile.

How Did We Do? Grade Us.

Thank you for choosing a Kaplan book. Your comments and suggestions are very useful to us. Please answer the following questions to assist us in our continued development of high-quality resources to meet your needs.

The title of the Kaplan book I read was: _____

My name is: _____

My address is: _____

_____

My email address is: _____

	Poor				Outstanding
What overall grade would you give this book?	Ⓐ	Ⓑ	Ⓒ	Ⓓ	Ⓕ
How relevant was the information to your goals?	Ⓐ	Ⓑ	Ⓒ	Ⓓ	Ⓕ
How comprehensive was the information in this book?	Ⓐ	Ⓑ	Ⓒ	Ⓓ	Ⓕ
How accurate was the information in this book?	Ⓐ	Ⓑ	Ⓒ	Ⓓ	Ⓕ
How easy was the book to use?	Ⓐ	Ⓑ	Ⓒ	Ⓓ	Ⓕ
How appealing was the book's design?	Ⓐ	Ⓑ	Ⓒ	Ⓓ	Ⓕ

What were the book's strong points? _____

How could this book be improved? _____

Is there anything that we left out that you wanted to know more about? _____

Would you recommend this book to others?   ☐ YES   ☐ NO

Other comments: _____

_____

_____

Do we have permission to quote you?   ☐ YES   ☐ NO

Thank you for your help.
Please tear out this page and mail it to:

Content Manager
Kaplan Publishing
1 Liberty Plaza, 24th floor
New York, NY 10106
or fax to 212-618-2497

KAPLAN

Thanks!

NOTES

NOTES

NOTES